THE PERSON OF CHRIST

DONALD MACLEOD

CONTOURS *of* CHRISTIAN THEOLOGY

GERALD BRAY
General Editor

InterVarsity Press
Downers Grove, Illinois

InterVarsity Press
P.O. Box 1400, Downers Grove, IL 60515
World Wide Web: www.ivpress.com
E-mail: mail@ivpress.com

Published in the United States of America by InterVarsity Press, Downers Grove, Illinois, with permission from Universities and Colleges Christian Fellowship, Leicester, England.

InterVarsity Press® is the book-publishing division of InterVarsity Christian Fellowship/USA®, a student movement active on campus at hundreds of universities, colleges and schools of nursing in the United States of America, and a member movement of the International Fellowship of Evangelical Students. For information about local and regional activities, write Public Relations Dept., InterVarsity Christian Fellowship/USA, 6400 Schroeder Rd., P.O. Box 7895, Madison, WI 53707-7895.

ISBN 0-8308-1537-6

Printed in the United States of America ♾

Library of Congress Cataloging-in-Publication Data

Macleod, Donald, 1940-
The person of Christ / Donald Macleod.
p. cm.
Includes bibliographical references and index.
ISBN 0-8308-1537-6 (paper)
1. Jesus Christ—Person and offices. I. Title.
BT202.M24 1998 *98-40356*
232'.8—dc21 *CIP*

17 16 15 14 13 12 11 10 9 8 7
12 11 10 09 08 07 06

In memory

of my parents, Donald and Alice Macleod,

my first, and best, tutors

in Christology

Contents

Series Preface

Contours of Christian Theology covers the main themes of Christian doctrine. The series offers a systematic presentation of most of the major doctrines in a way which complements the traditional textbooks but does not copy them. Top priority has been given to contemporary issues, some of which may not be dealt with elsewhere from an evangelical point of view. The series aims, however, not merely to answer current objections to evangelical Christianity, but also to rework the orthodox evangelical position in a fresh and compelling way. The overall thrust is therefore positive and evangelistic in the best sense.

The series is intended to be of value to theological students at all levels, whether at a Bible college, a seminary or a secular university. It should also appeal to ministers and educated lay-people. As far as possible, efforts have been made to make technical vocabulary accessible to the non-specialist reader, and the presentation has avoided the extremes of academic style. Occasionally this has meant that particular issues have been presented without a thorough argument, taking into account different positions, but when this has happened, authors have been encouraged to refer the reader to other works which take the discussion further. For this purpose adequate but not exhaustive notes have been produced.

The doctrines covered in the series are not exhaustive, but have been chosen in response to contemporary concerns. The title and presentation of each volume are at the discretion of the author, but the final editorial decisions have been taken by the Series Editor in consultation with IVP.

In offering this series to the public, the authors and the publishers hope that it will meet the needs of theological students in this generation, and bring honour and glory to God the Father, and to his Son, Jesus Christ, in whose service the work has been undertaken from the beginning.

Gerald Bray
Series Editor

Preface

For various reasons it has taken an inordinately long time to write this book. Indeed, that it has reached this stage at all is something of a miracle. Over the last ten years it has been taken up, laid down and resumed more times than I can remember.

This is part of my excuse for the fact that it does not take account of the most recent literature. It is a 1980s, rather than a 1990s, book. The other part of my excuse is that I am a theologian and therefore by definition a generalist. My task is not to be an expert in any particular field, but to take account of major developments across a wide range of disciplines and try to gather them into a coherent whole. The ongoing work of academic specialists is indispensable to theologians, but we have to wait till their findings are tried and tested before we can build on them. Current discussion as to the relations between Paul and Judaism and between Jesus and Ebionitism have thrown up little of relevance to Christology. The focus on the relation between Jesus and the Holy Spirit is more promising, provided it does not lose itself in adoptionism.

What greater privilege could a man have than an opportunity to write on such a theme as *The Person of Christ*? My prayer is that it will bring some honour to his Name.

Donald Macleod
March 1997

Abbreviations

ANF	*Ante-Nicene Fathers* (re-edition of *Ante-Nicene Christian Library* in 10 vols., Buffalo and New York, 1885–96, and Grand Rapids, 1950–51); new ed. (Grand Rapids: Eerdmans, and Edinburgh: T. & T. Clark).
KJV	King James Version.
NEB	New English Bible.
NPNF	*A Select Library of Nicene and Post-Nicene Fathers of the Christian Church*, First Series, ed. P. Schaff, 14 vols. (New York, 1886–90); Second Series, ed. H. Wace and P. Schaff, 14 vols. (New York, 1890–1900); new ed. (Grand Rapids: Eerdmans, and Edinburgh: T. & T. Clark, 1980).
RSV	Revised Standard Version.
TDNT	G. Kittel and G. Friedrich (eds.), *Theological Dictionary of the New Testament*, tr. and ed. G. W. Bromiley, 10 vols. (ET Grand Rapids: Eerdmans, 1964–76).

Introduction

This book is not a detached academic statement. It is written from within the Christian community by a member of that community and for the benefit of the community. As such, it reflects my personal belief that the gospels give us access to the real Jesus. It also reflects my belief that the great creeds, far from betraying the gospels, faithfully encapsulate their central concern to portray Jesus as the incarnate Son of God.

Yet it is easy to sympathize with scepticism, contemporary or otherwise. The claims made by the early church (and in my view by Christ himself) are staggering, and indeed offensive. At many points they require radical revision of our intuitive beliefs about God. Although I have personally moved beyond doubt and even uncertainty, I have not, I hope, forgotten how non-Christians think, and at every stage of the argument I have assumed that they are looking over my shoulder and challenging what I say. Many of those with whom I disagree profoundly have enriched my life by presenting me with new questions and offering fresh agendas.

There is no mandatory approach to Christology and at several points I had to make methodological decisions which can be challenged easily.

The most obvious is that against the contemporary current I have opted for a 'Christology from above'. This does not mean that I do not take the humanness of Christ seriously. I take it very seriously indeed. Some will think I take it too seriously altogether. But if I had opted for a Christology from below, it would have been a pretence. I am not starting from below. I am starting from faith, convinced before I put pen to paper (or finger to keyboard) that Jesus Christ is the eternal Son of God. This, it seems to me, is also where the gospels start. By the time they were written, Christ was already 'above', and the selection, arrangement and presentation of materials were determined by that fact. *Prima facie*, such an approach seems hopelessly biased. It is not more so, however, than that which insists that we must treat Christ as 'just an ordinary man' and the gospels as ordinary literature.

A substantial part of this study is historical, surveying the questions raised and the answers proffered by Christian thought from Tertullian to Barth (if Barth will excuse me for bracketing him with the North African father) and from Praxeas to Edward Irving. In the course of these discussions, most of the possible questions (and perhaps a few impossible ones) were formulated; and most of the possible answers were proposed. There are few new questions left, and even fewer new answers.

We can never be content with parrot-like repetition of the definitions of the past. Yet it would be presumptuous to speak before we have listened to the fathers. Men like Athanasius and Augustine, Basil and Calvin, are the Newtons and Einsteins of theology. By comparison, we are pygmies. Our only hope of far-sightedness is to stand on the shoulders of the giants.

This historical approach explains some of the peculiarities of this book. For example, it treats the Jesus of history after devoting three chapters to the basic New Testament material. My reason for doing so is that discussion of the Jesus of history began relatively late in the history of Christian thought. Besides, its fundamental concern was to challenge the authenticity of gospel material bearing on the deity of Christ. In particular, it challenged (and still challenges) the conclusion I try to establish in chapter 3, namely, that such titles as *the Son of God* can be traced back to Jesus himself.

Similarly, although it may seem obvious to treat the uniqueness of Christ at the very beginning, I have chosen to treat it last, in the context of contemporary discussion. We are too close to this period to assess it properly, but there can be little doubt that the crucial modern question is, What makes Christ different? For orthodoxy, the answer is clear enough. He is different because he is God incarnate. But what if, like Bultmann and those associated with *The Myth of God Incarnate*, we reject orthodoxy? In what sense can we still think him unique? And on what grounds can we continue to worship him?

Later in this book (page 155), I criticize Melanchthon's famous observation that 'to know Christ means to know his benefits'. Yet it contains an important truth. Though I write with the pen of men and of angels and have not the life of God in my soul, it profits me nothing.

Part One

"VERY GOD OF VERY GOD"— *From the Gospels to Nicea*

1

THE VIRGIN BIRTH

It is a virtual commonplace of modern Christology that we must begin with the humanity, not the divinity, of Jesus. As a result, the tide is set against a Christology 'from above' and is running strongly in favour of one 'from below'. Wolfhart Pannenberg is typical. Having asserted that 'the method of a Christology "from above" is closed to us', he goes on to say: 'Our starting point must lie in the question about the man Jesus; only in this way can we ask about his divinity.'[1]

Such an approach certainly cannot be dismissed out of hand. 'I have no fundamental objection to a Christological concept that starts "from below",' writes Klaas Runia: 'I believe that it brings out aspects of Jesus' person and work that are easily overlooked in a Christology "from above". Moreover, it is the very same way along which the apostolic church came to its confession of Jesus as Messiah, as Lord, as the Son of God.'[2] There is no doubt that the church neglected the humanity of Christ and focused too exclusively on 'the Lord from heaven'. It is also arguable, as Runia suggests, that the early Christians, on their journey to faith, started out 'from below': they first encountered him in his humanness and progressed from that, more or less rapidly, to apprehension of his deity.

On the face of things, the problem of 'from above' or 'from below' is only one of method. If so, we can walk away from it, saying, simply, *methodus est arbitrarius*. All we want is an arrangement which enables us to handle the facts. But then we come up against one awkward fact: the New Testament, almost unanimously, presents us with a Christology from above. It starts from the side of his deity, not from that of his humanity. There is probably good reason for this. The New Testament is looking at Christ in the light of the resurrection; and if we are articulating our theology from the standpoint of faith, we cannot but do the same. To regard the resurrection as an open question is itself a judgment against faith. Furthermore, historically the movement described by the New Testament is from God to man and, if we begin from below (from the human side), it may be fatally difficult to recover this perspective. It is not without significance that since the approach 'from below' came into vogue there has been a rash of adoptionist Christologies setting Christ forth not as God become man but as man becoming, in some sense, God. In such an ethos, the humanness becomes not only an axiom but a limiting factor: we can assert nothing of Christ which we cannot assert of man. Not surprisingly, many theologians are finding it impossible to move from this starting-point to belief in the deity of Christ.

Whatever the reasons, the fact itself is clear: the New Testament starts from above. This is most obvious in the Gospel of John. Not that John is not a firm believer in the humanness of the Lord: quite the contrary. He it is who speaks of the *Logos* becoming flesh (Jn. 1:14), portrays the Lord sitting wearily at Jacob's well (Jn. 4:6) and specifically mentions that when the spear pierced his side there came out blood and water (Jn. 19:34). In fact, in his first epistle, John makes denial of the physical manhood of Jesus the very mark of antichrist (1 Jn. 4:2f.). That Christ lived a genuinely human life, and lived it below, is the very core of John's message.

However, it is not his starting-point. Entry into John's Christology is only through his Prologue with its sustained emphasis on the deity of Christ. What we meet on the threshold is not a statement about anything below, but the magnificent words, 'In the beginning was the Word, and the Word was with God, and the Word was God' (Jn. 1:1). Everything here is from above. In the beginning, when God created the heavens and the earth (Gn. 1:1), Christ was already in existence. All things were made by him. He existed face to face with God. And he was God. He is among men only because, being already God, he became flesh; and even in his incarnateness, when men looked at him, and saw him truly, what they saw was the glory of God's only begotten Son (Jn. 1:14). Even the idea that the disciples' progress to a high view of Christ was gradual is somewhat shaken by the fact that on his very first encounter with Jesus, Nathanael is already exclaiming, 'Rabbi, you are the Son of God; you are the King of Israel' (Jn. 1:49).

The Christology of Hebrews follows the same pattern. As in John, there is a firm emphasis on the fact of the incarnation: 'Since the children have flesh and blood, he too shared in their humanity' (Heb. 2:14). Furthermore, throughout the epistle, Christ's humanness is taken with the utmost seriousness. He had a real experience of death, tasting it (2:9); it was through suffering that he was made perfect (2:10); he was subject to the same temptations as ourselves (4:15); he sympathizes with us in our weakness; and he learned obedience through the things he suffered (5:8).

All of these points are of incalculable importance. But none of them is said first. What is said first is that when God spoke through Christ he spoke through a Son (Heb. 1:2). This Son was the heir of all things and the creator of all things (Heb. 1:2). He was the effulgence of the Father's glory and the express image of his being (Heb. 1:3). As far as the highest beings in creation were concerned, he was their infinite Superior. What angel did God ever address as Son? Even more, what angel ever received the title God (Heb. 1:8)?

Whatever the writer to the Hebrews goes on to say of the earthly life and sufferings of Jesus (and he says a great deal), it is all said against this background. Christ is the heavenly Son of God and he is vulnerable to the experiences of this life only because he chose to become, for a time, a little lower than the angels.

Paul is no different. For him, too, Christ is the Lord, a being whose origin lay before time and beyond this world. This probably reflects Paul's experience at his conversion. His introduction to the grandeur of Christ had not been at all gradual. On the Damascus Road itself, Paul had seen the risen Christ and the vision had blinded and disabled him (Acts 9:3ff.). God had revealed Jesus to him as his Son (Gal. 1:16) and that conviction was forever afterwards his starting-point in describing him. This is true, for example, of his teaching in Galatians, probably the earliest of his epistles (written before the Council of Jerusalem made an authoritative pronouncement on the very issues in dispute between the apostle and Judaism): 'when the time had fully come, God sent his Son, born of a woman, born under law' (Gal. 4:4). Here Christ's presence in the world and under the law is the result of a movement from heaven initiated on God's side. 2 Corinthians 8:9 moves in the same direction: 'For you know the grace of our Lord Jesus Christ, that though he was rich, yet for your sakes he became poor.' The movement is not from poverty via the resurrection to riches, but from the riches of pre-existent glory to the poverty of his earthly life with its homelessness, its friendlessness and, at last, its Godlessness.

The dynamics of Paul's Christology are seen most clearly, however, in Philippians 2:5–11. Even if Paul himself did not actually compose the passage but quoted it from an earlier hymn, he obviously endorsed its teaching. Here again the starting point is the pre-existence of Christ. The idea is already implied in the word *hyparchōn* ('existing') and reinforced by the whole context. Before Christ took the great step of *kenōsis*, he already existed as one who shared God's form and was in all respects his equal.

When we turn to the synoptic gospels, however, do we not see a very different picture? Surely here we do have a Christology from below? By no means! Mark's starting-point is the same as John's: 'The beginning of the gospel about Jesus Christ, the Son of God.' Admittedly, the text is disputed. The phrase 'the Son of God' is lacking in some manuscripts and Westcott and Hort omitted it from their edition of the New Testament (1885). Recent commentators have not followed their example, however. 'There are strong reasons', wrote Vincent Taylor, 'for accepting the phrase as original in view of its attestation, its possible omission by *homoioteleuton* and the use of the title in Mark's Christology.'[3] C. E. B. Cranfield takes the same view: 'There are very strong reasons for regarding it as original.'[4] Dennis Nineham is less sure: 'It is hard to decide whether the words are original,' he writes, adding, 'But the question is not of great moment since Saint Mark certainly believed that Jesus was the Son of God and that belief underlies the whole gospel.'[5]

There is therefore little textual-critical reason for omitting the words 'the Son of God' from Mark's text. He is declaring his conviction (and his thesis) at the very outset of his gospel and all that follows is confirmation and illustration of it.

The phrase should not, however, be made to stand alone. As Nineham indicates,[6] the concern of the whole introductory section (verses 1–11) is to establish Jesus' identity and credentials. One way in which this is done is by describing the relationship between Jesus and John the Baptist. John, for all his eminence, is only the forerunner of Jesus. At one level, the difference is merely functional: 'I baptise you with water, but he will baptise you with the Holy Spirit' (Mk. 1:8). But the difference is also ontological: 'After me will come one more powerful than I' (Mk. 1:7). This difference in status becomes even more apparent when we ponder the significance of Mark's quoting Malachi 3:1. In the original context, Yahweh himself is the Coming One, and Mark's application of the passage (and the title) to Jesus is a clear indication of the unique position he conceives Jesus as occupying.

Jesus' identity and credentials are asserted equally clearly, but more dramatically, in the story of his baptism. Not only is he then visibly anointed with the Holy Spirit, but he is attested as God's Son (and Servant) by the Voice from heaven: 'You are my Son, whom I love; with you I am well pleased' (Mk 1:11). Clearly, Mark is not allowing the deity of Christ to emerge only gradually from his narrative. He is ensuring that the reader, in his very first encounter with Jesus, is left in no doubt as to his being from above. He is also indicating, of course, that Jesus himself entered upon his work already possessing the assurance that God was, in a unique sense, his Father.

The birth narratives

When we come to the gospels of Matthew and Luke we encounter 'Christology from above' in a very special form: the story of the virgin conception. The birth of Jesus was perfectly normal. The narratives do not indicate virginity in birth (there is no mention of the absence of the usual pains of parturition, for example). Even less do they imply that Mary remained ever a virgin (*semper virgo*). They teach simply that Mary became pregnant without sexual intercourse. In Matthew's Gospel, this is expressed in the words, 'before they came together' (*prin ē synelthein autous*), that is, before the marriage was consummated. Joseph's reaction was natural: he resolved to divorce her. In a generous attempt to lessen Mary's humiliation, however, he planned to do it quietly (Mt.1:19). At this stage the angel of the Lord intervened to dissuade him: 'do not be afraid to take Mary home as your wife, because what is conceived in her is from the Holy Spirit' (Mt. 1:20). The virgin conception is affirmed later in verse 25: 'he [Joseph] had no union with her until she gave birth to a son'. The words *ouk eginōsken autēn* ('had no union with her') clearly imply that he had no sexual intercourse with her prior to the birth. The words 'until [*heōs*] she gave birth' equally clearly imply that he did afterwards. Verse 25 is also interesting, because it informs us that it was Joseph who 'called his name Jesus'. As Cranfield points out, to name the child was to accept him as his own son.[7] It was an act of adoption, conferring on Jesus all the rights of legitimate sonship.

Matthew sees the birth of Jesus as a fulfilment of Isaiah 7:14: 'The virgin [*'almâ*] will be with child and will give birth to a son, and will call him Immanuel.' According to the lexicographers, the Hebrew word *'almâ* means not strictly a virgin but a young, unmarried woman.[8] The point is rather academic since young, unmarried women would be expected to be virgins. If they were not, their prospects of marriage would be seriously compromised (Dt. 22:13ff.). The translators of the Septuagint certainly understood *'almâ* to mean 'virgin' (in Greek, *parthenos*). Indeed all the Jewish Greek versions rendered it *parthenos* until Aquila (*c.* 130 AD), who used *neanis* ('young woman') instead. We can be confident, however, that Aquila was driven by a concern to deprive Christians of a proof text.[9]

Several comments may be made on Matthew's use of Isaiah 7:14.

First, whatever the merits of Matthew's exegesis, his assertion of the virgin birth is quite independent of it. Isaiah 7:14 may be difficult to interpret. Matthew 1:18, 25 are not.

Secondly, Matthew cannot be accused of trying to accommodate the truth to the expectations of his readers. The Jews never applied Isaiah 7:14 to the Messiah: not even after the Septuagint had rendered *'almâ* by *parthenos*.

Thirdly, it is difficult to understand why, if Matthew simply wanted to invent a spectacular birth for the Lord, he should have sought inspiration in such an obscure and difficult passage as Isaiah 7:14. There were other more obvious Old Testament sources, such as the birth of Samuel (1 Sa. 1:1–20) and the birth of Isaac (Gn. 21:1–7; *cf.* Romans 4:18ff.). The motif of barrenness, which is prominent in both of these narratives, also occurs in the story of John the Baptist. The motif was hallowed by the fact that the Jewish nation owed its very existence to a miracle related to this very affliction and if Matthew had merely wanted an apologetical lever, this was the theme to go for.

Finally, while Isaiah 7:14f. contains enough problems to drive any exegete to distraction, the reference to a miraculous birth is probably the one certainty in the passage. The natural meaning of *'almâ* points this way. So does the whole context. The birth was to be a sign (verses 11, 14). It is difficult to see how a birth from 'a young woman' (RSV) could effect this. A sign required some unusual circumstance: and what more unusual than that the child should be born from one who was an *'almâ/parthenos* in the natural meaning of these terms?

Luke's account of the birth of Christ is not significantly different from

Matthew's. It retains even his Jewish flavour. More attention is given to the response and attitude of Mary and there is a firmer emphasis on the glory of her Son: he is the Son of the Most High and the Son of David (Lk. 1:32); the ruler of an eternal kingdom (1:33); and the Son of God (1:35). But the core of the message remains the same: when she became pregnant, Mary was not Joseph's wife, but only his betrothed; and she was still a virgin (1:27). Her pregnancy is an act of divine grace, explicable not in terms of human insemination (nor of a mythical act of divine begetting) but in terms of the creative power of the Holy Spirit.

For centuries, this doctrine was accepted unquestioningly by Christians. It figured prominently in the early creeds and in the doctrinal standard of the Greek, Roman and Protestant churches. In 1892, however, a German pastor named Schrempf refused to use the Apostles' Creed in baptism because it affirmed this article, and during the twentieth century even relatively conservative theologians have dismissed it as legendary. Hans Küng, for example, writes: 'Today it is admitted, even by Catholic exegetes, that these stories are a collection of largely uncertain, mutually contradictory, strongly legendary and ultimately theologically motivated narratives.'[10] Emil Brunner sees the virgin birth as an attempt to turn a miracle of salvation into a metaphysical problem: 'the existential question: What took place? is turned into the inquisitive enquiry: How did it take place? From the very outset to ask how it is possible that God should become man is a wrong question.'[11] Wolfhart Pannenberg sees it as a legend which emerged in circles of the Hellenistic Jewish community and which, so far as its content is concerned, 'stands in an irreconcilable contradiction to the Christology of the incarnation of the pre-existent Son of God found in Paul and John'.[12] Edward Schillebeeckx appears to share the basic standpoint of Brunner: 'What we have here is a theological reflection, not a supply of new informative data, as the New Testament texts themselves show quite clearly.'[13] Nearer home, William Barclay regards the evidence as inconclusive and declares: 'The supreme problem of the virgin birth is that it does quite undeniably differentiate Jesus from all men; it does leave us with an incomplete incarnation.'[14] John Robinson is predictably decisive, arguing that the doctrine of the virgin birth and the doctrine of pre-existence are alternative and mutually exclusive ways of speaking about Christ. We cannot speak of them both; neither can be taken literally, or descriptively; and each is so misleading as to be unusable today.[15]

These denials are supported by several lines of argument.

Difficulties in the birth narratives

First, there are objections to the actual narratives themselves. The most important of these are directed against Luke's account. It is claimed, for example, that this story contains two quite different concepts of the divine sonship. According to verse 32, the sonship is linked to the Messianic kingship: he is Son because he is Messiah. According to verse 35, however, the sonship is linked to the miraculous conception. He is Son because he is born by the power of the Most High.

It is difficult to see any inconsistency between the two views. The Davidic sonship is surely no more incompatible with the divine sonship than it is incompatible with his being David's Lord. To invoke the idea that verses 32f. and 34f. represent two different sources is a desperate expedient. It is reasonable to assume that any discrepancy would have been as obvious to Luke as to modern scholars: and certainly difficult to believe that something so obvious would have taken 2,000 years to discover.

More serious is the problem presented by verse 34 itself: '"How will this be," Mary asked the angel, "since I am a virgin?"' She was betrothed to Joseph: why should she have thought a pregnancy so unlikely? To claim that her words indicate a previous vow of perpetual virginity is to introduce an idea utterly alien to the context (and to the entire New Testament). In any case, if she had made such a vow why was she betrothed? On the other hand, to claim that Mary understood the angel to be referring to an immediate conception is also precarious. The words of verse 31 contain no indication of time. There is nothing in them to make Mary rule out the thought of her becoming pregnant *after* her marriage (which was still in the future).

Why then her question and its implied surprise? It is unnecessary to assume that it is merely a literary device of Luke's giving an opportunity to introduce the angel's prophecy.[16] The most likely explanation is simply that at the time Mary was not thinking clearly. The subject, after all, was not the kind she would normally discuss; the being addressing her was an angel; and the news he had given her was a bombshell. In fact, throughout Scripture, few people appear to have been able to think (or speak) clearly when visited by angels. In Luke 1:12, Zechariah is said to have been *troubled* (RSV). John (Rev. 22:9) instinctively falls at the feet of his heavenly visitor, mistakenly offering him worship. Mary's mental state, when she spoke, was probably akin to that of Peter on the Mount of Transfiguration, when he blurted out, '"Let us put up three shelters" – one for you, one for Moses and one for Elijah." (He did not know what he was saying.)' (Lk. 9:33). Mary has not been listening all that attentively; she has not put the various bits of information together logically; and the one thing registering in her mind is that it is strange to be talking about children when she is not yet married.

The silence of the rest of the New Testament

The second line of objection is more formidable: that outside the birth narratives of Matthew and Luke, the rest of the New Testament is silent about the virgin birth and shows no interest in it whatsoever.

Few scholars would deny the facts upon which this objection proceeds. There are, at the most, only three New Testament passages in which even the most zealous would find allusions to the virgin birth.

The first of these is John 1:13. The commonly accepted text of this verse reads, 'children born not of natural descent, nor of human decision or a husband's will, but born of God'. Some manuscripts of the Old Latin, however, had a different reading, applying the words to Christ and, more particularly, to his birth: 'who *was* born not of natural descent ... but of God.' This reading was favoured by Tertullian and appears in some of the patristic quotations of the passage. For all that, however, the manuscript evidence for it is hopelessly inadequate and even such a staunch defender of the virgin birth as J. G. Machen concludes, 'We are not inclined to lay any great stress upon John 1:13 as a testimony to the virgin birth of Christ.'[17]

The same might be said of Galatians 4:4: 'God sent his Son, born of a woman, born under law'. It is highly unlikely that the phrase 'born of a woman' points to anything special in the birth of our Lord. It occurs, for example, in Matthew 11:11, 'Among those born of women there has not risen anyone greater than John the Baptist.' We find it, too, in Job 14:1: 'Man born of woman is of few days and full of trouble.' These passages strongly suggest that nothing is implied in Galatians 4:4 beyond the fact that our Lord had a true, human mother.

It is worth noting, however, that there is a significant difference in wording between Galatians 4:4 and the apparent parallels. In both Matthew 11:11 and Job 14:1, the word used is 'born' (*gennētos*). In Galatians 4:4 the word is *genomenos* ('become'). The variation suggests a point to which we shall return later: even while not explicitly asserting the virgin birth, the New Testament writers describe the Lord's advent into the world in terms which are highly unusual. In the meantime, suffice it to say that if Paul had wanted to avoid contradicting the doctrine of the virgin birth, he could not have chosen his language more felicitously than he does in Galatians 4:4.

The third passage is Romans 1:3, which declares that Christ was, according to the flesh, the Son of David. In the genealogies of Matthew and Luke, this descent is traced, not through Mary, but through Joseph. It would be hasty, however, to conclude that this palpably contradicts the virgin birth. If it did, the evangelists themselves would surely have spotted it. Apart altogether from the possibility that Mary herself belonged to the house of David, Joseph had adopted Jesus as his own son and thus placed him legally within the Davidic line. Furthermore, here, as in Galatians 4:4, Paul uses the verb *ginesthai* ('to become') rather than *gennasthai* ('to be born'). As C. E. B. Cranfield points out, this may reflect Paul's knowledge of the tradition of the virgin birth.[18] His language is certainly fully consonant with it: and very difficult to account for otherwise.

The fact remains, however, that apart from the birth narratives of Matthew and Luke, the New Testament makes no explicit reference to the virgin birth. But that is far from being as damning as it looks.

Firstly, the New Testament nowhere contradicts or denies the virgin birth.

Secondly, the stories of Matthew and Luke are the only accounts we possess of the birth and infancy of our Lord. At this rate, the miraculous conception receives 100% attestation from the available records.

Thirdly, John is silent, not only about the virgin birth but also about such incidents as the temptation, the transfiguration, the last supper and the agony in the garden. He probably saw no point in duplicating the accounts of these events given in the synoptic gospels, and his silence on the virgin birth can be explained by the same consideration. After all, he does say that if he had written down all he knew, the world could not contain all the books he would have had to write (Jn. 21:25).

Fourthly, if the story of the virgin birth were legendary, John, writing thirty or forty years afterwards, would surely have denied it and set the record straight. He does not hesitate to correct other erroneous traditions (such as that Jesus had said that John himself would not die, Jn. 21:23). He would have been even more likely to correct a story involving the risk of scandal to Mary, for whom he had a special responsibility (Jn. 19:27). This would have been reinforced by the fact that on the face of things the virgin birth seemed to qualify and limit the humanity of the Lord and thus to play into the hands of those heretics who denied that Christ had come in the flesh (1 Jn. 4:2).

So far as Paul is concerned, it is worth remembering that he was Luke's travelling companion and that it is highly unlikely that there would be any fundamental divergencies in the traditions they proclaimed. It is also very unsafe to assume that if Paul believed something, or knew of something, he was therefore bound to mention it. In fact, he is very sparing in his references to details in Jesus' life. For example, he never mentions either Joseph or Mary. Does this mean that he knew nothing of Jesus' parents (or denies that they existed)? He is equally silent on the baptism, the temptation, the transfiguration and Gethsemane. He mentions none of the parables or miracles of Christ. The only reason he mentions the Lord's Supper is that special problems had arisen in connection with it in the church at Corinth: problems which could be resolved only by recalling the precise words and actions used by Jesus in instituting it. No problem ever arose requiring allusion to the virgin birth and that is probably the total explanation of the apostle's silence on the matter.

Yet his silence is not uncomplicated and one has the impression more than once that the virgin birth is at the back of Paul's mind, imposing its own contours on the way he writes. As James Orr points out, 'There is hardly an allusion to Christ's entrance into our humanity in the Epistles which is not marked by some significant peculiarity of expression.'[19] As we look at the language of Romans 1:3, Galatians 4:4 and Philippians 2:7 (being made, *genomenos*, in the likeness of men), it is only natural to ask, 'Is this how one is accustomed to speak of a natural birth?'[20]

Three further points may be made.

First, of all the evangelists, Luke is the most self-conscious historiographer. His preface indicates that he had access to written sources and to the eye-witness accounts of those who had been with the Lord from the beginning. It also brings out that he himself had 'carefully investigated everything' and that his concern was to present an orderly account which would confirm to Theophilus the truth of the things he had heard. It is difficult to believe that, having said that, he would proceed immediately to deal in legends. He was obviously not credulous, and was unlikely to practise deliberate deception. He must have been personally convinced that the tradition of the virgin birth was well attested.

Secondly, in the very nature of the case, the virgin conception would have been a closely guarded secret. At the time of Jesus' birth, Mary and Joseph were among strangers and suspicions that the child had been conceived out of wedlock would have been unlikely to arise. Psychologically, Mary would obviously have been reluctant to discuss the details with any but her closest friends. The details were too intimate and potentially embarrassing. We are told more than once that Mary kept these things to herself. This would largely explain the church's silence. Few would know the truth, and on the rough mission-fields of the empire few of those who did would have thought it wise to proclaim it.

Thirdly, in some ways the fact that the rest of the New Testament is silent is an argument in favour of the doctrine put forward by Matthew and Luke. It shows that, like the title 'Son of Man' and the phrase 'the kingdom of God' the doctrine of the virgin birth did not figure in the preaching of the early church. Obviously, then, Matthew and Luke were not simply reading back the message of the Christian community into the earlier history. Nor, as we have seen, did the doctrine have any apologetic value. There was no Jewish expectation that the Messiah would be born of a virgin (as there was that he would be the Son of David). The only motive for recording such a doctrine was that they believed it to be true; and they recorded it even though it was open to gross misunderstanding by pagans and to refutation by people like John who were in a position to know the truth.

Theologically motivated?

The third line of objection to the virgin birth is that it is theologically motivated. The birth narratives reflect not the truth but a desire to provide an explanation for calling Jesus the Son of God. Indeed, according to Küng[21] Luke says so himself: 'therefore the child to be born will be called holy, the Son of God' (1:35, RSV).

It might be said, in response, that a man is not telling a lie simply because he is giving an explanation. If Jesus was Son of God, some explanation was appropriate and the virgin birth (along with later concepts such as eternal generation) might be part of that explanation. Jesus was Son of God by eternal generation and by the resurrection and by the virgin birth. A comprehensive Christology would have to do justice to all those elements.

On the other hand, it may be that what Luke is doing is not explaining the sonship by the virgin birth, but the virgin birth by the sonship. Like many another believer, he may be facing the questions, Why the virgin birth? What is its significance? and replying, It is a sign of the sonship of Christ: a unique form of entrance into human life, consonant with his unique divine standing.

It is also worth noting that Luke's explanation of Christ's sonship is given in terms of the Holy Spirit. There is no emphasis on the absence of human paternity; nor on the activity of God the Father. In fact, one has the impression of a studied avoidance of any language which might suggest that Mary's child was *begotten* by God. Luke uses the language of creation, not of generation: 'The Holy Spirit will come upon you, and the power of the Most High will overshadow you.' The result is not so much that the child is the Son of God as that he is 'holy' (verse 35).

The objection is put in a slightly different form by Emil Brunner: 'The idea of a parthenogenesis is an attempt to explain the miracle of the Incarnation.'[22] Curiously, however, the narrative has made the exactly opposite impression on some scholars. James D. G. Dunn, for example, regards the Christology of the birth narratives as inconsistent with the doctrine of the incarnation, which implies the pre-existence of Christ.[23]

Assuming, however, that Luke is at least consistent with the incarnation, it is very difficult to believe that he is arbitrarily putting forward a theory as to how it occurred. He was not working in a vacuum. Apart from anything else, he had to consider the feelings of Mary, and this alone would have made it impossible to give free rein to his imagination. Besides, as an explanation of the incarnation, the doctrine of the virgin birth is a complete failure. It is itself as big a mystery as what it sets out to explain. Even after the birth narratives we are still asking, How did the Holy Spirit come upon her? How did the power of the Most High overshadow her? These questions are not essentially different from, How did he become incarnate?

There is no need to believe that Matthew and Luke wrote what they did for any other reason than that they believed that that was how things actually happened.

Theologically untenable?

Critics of the virgin birth have not been content, however, to argue that the birth narratives are theologically motivated. They have gone on to say that the doctrine itself is theologically untenable. This argument has taken more than one form.

According to some scholars, the virgin birth is inconsistent with the pre-existence of Christ. Dunn, for example, claims that the birth narratives portray the virgin conception as 'Jesus' origin, as the begetting (= becoming) of Jesus to be God's Son'.[24] A little later he writes to the same effect: 'It is a begetting, a becoming which is in view, the coming into existence of one who will be called, and will in fact be, the Son of God, not the transition of a pre-existent being to become the soul of a human baby or the metamorphosis of a divine being into a human foetus.'[25] Pannenberg, as we saw, takes the same position: the virgin birth is inconsistent with the idea of the incarnation of a pre-existent being.[26]

We should note, however, that the birth narratives, especially

Matthew's, contain clear hints of the absolute deity of Christ. He is called *Immanuel* ('God with us') in Matthew 1:23. The name 'Jesus', too, is significant. The important point here is not the etymology ('Jehovah saves'): too many Jewish boys carried this name to allow us to build a theory on this fact alone. What is important is the statement in Matthew 1:21 that those he saves are *his own* people. Matthew's assumption is the same as Mark's who, at the beginning of his gospel portrays the advent of Christ as the fulfilling of the Old Testament prophecy that the Lord (Jehovah) would come to *his* temple (Mk. 1:3).

Moreover, the most that can be said against the birth narratives is that they do not specifically teach the pre-existence of Christ. They do not deny it; nor do they teach anything inconsistent with it. Why should we expect the evangelists to cram the whole of their Christology into every single reference to Jesus? Besides, any statement about the Lord's human existence can be made to appear inconsistent with his deity if detached from its theological context. No New Testament writer has a higher Christology than the writer to the Hebrews. Yet he proclaims Christ as tempted (Heb. 4:15), learning obedience (5:8) and tasting death (2:9). On the face of it no person of whom these things are true could be divine. Nor could one simultaneously be the Son of God and be born of a woman (Gal. 4:4). According to Matthew, Jesus, the King of the Jews, was born; according to Luke, the Son of God was born. Sixteen hundred years passed before anyone began to suspect that there was something in these words incompatible with the Christology of Chalcedon.

Emil Brunner raises a different theological objection: the virgin birth is inconsistent with the genuine humanity of Christ (we cannot but notice in passing how mutually contradictory the various objections are: one critic sees the doctrine as inconsistent with pre-existent deity, another regards it as incompatible with real manhood). The particular point which Brunner has in view is that procreation by a human father is part of what it means to be a man: 'The Son of God', he writes, 'assumed the whole of humanity; thus he took on himself all that lies within the sphere of space and time. Procreation through the two sexes forms part of human life.'[27]

Here, Brunner is guilty of a procedure he often condemns in others: making an *a priori* assumption as to what, in God's judgment, would constitute a genuine incarnation. As he sees it, God could become incarnate only by means of human procreation. But this can never be more than an assumption: and one far too flimsy to justify a Christian theologian repudiating the clear teaching of Scripture. Furthermore, what, on Brunner's assumptions, are we to make of Adam and Eve? They were not procreated by union between the sexes. Brunner, of course, does not accept the historicity of Adam. Even so, the first man, whoever he was, could not have come into existence through an act of sexual intercourse between two human beings.

Besides, Brunner's argument has been overtaken by events. Artificial insemination and *in vitro* fertilization have eliminated the need for sexual intercourse. Ectogenesis may eliminate ordinary gestation; and cell division may one day replace ovum and sperm. Whatever the ethical merits of these procedures they completely nullify the argument that ordinary procreation is essential to genuine humanness. The decisive question is whether the cell or gene is a human one. How it came into existence is immaterial.

Brunner also offers another argument, almost beguilingly attractive. The Son of God must have entered the world in an unworthy way; and the virgin birth, by denying this, is docetic. 'Even his origin had neither form nor beauty. It also took place in the form of a servant.'[28]

Here again, Brunner is imposing his own logic on the divine procedure. Everything must have an anti-Docetic motif. Everything that is 'not unworthy' must be eliminated including, surely, the voice from heaven heard at baptism, the transfiguration, the miracles and even the resurrection itself. What is the point of avoiding the Scylla of Docetism if we end up in the Charybdis of Arianism? In any case, the birth narratives do not tend consistently in the direction of exalting Jesus. Not only do they highlight his humble origins and poor circumstances, but they raise, almost unnecessarily, the scandal that his birth was premature and that Joseph was not his father. Furthermore, the miraculous birth itself is offensive to many, although if it were absent from the narrative, many of the very scholars who now object to it would then be objecting to its omission. How, they would be asking, could one who was born in the ordinary way of ordinary human parents be the Son of God? The truth is, man will always find God's procedure offensive.

The doctrine of the virgin birth is indubitably taught by Matthew and Luke, and the birth narratives were an integral part of these gospels from the very first. Brunner attempts to discount this with a cheap jibe: 'In earlier days this discussion used to be cut short by saying briefly, "It is written"; that is with the aid of the doctrine of verbal inspiration. Today we can no longer do this, even if we would.'[29] This is totally unfair. What is at stake here is not verbal inspiration, but canonicity. The issue does not hang on textual and exegetical minutiae but on two substantial blocks of biblical teaching dealing with matters purely theological and propounding a message whose essential meaning is beyond dispute. Even minimal respect for the authority of Scripture should command respect for this doctrine, or at least preclude the contemptuous tones in which too many Christians allow themselves to speak of it.

The theological significance of the virgin birth

Assuming it to be true, however, what is the theological significance of the virgin birth? It may, of course, be true and have no significance beyond itself. But many theologians have argued that important theological issues are involved in its affirmation or denial.

Karl Barth, for example, has argued persuasively that the virgin birth has a special status as a sign: 'It is the sign which accompanies and indicates the mystery of the incarnation of the Son, marking it off as a mystery from all the beginnings of other human existence.'[30] In an earlier volume he had spoken of the virgin birth as the negative side of the miracle of Christmas, the sign of the inconceivable,[31] and concluded: 'The Virgin Birth at the opening and the empty tomb at the close of Jesus' life bear witness that this life is in fact marked off from all the rest of human life, and marked off, in the first instance, not by our understanding or our interpretation, but by itself.'[32]

Barth's position harmonizes well with several aspects of biblical teaching. For example, the idea of a sign is important in connection with the resurrection. This is clear from such a passage as Acts 17:31: 'he has fixed a day on which he will judge the world in righteousness, by a man whom he has appointed, and of this he has given assurance to all men by raising him from the dead' (RSV). It is also hinted at (though no more than that) in Romans 1:4: 'declared with power to be the Son of God, by his resurrection from the dead'.

On a broader front, the concept of sign was also important in connection with miracles in general. They were not only mighty acts (*dynameis*) and wonders (*terata*), but also signs (*sēmeia*). The precise function they performed in this connection is indicated in Acts 2:22 (RSV): 'Jesus of Nazareth, a man attested to you by God with mighty works and wonders and signs, which God did through him in your midst.' The miracles attested Jesus as God's man.

So far as the virgin birth itself is concerned, the prophecy of Isaiah 7:14 spoke unmistakably of a sign: 'Therefore the Lord himself will give you a sign. Behold, a young woman shall conceive and bear a son'

(RSV). The miraculous birth showed that God was still with his people.

Clearly, then, Barth is pursuing a valid biblical theme. But to what is the sign of the virgin birth pointing?

First, it is highlighting the essentially supernatural character of Jesus and the gospel. Alluding to Barth again,[33] the virgin birth is posted on guard at the door of the mystery of Christmas; and none of us must think of hurrying past it. It stands on the threshold of the New Testament, blatantly supernatural, defying our rationalism, informing us that all that follows belongs to the same order as itself and that if we find it offensive there is no point in proceeding further. If our faith staggers at the virgin birth what is it going to make of the feeding of the five thousand, the stilling of the tempest, the raising of Lazarus, the transfiguration, the resurrection and, above all, the astonishing self-consciousness of Jesus? The virgin birth is God's gracious declaration, at the very outset of the gospel, that the act of faith is a legitimate *sacrificium intellectus*. 'It eliminates', writes Barth, 'the last surviving possibility of understanding the *vere deus vere homo* intellectually. It leaves only the spiritual understanding, that is the understanding in which God's own work is seen in God's own light.'[34]

Secondly, the virgin birth is a sign of God's judgment on human nature. The race needs a redeemer, but cannot itself produce one: not by its own decision or desire, not by the processes of education and civilization, not as a precipitate of its own evolution. The redeemer must come from outside. Here, as elsewhere, 'all things are of God'. He provides the lamb (Gn. 22:8). Barth is exactly right: 'Human nature possesses no capacity for becoming the human nature of Jesus Christ.'[35]

Thirdly, the virgin birth is a sign that Jesus Christ is a new beginning. He is not a development from anything that has gone before. He is a divine intrusion: the last, great, culminating eruption of the power of God into the plight of man: 'Man is involved only in the form of non-willing, non-achieving, non-creative, non-sovereign man, only in the form of man who can merely receive, merely be ready, merely let something be done to and with himself.'[36]

There are two areas, however, where the virgin birth is more than a sign and where in fact it appears to be part of the internal logic of the doctrines themselves. These are the divine sonship of Christ and the sinlessness of Christ. Indeed, Luke himself explicitly connects these doctrines with the virgin birth:

> The Holy Spirit will come upon you,
> and the power of the Most High will overshadow you;

> therefore the child to be born [of you] will be called holy,
> the Son of God.
>
> (Lk. 1:35, RSV)

It is difficult to lay down, dogmatically, that there could be no incarnation without a virgin birth. What we can say, however, is that there would be something profoundly incongruous in a non-miraculous advent. In Hebrews 2:10, the writer speaks of the fittingness of the Captain of Salvation being made perfect through sufferings. There is surely a similar fittingness in the manner of our Lord's birth as described by Matthew and Luke.

Is it possible to define more exactly the incongruities involved in an incarnation which was the result of normal sexual intercourse? Three points suggest themselves.

First, it would be very difficult to avoid some form of adoptionism because on this construction God would make the human nature of Christ his own only after it had been brought into existence by some other agency. According to the doctrine of the virgin conception, however, the human nature of Christ does not exist for a single moment except as the humanity of God. It never *becomes* God's human nature. It comes into existence united to God.

Secondly, refutation of the virgin birth would mean that the Lord had a double paternity: a divine Father, God; and a human father, Joseph. This is not impossible, but it is incongruous and seems to be studiously avoided by the New Testament, as in Luke 3:23 (RSV): 'being the son (as was supposed) of Joseph'. In fact, the difficulty is felt by many of those who deny the virgin birth, since they often proceed to deny the pre-existence and divine personality of Christ as well. Dismissal of the virgin birth is seldom the end of an individual's theological pilgrimage.

Thirdly, without the virgin birth, the incarnation becomes a matter of mere human initiative. Let us recall John 1:13: 'who were born, not of blood nor of the will of the flesh nor of the will of man, but of God' (RSV). We have already seen that this passage cannot be cited as direct evidence for the virgin birth, but it is difficult to disagree with Abraham Kuyper when he writes: 'John undoubtedly borrowed this glorious description of our higher birth from the extraordinary act of God which scintillates in the conception and birth of Christ.'[37] At the very least, we must concede that in the act of incarnation God moves with the same freedom and independence as he enjoys in the work of the new birth. There, dependence on the will of man is expressly excluded. It would be incongruous to yield more to it in the delicate area of incarnation.

Furthermore, there can be no doubt that the birth narratives relate Jesus' divine sonship to the fact that God was involved in a peculiarly direct and intimate way in the creation of his humanity. To deny the virgin birth and introduce instead human sexual activity is to distance God unacceptably from the production of the Holy One (Lk. 1:35).

When it comes to the connection between the virgin birth and the sinlessness of Jesus, we must proceed with care. The New Testament never sets forth the miraculous conception as an explanation for his sinlessness. Nor would the elimination of the male factor in the conception of our Lord by itself explain his sinlessness. Mary, too, was sinful (unless we accept the Roman Catholic dogma of the immaculate conception) and there is no evidence that sin is transmitted only through the male. Moreover, Mary's own behaviour at the point of the annunciation and conception cannot be deemed sinless. When we have said all we can about Mary's faith and submissiveness and acquiescence to the will of God, we have to go on to admit that her response (even her passivity) was a human one and, as such, tainted. 'All our righteous acts are like filthy rags' (Is. 64:6). Besides, elements in Mary's subsequent behaviour make it clear that she remained largely uncomprehending (Lk. 2:48ff.) and this should warn us against speaking too glibly of the faith which served as the human matrix to the divine promise.

Nor can we allow ourselves to think that the transmission of sin is linked to the libidinousness of the sex act itself. Augustine rejoiced that 'the conception was not according to the law of sinful flesh (in other words, not by the excitement of carnal concupiscence)'.[38] And there have always been strands in the Christian tradition which have regarded the sexual act as itself sinful and virginity as specially virtuous. But none of this owes very much to the teaching of Scripture, and in this area, at least, Barth is a safer guide than Augustine:

> It is not as if virginity as a human possibility constitutes the point of connection for divine grace ... The sinful life of sex is excluded as the source of the human existence of Jesus Christ, not because of the nature of sexual life, nor because of its sinfulness, but because every natural generation is the work of willing, achieving, creating, sovereign man.[39]

Yet, the virgin birth does shed significant light on the sinlessness of Christ.

It does so, first of all, by emphasizing the role of the Holy Spirit. There are, however, difficulties in the way this has usually been formulated in orthodox theology. Almost invariably those who treat the subject speak of Christ's human nature being sanctified or purified by the Holy Spirit. The idea is at least as old as Augustine: 'For what he took of flesh, he either cleansed in order to take it, or cleansed by taking it.'[40] Calvin spoke in the same vein: 'we make Christ free of all stain not just because he was begotten of his mother without copulation with man, but because he was sanctified by the Spirit that the generation might be pure and undefiled as would have been true before Adam's fall'.[41] This became the standard way of explaining the Lord's sinlessness.[42]

The motive behind such language, obviously, is to find some way around the difficulty arising from the sinfulness of the Virgin herself. That is perfectly laudable; and one hesitates to confront such a formidable battery of theological talent. But there are questions to be asked. What was sanctified, and when? Was it the unfertilized ovum? Surely not. It makes little sense to speak of sanctifying a piece of tissue. Was it the fertilized ovum: the foetus itself? It seems impossible to speak of this being sanctified without implying that prior to such sanctification it was impure or sinful. That this leads us into serious theological trouble is clear from Shedd, probably the most forceful advocate of the idea that Christ's human nature was sanctified in its conception. Shedd finds himself having to argue that Christ's human nature was *justified* as well: and justified on the grounds of the atonement. 'Christ's human nature', he writes, 'was both justified and sanctified before (*sic*) it was assumed into union with the Logos; justified proleptically, as were the Old Testament saints, on the ground of an atonement yet to be made.'[43] There is a similar statement a few pages later:

> Any nature that requires sanctification requires justification; because sin is guilt as well as pollution. The Logos could not unite with a human nature taken from the Virgin Mary, and transmitted from Adam, unless it had previously been delivered from both the condemnation and the power of sin.[44]

These are hair-raising statements, which not only suggest that the humanity of Christ existed for a time un-united to the *Logos*, but even portray the Lord as standing in need of his own atonement.

It seems best to avoid altogether language which involves us in such difficulties. We need say no more than that the humanity of Christ was created by the Holy Spirit, rather than procreated by sexual intercourse, and that as such it partook of the essential character of all that God creates: it was very good. If the emphasis falls upon the divine creativity then any sinfulness adhering to the humanity of Christ would have to be attributed to the Holy Spirit, its Creator, which is unthinkable. The only refinement it would be wise to add is to speak of the Lord's holiness as con-created. This would mean that it was given in and with the creation of the humanness itself. Just as God made the first man upright, even though he was formed from the dust of the ground (Gn. 2:7), so he makes the Last Man upright, even though he was born from a sinful mother.

The second connection between the virgin birth and the sinlessness of Christ is that it helps us understand how Christ can stand outside the guilt of Adam. As Abraham Kuyper points out, 'everything depends upon the question whether the original guilt of Adam was imputed also to the man, Christ Jesus'.[45] Assuming for the present the doctrine of Adamic guilt as defined in traditional dogmatics, it is clear that such guilt was not imputed to Christ. The only factor available to help us understand this immunity is the virgin birth. Adam begot a son in his own image (Gn. 5:3). But Adam did not beget Christ. The Lord's existence has nothing to do with Adamic desire or Adamic initiative. As we have already seen, Christ is new. He is from outside. He is not a derivative from, or a branch of, Adam. He is parallel to the first man, a new departure, and as such not involved in the guilt which runs in the original stream. In saying this, however, we must not forget that he voluntarily assumed this guilt, laying hold of it (Heb. 2:16). Even here, however, the language of Hebrews relates Christ not to the *seed of Adam*, but to the *seed of Abraham*.

The argument that there is some connection between the virgin birth and the sinlessness of Christ is reinforced by the fact that a sinless humanity is impossible without a miracle. The first man was holy because God made him so; the new man (the Christian) is holy because God makes him so; the Last Man is holy because God makes him so. Holiness can exist in human life only by virtue of divine action and so far as Jesus Christ is concerned that action occurs in the very commencement of his existence.

Positive roles

Expositions of the virgin birth can easily degenerate into mere negatives, as if the doctrine involved only the exclusion of human paternity. In fact it also involves highly positive roles for both Mary and the Holy Spirit.

Dealing first with the role of the Holy Spirit, the language of Luke 1:35 is highly significant: 'the power of the Most High will *overshadow* you'. The verb *episkiazein* is reminiscent of the transfiguration when a cloud came and *overshadowed* them (Lk. 9:34, RSV). Like the clouds of Sinai (Ex. 24:15) and the clouds of the *parousia*, it suggests theophanic presence. It also reminds us that although the conception of Christ was miraculous it is not inexplicable. It is explained by the power of the Holy Spirit, just as the existence of the cosmos itself is explained by the fact that the Holy Spirit moved on the face of the waters (Gn. 1:2). One thing is carefully avoided, however: any suggestion that the Holy Spirit was Jesus' Father or that his birth was the result of sexual union between Mary and the deity. Christ's human nature was not *begotten* from the essence of God, but created from the substance of the Virgin. If we may reverently probe a little further, we may say that an ordinary ovum, produced in the ordinary way, was miraculously fertilized by the power and benediction of the Spirit. John of Damascus[46] was therefore correct, if a little quaint, when he described Mary's ear (her believing response) as the bodily organ of the miraculous conception.

In the interests of accuracy, and to avoid misunderstanding, it would be better to avoid speaking of God as Father of the human nature of Christ. It is probably not even helpful to speak of him as Father of the divine nature. He is the Father of the Eternal Person, the Son of God. Since Christ does not change or renounce his identity when he becomes flesh, God is the Father of the incarnate Son as well as of the pre-existent Son. But he is not the *Father* of his human nature. He is its *Creator*.

Mary's role, too, was a positive one. Christ's humanness was created not *ex nihilo* but *ex Maria*: of her substance.[47] She contributed to him exactly what any human mother contributes to her child: ovum, genes, ordinary foetal development and ordinary parturition. He was, in an entirely proper sense, 'the fruit of her womb' (Lk. 1:42, RSV). There is no reason, wrote John Pearson, to deny to Mary, 'whatsoever is given to other mothers in relation to the fruit of their womb; no more is left to be attributed to the Spirit than what is necessary to cause the Virgin to perform the actions of a mother'.[48]

Mary's contribution did not end with the birth. She provided the home, the environment and the nurture within which Jesus grew up and may well have had to do so as a single parent. The total lack of reference to Joseph during the public ministry strongly suggests that by that time he had died. Under his mother's care, Jesus grew physically, intellectually, socially and spiritually (Lk. 2:52), and even though at times she was uncomprehending, her loyalty to him never faltered. She was with him to the end (Jn. 19:26), and her love, support and early guidance contributed inestimably to making him the man he was. That does not mean that she merits adoration. But she does deserve our gratitude

2

THE PRE-EXISTENCE OF CHRIST

The pre-existence of Christ is clearly affirmed in the Nicene Creed: he was 'begotten of the Father before all worlds'. The doctrine clearly implies that originally Christ was not like us; that he came to be like us only by voluntarily sharing our life; that, as the particular individual he was, he existed before creation; and that his existence as a man was continuous with his earlier existence as a heavenly being.

Pre-existence in John

During the twentieth century this doctrine has been strongly challenged even from within the church itself. But there is one thing on which most are agreed: the doctrine is taught in the Gospel of John. We encounter it in the Prologue and indeed in the opening words: 'In the beginning was the Word.' The verb is significant. *Was* contrasts with *became* (in verse 14). The Word never *became* in the sense of coming into being. He simply *was*. John uses the imperfect tense (again, note the contrast with the aorist of verse 14) to indicate not so much the continuousness as the open-endedness of this state of existence. It corresponds to the *I am* of John 8:58 ('before Abraham was born, I am') and to the *ho ōn* ('the Being One', Rev. 1:8) of the Apocalypse. It is interesting, too, that John links this (surely not accidentally) to the opening words of Genesis, 'In the beginning'. He clearly wants to stress that, 'In the beginning', when everything created came into being, the Word did not come into being. He already was in being.

In the remainder of John's Gospel there are frequent allusions to the pre-existence of Christ. In John 8:57–58, for example, the Jews challenge Jesus: 'You are not yet fifty years old, and you have seen Abraham!' Jesus replies that he has seen Abraham, because 'before Abraham was born [*genesthai*], I am [*egō eimi*]!' The present tense is remarkable, both because it emphasizes the ageless open-endedness of Christ's existence and because it brings out the continuity between his incarnate life and his pre-incarnate past. It also relates him most strikingly to 'the God of your fathers' who, when Moses enquired as to his name, replied, 'I am who I am. This is what you are to say to the Israelites: "*I AM* has sent me to you"' (Ex. 3:14).

That Jesus would have made such a public claim to divinity is dismissed as highly unlikely by many scholars.[1] However, surely some such claim is necessary to explain the crucifixion? Jesus must have said and taught something deeply offensive to the Jewish rulers: something that singled him out as more than a mere social or political reformer. According to Mark 16:62 he was condemned for blasphemy. To Jewish ears, such words as those of John 8:58 would certainly come into that category.

The best window we have into Jesus' own self-consciousness is the prayer of John 17. It has a special intimacy both because of the circumstances (on the threshold of Calvary) and because of the company (none present but the disciples). For our present purpose the most striking words are those of verse 5: 'And now, Father, glorify me in your presence with the glory I had with you before the world began.' The doctrine of Jesus' pre-existence shines through these words unambiguously. Jesus had glory before the world was: and he had it in the presence of the Father (*para soi*, 'with you'). His prayer is that he will return to the position he enjoyed before the incarnation.[2]

There are also the Son of Man sayings in John. In two of these the idea of pre-existence is strongly asserted. One is John 3:13, 'No-one has ever gone into heaven except the one who came from heaven – the Son of Man [who is in heaven].' Even if, with some editors, we omit the last clause, the position is clear: the Son of Man is present on earth only because he has come down from heaven. The other relevant Son of Man saying is John 6:62: 'What if you see the Son of Man ascend to where he was before!' The thought here is similar to John 17:5. The ascension does not mean access to a new and unknown kind of existence, but a return to what the Lord had been familiar with before.

One of the few writers to question whether John really taught the personal pre-existence of Christ is John A. T. Robinson. The essence of his argument is that, for all John's stress on Jesus' otherness, 'the language he uses to designate Christ in his profoundest relationship to the Father is the *same* language that he applies in a weaker and more general sense to men in general'.[3] For example, the idea of 'coming into the world' is used identically of Jesus, 'the prophet', the Messiah and 'every man'. The designation 'of God' (*para theou*) applies not only to Jesus but to 'anyone who is devout and obeys [God's] will' (Jn. 9:31–33, NEB). The designation *Son of God* ought to apply to every man: and even the designation *gods* was applied by the Old Testament to some men (Ps. 82:6).

But this is very special pleading. The language John uses of Jesus, says Robinson, is the same in *a weaker and more general sense* as he uses of man universally. How much *weaker and more general* can it be before it ceases to be the same? Furthermore, the examples cited are highly selective. Robinson omits nearly all the classical proofs of pre-existence. Of which other man does John say that he was in the beginning, that he was with God and that he was God? Or that he made the world and had glory with the Father before the world was? On which human lips does he place the words of the eternal *I AM*? Of which human being does he say that he descended from heaven and after death would ascend to where he was before? Certainly, John uses exceedingly exalted language of believers, as indeed does Paul. But the key to such language in both instances is not ontological equality but the principle of *koinōnia* ('fellowship').

There is, in reality, little room to doubt that the Gospel of John teaches the pre-existence of Christ and traces that doctrine back to Jesus' own self-consciousness. But how credible is John's testimony? 'Can we assume', asks Dunn, 'that John's intention was to give these various expressions as utterances of the historical Jesus?'[4] Dunn is sceptical: the classical Christology of H. P. Liddon[5] depended on the fourth gospel 'to a critical degree', but the work of Strauss and Baur made such a reliance impossible (except for a few benighted conservatives). According to Dunn, because of its patently theological character the fourth gospel is hopelessly suspect as a straightforward historical source: 'It would be verging on the irresponsible to use the Johannine testimony on Jesus' divine sonship in an attempt to uncover the self-consciousness of Jesus himself.'[6]

There is of course nothing unusual, by today's standards, in Dunn's position. It is the current orthodoxy. But we must not ignore its implications. The fourth gospel is canonical and has been accepted as canonical from the first. Furthermore, its authority was never challenged in the early church, although, as J. B. Lightfoot pointed out, it made life difficult for orthodox and heretic alike 'because the language of this gospel has a very intimate bearing on numberless theological controversies which started up in the second, third and fourth centuries of the Christian era: and it was therefore the direct interest of one party or other to deny the apostolic authority, if they had any grounds for doing so'.[7] Dunn himself is a fine example of Lightfoot's principle. He has a theological and academic interest in denying the validity (or at least the primitiveness) of the doctrine of pre-existence. The Gospel of John stands in his way and its evidence must be got rid of. Dunn therefore dares to do what none dared in the early church. He makes no explicit denial of John's canonicity. But the implicit denial is emphatic: it is irresponsible to rely on John. One must surely ask: If it is irresponsible for a Christian theologian to rely on the unambiguous witness of an indisputably canonical book, what criterion is left?

But even this is not the full extent of the problem. There can be no doubt that the fourth gospel exercised a momentous influence on subsequent Christology. The link between it and Nicea and Chalcedon is a very direct one. Nor is this merely a matter of dogma. John's Gospel had an equal influence on Christian life and devotion. Here discipleship found the greatest extant utterances on the divine love. Dunn is aware of all this: 'In a real sense the history of theological controversy is the history of the church's attempt to come to terms with John's christology.'[8] Yet Dunn also contends that 'the weightier Johannine sayings are a development from the earlier tradition *at best tangential to the earlier tradition*'.[9] If tangential at best, what at worst? Does he mean that throughout the last two thousand years the church, in trying to come to terms with John's Christology, has been going off at a tangent? Is he saying that we must roll the theological carpet back all the way to Chalcedon, pass beyond it through John's Gospel to the Christology of Mary Magdalene and begin all over again?

The impression is too often given that Liddon's classic, *The Divinity of our Lord,* was born out of due time, rendered immediately obsolete by the rise of modern critical scholarship, just as the Caledonian Canal was by the advent of the great steamships. Certainly, Liddon speaks with 'majestic certainty'.[10] But this is not because he was unaware of the issues or because he was pre-critical. His Bampton Lectures were delivered in 1866, thirty-one years after Strauss' *Life of Jesus* (1835, ET 1846) and nineteen years after F. C. Baur's *Kritishe Untersuchungen Uber Die Kanonische Evangelien* (Tubingen, 1847). Liddon was fully aware of the position taken by these scholars on the fourth gospel and observed perceptively that St John's Gospel had become the battlefield of the New Testament.[11] He also observed that,

> it is no question of mere *dilettante* criticism that is at stake when the authenticity of St. John's Gospel is challenged. The point of this momentous enquiry lies close to the very heart of the creed of Christendom ... For St. John's Gospel is the most conspicuous written attestation to the Godhead of Him whose claims upon mankind can hardly be surveyed without passion, whether it be the passion of adoring love, or the passion of vehement and determined enmity.[12]

Which, being interpreted, means: It is only because 'the elemental powers of the universe' (Gal. 4:9, my translation) know full well the strategic importance of the fourth gospel that they have concentrated their attack upon it.

Within the limits of his lecture programme Liddon met Strauss and Baur competently on their own ground. Five years later, Britain's greatest New Testament scholar, J. B. Lightfoot, delivered a magisterial lecture on *Internal Evidence for the Authenticity and Genuineness of St. John's Gospel.*[13] The abiding value of Lightfoot's contribution is that he shows, even to the point of over-kill, that John was no 'unearthed theologian'. His gospel abounds in historical, biographical, geographical and topographical details. Lightfoot concludes: 'The evangelist is not floating in the clouds of theological speculations. Though with his eye he peers into the mysteries of the unseen, his foot is planted in the solid ground of external fact.'[14] This point of view has commanded growing support, represented by C. H. Dodd's study, *Historical Tradition in the Fourth Gospel,*[15] J. A. T. Robinson's posthumously published Bampton Lectures,[16] and on a lesser scale by Robinson's essay, *His Witness is True: A Test of the Johannine Claim.*[17]

John clearly had an interest in facts, clearly thought they were important and clearly intended to relate them. *A priori,* we should expect this attitude to spill over into his recording of the words of

Christ. A man who wants to give the precise location of Gethsemane, the precise identity of those who arrested Jesus, the precise time it took to build the temple and the precise timing of the crucifixion is not lightly going to invent words to put into the mouth of the One he regards as the Truth.

Dunn, of course, is not unaware of more conservative trends in biblical scholarship. He is hospitable to the idea that the fourth gospel was written prior to AD 70 and fully aware of 'the renewal of interest in the Fourth Gospel as a historical source for the ministry of Jesus'.[18] But he is still not prepared to admit that what we find in John is authentic tradition, or at least authentic reflections of the self-consciousness of Jesus.

There are two reasons for his position. First, there is, he says, a vast difference of style between the teaching of the synoptics and the discourses recorded by John. But are these differences really surprising? Matthew and Luke deliberately used the work of their predecessors, and this left little room for either to exercise originality. John, however, deliberately chooses to cover different ground, focusing on the Jerusalem ministry and on Jesus' discourses, rather than on the outward events of his ministry. These discourses themselves had a different audience (Jerusalem rabbis and the intimate circle of disciples) from that which witnessed the Galilean ministry; and they were delivered in Aramaic, which John would have had to translate (without the help of predecessors). Above all, John had to compress and condense them, and he would have done so according to his own intention and situation, against the background of his own preaching and within the limitations of his own personality. The summary would be as much his as Matthew's summary of the Sermon on the Mount or Mark's précis of the Little Apocalypse (Mk. 13:5–37). But this is not the same as saying that new ideas such as pre-existence and claims to deity could be placed on the lips of the Lord. Such ideas would not represent an evolution of Jesus' thought, or even be merely tangential to it, as Dunn suggests. They would revolutionize it and make John a false witness. In the abstract, of course, scholarship may come to that very conclusion. But the Christian church cannot: at least not while retaining the Gospel of John in its canon.

Dunn argues, secondly, that there is a complete lack of real parallels in the earlier tradition to John's insistence on a pre-existent divine sonship. In other words, the doctrine of pre-existence does not appear in the Pauline epistles, in Peter or James, in the synoptic gospels or even in the epistle to the Hebrews.

We must be clear as to the implications of Dunn's contention. A rapid inventory of texts traditionally deemed to teach the doctrine of pre-existence includes the following: Matthew 18:11; 20:28; Mark 1:1–3; 12:1ff.; Romans 8:3; 1 Corinthians 10:4; 2 Corinthians 8:8; Galatians 4:4; Philippians 2:6; Colossians 1:15–17; 1 Timothy 1:15; 3:16; 2 Timothy 1:10; Hebrews 1:1–14; 7:3 and 1 Peter 1:20. This is an impressive catena, clearly suggesting that the strength of the doctrine lies not merely in individual texts, but in the cumulative force of the evidence. Dunn's approach to these passages is highly problematical. For one thing, he attacks each one in isolation from the others. More seriously, he appears to be applying an untenable hermeneutic. Focusing not on the natural, but on the necessary meaning he asks, 'Could the words *possibly* bear another meaning?' and answers, in every instance, 'Yes!' The dangers of this approach become apparent immediately when we look at the phraseology in which Dunn expresses his conclusions: 'it may indeed be the case'; 'Peter may well mean'; '*phanerousthai* may well be used here in the sense …'; 'perhaps the thought is simply'.[19] Earlier (p. 47), we have such statements as, 'Mark left his account open to the interpretation'.

If we were to apply such canons of interpretation to everyday statements, we would quickly find ourselves enmeshed in absurdity. Take, for example, the proposition, 'Scotland beat England at Hampden.' Its natural meaning (to us) is that Scotland's soccer team scored a victory over England's soccer team at Hampden Park, Glasgow. But that is not its necessary meaning. It may well mean something else. It 'leaves itself open to other interpretations', especially if each word is isolated and the passage interpreted atomistically. *Scotland* may mean the Scottish army, the Scottish hockey team or the Scottish ladies' bowls team. *Beat* may mean *beat with sticks*. And *Hampden* may be a scribal error for *hampton*: which in turn may be an abbreviation for Hampton Court, Southampton or Northampton. We might therefore conclude that the original statement 'may well mean' that the Scottish ladies' bowls team beat the English hockey team with sticks at Northampton.

The only way to avoid such absurdities (especially in interpreting documents from which we are separated by enormous linguistic, cultural and historical barriers) is to insist that words must bear their natural, not their necessary, meaning and that sentences and paragraphs must be interpreted holistically, not atomistically. The spectacle of a Christian scholar building his own case by pointing out minute verbal ambiguities in every one of sixteen arguments which have moulded the faith and worship of the church for two thousand years is neither convincing nor edifying.

Another problem is Dunn's use of the concept, 'the first century context of meaning'. His argument here is that in the thought-world of the first century such designations as *Son of God, Son of Man* and *Spirit of God* never indicated a personal, pre-existent redeemer and therefore cannot bear that meaning when applied to Christ. There is a typical instance of this kind of logic in Dunn's discussion of Galatians 4:4:[20] 'Paul has no intention here of arguing a particular Christological position or claim, incarnation or otherwise.' Why? Because there is little precedent for such an idea of incarnation. Indeed, there is a surprising absence in 'the first century context of meaning' of the idea of a Son of God or divine individual who descends from heaven to earth to redeem men. Consequently, if Paul had intended to teach a doctrine of incarnation, this would have been a radical new departure which would have been (a) impossible for a Jew and (b) unintelligible to his hearers.

But can we seriously entertain the suggestion that Christology can rise no higher than its first-century context of meaning, that it must contain nothing radical and nothing strange to the hearers' ears, that the Son of Man in the synoptics can mean no more than it does in IV Esdras, that *Spirit* cannot transcend its meaning in Wisdom and that *Son of God* cannot rise above its significance in Philo and Josephus? This is surely nonsense. All the divine titles are transformed when applied to Christ. Besides, the gospel is in its very nature a *mystery*. It is not something already present in the hearers' culture and environment, but something new and astonishing: good news which almost defies belief. Does Paul himself not exclaim,

> No eye has seen,
> no ear has heard,
> no mind has conceived
> what God has prepared for those who love him.
>
> (1 Cor. 2:9)

And surely, too, the very reason that the Jews crucified Christ and the Athenians mocked the gospel and the Empire persecuted the church was that Christianity so manifestly transcended its first-century context of meaning?

Pre-existence in Hebrews

If we turn to the pre-Johannine tradition in more detail, the best starting-point is the teaching of the epistle to the Hebrews, especially

Hebrews 1:1ff. and Hebrews 7:3, supplemented by Hebrews 2:9 and Hebrews 10:5. Whether or not the doctrine of Christ's pre-existence is true, it is very difficult to believe that it is not taught in these passages. Christ is a Son (without the definite article, Heb. 1:1), not in the same sense as the prophets, but in a sense that sets him apart and alone. Furthermore, he is the One through whom God made the world, not in this case *ton kosmon* but *tous aiōnas* ('the ages', Heb. 1:2): it is difficult to escape the conclusion that the One through whom the successive ages of history were called into being himself existed before these ages. In Hebrews 1:10, in a quotation from Psalm 102, the Son is described as the One who established the earth (and therefore pre-dated it); and in Hebrews 1:3, the present participles *ōn* ('being') and *pherōn* ('sustaining') strongly suggest the unending continuousness, if not quite the eternalness, of the Son's existence and activity.

Turning to Hebrews 2:9, what is interesting is the way it speaks of (lit.) Christ 'having been made lower' than the angels. That, clearly, was not his natural or original status. In Hebrews 7:3, it is not Christ but Melchizedek who is directly in view. However, Melchizedek is said (lit.) 'to be made like' (*aphōmoiōmenos*) the Son of God. The historical Melchizedek ante-dates the historical Jesus by many centuries: yet Christ is the pattern for Melchizedek, not *vice versa*. This 'being made like' must include being 'without beginning of days' as surely as it does his 'ever living' (*pantote zōn*, Heb. 7:25).

Dunn recognizes the force of such passages, conceding that 'Hebrews describes Christ as God's Son in language which seems to denote pre-existence more clearly than anything we have met so far'.[21] But he has a ready explanation. This language of apparent pre-existence has to be set in the context of its writer's indebtedness to Platonic idealism, and interpreted with cross reference to the way in which Philo treats the *Logos*: 'What we may have to accept (*sic*) is that the author of Hebrews ultimately has in mind an *ideal* pre-existence, the existence of an idea in the mind of God, his divine intention for the last days.'[22] This is surely highly unlikely. We have little evidence that the writer to the Hebrews had any contact with Platonism, and none at all of any indebtedness. Verbal parallels are not proof of literary dependence, far less of ideological identity. Besides, what sense would it make to substitute 'an idea in the mind of God' for *the Son* in Hebrews 1 and 2? Did God in these last days speak to us through an idea in his own mind? As G. W. H. Lampe points out, in Hebrews and John the pre-existent *Logos*/Wisdom, although not explicitly said to be a person, is identified with the personal figure of the historical Jesus, whose personality is then retrojected upon the hypostatized *Logos*/Wisdom.[23] Lampe probably intends this as a criticism, but the perception itself is accurate enough. The pre-existent Son of Hebrews 1:1 is the very same person who cried to God with strong crying and tears (Heb. 5:7); and in his pre-existent state he is as personal as the God with whom he is compared and the prophets with whom he is contrasted.

Pre-existence in Paul

When we turn to the Pauline writings we are not conscious of entering a world any different from that of John and Hebrews. He might well have said in this connection what he said in another, 'those men added nothing to my message' (Gal. 2:6). His Christology is as high as theirs and at least equally emphatic in its assertion of Jesus' pre-existence.

Probably the most important single passage is Galatians 4:4, 'But when the time had fully come, God sent his Son, born of a woman, born under law, to redeem those under law.' These words appear to be saying the same thing as Cecil Francis Alexander:

He came down to earth from heaven,
Who is God and Lord of all.

Christ was God's Son before his mission and was despatched as God's delegate and representative. Dunn objects, however, that the verb *exapesteilen* ('sent forth') is ambiguous and implies nothing as to the origin and status of the one sent. Angels were sent. Moses, Gideon and the prophets were sent. He writes:

> It is evident from this that *exapesteilen* when used of God does not tell us anything about the origin or point of departure of the one sent; it underlines the heavenly origin of his commissioning but not of the one commissioned. So far as its use in Galatians 4:4 is concerned, therefore, all we can say is that Paul's readers would most probably think simply of one sent by divine commission.[24]

But is there not some confusion here? It is indeed true that *exapesteilen* is commonly used in later Greek of any kind of mission and that we therefore cannot tell from the verb itself whether the person sent was prince or pauper, god, ambassador or postman. However, that is not the point at issue. The question is not whether Christ was God before he was sent but whether he existed before he was sent. It is very difficult to find an instance of *exapesteilen* referring to a birth, and the instances cited by Dunn do not really help his case. The angels existed before they were sent. So did Moses, Gideon and the prophets. There is a presumption in favour of the same being true of Christ. He is sent forth as one who already has being, not as one who comes into being by being sent.

There is an even more important issue, however. Dunn himself raises the question, 'Would the fact that it was *his Son* who was sent not resolve the ambiguity of the verb?' Unfortunately, he does not give any satisfactory answer. Yet the idea of a special relationship between Jesus and God is no isolated occurrence confined to this passage alone. It occurs, for example, in two other passages in Paul: Romans 8:3 and 8:32.

In Romans 8:3, he writes, 'For what the law was powerless to do in that it was weakened by the sinful nature, God did by sending his own Son in the likeness of sinful man to be a sin offering.' The passage has two interesting peculiarities. First, Paul is not content to say *his Son* but his *own* Son ('the Son of himself'), emphasizing the special intimacy of the bond between him and the Father. The emphasis would be practically meaningless if the bond did not exist before he was sent. Secondly, Paul says that God sent him forth *in the likeness of sinful man*. This refers, of course, to the Lord's humanness. But why refer to it at all? Aren't we all sent forth in flesh? And why express it in such an extraordinary way: 'in *the likeness* of sinful man? Clearly, there was a felt need to say that Jesus was human. Equally clearly, there was a need to define very precisely the kind of humanity he actually possessed. All this is fully consonant with his uniqueness as pre-existent and divine; and very difficult to explain without it.

Romans 8:32 reads: 'He who did not spare his own Son, but gave him up for us all – how will he not also, along with him, graciously give us all things?' Whatever the precise meaning of *not sparing* and *delivering*, one thing is clear: there was a very special relationship between the Father and the Son. He was *his own Son*, so precious that if he did not withhold him, then, *a fortiori*, he would withhold nothing. In fact the language here is strongly reminiscent of John 3:16, 'God gave his only begotten Son' (KJV).

This brings home very forcibly the gravity of the issues involved in denial of the pre-existence of Christ. The glory of God the Father's loving initiative is the greatest theme of the New Testament. The supreme manifestation of that love is the giving, sending and sacrificing of his Son: but it depends for all its force on the special relationship between Christ and the Father. This is why in both John 3:16 and Romans 8:32 the writers use language reminiscent of Abraham sacrificing Isaac: 'Take your son, your only son, Isaac, whom you love' (Gn. 22:2). The whole marvel of the Patriarch's devotion lies in the unique preciousness of Isaac, and the whole marvel of Calvary, considered (as it must be) as an act of God the Father, lies in the unique preciousness of Christ. The *sending* is immeasurably diminished if there was no love before. The *delivering up* loses most of its majesty if the relationship between 'father' and 'son' was of only a few years' standing. Calvary might still stand out as a monument to the heroism of Christ, but it would cease to speak to us of the Father's love. Curious as it may sound, John 3:16 and Romans 8:32 depend for all their force on the *homoousios* ('one substance') of Nicea. According to Nicea God gave up his Own. According to those who deny the pre-existence, God gave up Another.

Our next classical Pauline text on the pre-existence is 2 Corinthians 8:9: 'For you know the grace of our Lord Jesus Christ, that though he was rich, yet for your sakes he became poor.' These words have a clear practical concern. The motive to liberality is what Christ did *for you* (*di hymas*, for your sake): he made himself poor. He *was* rich, precisely as God is rich, in glory (Phil. 4:19). But he *made himself* poor. This was not a gradual process, but a decisive moment, signified by the aorist tense. As applied merely to the historical Christ this makes no sense. When was the post-nativity Christ rich? 'He was not like Moses, who renounced the luxury of the palace in order to serve his brethren; he never had any earthly riches to renounce.'[25] What Paul is saying is that whereas for the Christian prior poverty gives way to riches, for Christ prior riches gave way to poverty. Moreover, this understanding of Jesus' mission is no novelty to the Corinthian Christians. It is something with which they are perfectly familiar: 'For *you know* the grace of our Lord Jesus Christ ...'

In Colossians 1:15ff. we are back in the atmosphere of John 1:1–4 and Hebrews 1:2–4 with their emphasis on the pre-temporal cosmic significance of the Lord. This is all the more remarkable if, as some scholars argue, the passage is a pre-Pauline hymn. It would then reflect primitive Christian tradition even more directly.

The key statement is verse 17, 'He is before all things.' Paul does not say *was* but *is* (*estin*). In form, at least, this is exactly similar to John 8:58, 'Before Abraham was, I am (*egō eimi*)'. It is difficult to believe that by the phrase *before all things* superiority of rank rather than priority of existence is intended. The natural way to express superiority would not have been *pro pantōn* but *epi pantōn* (Rom. 9:5; Eph. 4:6) or *hyperanō pantōn* (Eph. 1:21; 4:10) or *hyper panta* (Eph. 1:22). Besides, the preceding context makes plain that Paul had pre-existence in mind: 'by him all things were created ... all things were created by him and for him'. If everything that was created was created by him, then manifestly he himself was not created.

But what about the words of verse 15: 'He is ... the firstborn over all creation'? Do they not suggest that Christ was a creature, albeit the earliest? The words were certainly put to this use by Arians in support of their doctrine that 'there was when he was not' (*ēn pote ouk ēn*). It should be borne in mind, however, that Paul (or whoever the original author was) does not say *prōtoktistos* ('first-created') but *prōtotokos* ('first-born'). Furthermore, the Septuagint had used *prōtotokos* in Psalm 89:27, 'I will also appoint him my firstborn' and, as a result, *prōtotokos*, used absolutely, had become a recognized Messianic title.[26] This had been facilitated by its application to Israel in, for example, Exodus 4:22, 'Israel is my firstborn son'.

The strongest suggestion in the title *prōtotokos* is primogeniture (in fact, the Vulgate translates it *primogenitus*), which in turn carries with it the ideas of sovereignty over the household and the right to the inheritance. The idea of sovereignty is already linked with the word in Psalm 89:27, 'I will also appoint him my first-born, the most exalted of the kings of the earth.' In Hebrews 1:2 the divine sonship is clearly linked to inheritance and in Hebrews 12:23 all the people of God are subsumed under the designation 'the church of the firstborn'. In the Christian community every member has rights of primogeniture: we are 'heirs of God and co-heirs with Christ' (Rom. 8:17). It is worth noting, too, that both Lightfoot[27] and Bruce[28] are able to cite two instances from a Rabbinic source where the title *prōtotokos* is given to God himself, and where there can certainly be no thought of portraying God as part (even the first part) of the world.

Pre-existence in the synoptic gospels

The synoptic gospels are less explicit about the pre-existence of Christ than the Pauline epistles, and this is something of a puzzle. We must remember the following, however: that the gospels do not represent an earlier phase of tradition than, say, Galatians; that they portray Christ in terms of deeds rather than of propositions; and that no formal distinction can be drawn between deity and pre-existence. The synoptics contain abundant evidence of the former and it surely implies the latter.

The evidence we do have for pre-existence is fourfold.

First, there is the use of the title *Lord*, especially in such passages as Mark 1:2–3. Here John is represented as the forerunner of the *Lord*, but Mark intensifies the force of the whole statement by representing it as a fulfilment of Malachi 3:1 and Isaiah 40:3. In the former passage, it is Yahweh himself who comes as the messenger of the covenant. In the latter, it is for Yahweh that the way must be prepared. If Mark saw Christ as the *Lord* (as the One who was coming to his own temple), then surely he saw him as one who existed prior to his coming?

The second piece of evidence is the implications of the claim, 'The time has come. The kingdom of God is near' (Mk. 1:15). The connection between Jesus and the kingdom is an intimate one: so much so that we can even say that the only reason the kingdom has come is that in Jesus the King himself has come. There is nothing at all novel in such an interpretation. Cranfield[29] is able to quote Marcion to the effect that, 'In the gospel, Christ himself is the kingdom of God.' Origen expressed himself similarly: 'As he is the wisdom itself and the truth itself, so maybe he is also the kingdom itself.' Cranfield expresses his own view as follows: 'We may actually go so far as to say that the kingdom of God *is* Jesus and that he *is* the kingdom.'[30] Nor does this mean merely that he is the supreme blessing and gift of the kingdom. In the light of Mark 1:2f. it must mean that he is the King. The kingdom has come because the King has come: and the King has come because Yahweh has come. This was what the Old Testament expected:

> Then all the trees of the forest will sing for joy;
> they will sing before the LORD, for he comes,
> he comes to judge the earth.
>
> (Ps. 96:12–13; *cf.* Ps. 98:9)

From this point of view the nativity itself is already a *parousia*, rendered possible only by the pre-existence of Christ.

The third line of synoptic evidence for the pre-existence of Christ is Jesus' use of the title *the Son of Man* as his preferred self-designation.[31] C. F. D. Moule[32] regards the doctrine of the pre-existence of Christ as post-dominical and claims that the idea of pre-existence attached itself to the Son of Man sayings only in the writings of John. There is certainly a degree of explicitness about the Johannine sayings which goes beyond anything in the synoptics. But Moule ignores the possibility that the idea of pre-existence is involved in the very designation itself. By calling himself *the Son of Man,* was Jesus claiming, among other things, pre-existence? This used to be answered with a confident affirmative on the basis that in the *Similitudes of Enoch* the Son of Man is a pre-existent divine figure. George Eldon Ladd, for example, writes: 'In Enoch, the Son of Man is clearly a pre-existent, heavenly (if not divine) being who comes to earth to establish the reign of God. Jesus' very use of the term Son of Man involved an implicit claim to pre-existence.'[33] There is now considerable doubt as to the date of the *Similitudes* and the consensus among scholars appears to be that they are post-Christian.[34] This does not altogether deprive Enoch of evidential value for the time of Christ, but it does make it impossible to argue that Jesus' original hearers would have understood him at once as making the precise claims which appear in the Similitudes.

It still seems safe, however, to argue that the Son of Man sayings must be interpreted in the light of Daniel 7:13ff. If this is so, it has a direct bearing on the question of the teaching of the synoptics as to the pre-existence of Christ, because Daniel's Son of Man is almost certainly a divine figure. He is superhuman (not *a* son of man, but *like* a son of man); he exercises a dominion which is universal and eternal; and he comes 'with the clouds of heaven' (verse 13). As Joyce Baldwin points out, 'a concordance will reveal how frequent is the reference to clouds in connection with the presence of the Lord, not only in the Pentateuch but throughout the Old Testament poetry and prophetic literature'.[35] We might cite as examples the glory of God on Mount Sinai (Ex. 24:16), the pillar of cloud (Nu. 9:16) and the cloud which filled Solomon's temple (1 Ki. 8:10). The symbolism continues in the New Testament in connection with the transfiguration (Mk. 9:7) and the *parousia* (Mk. 14:62). Jesus' returning with the clouds of heaven is synonymous with his returning in the glory of his Father.

If Jesus was *this* Son of Man, then he was royal, superhuman and divine, and the claim to pre-existence is already implicit in these others. Jesus could hardly claim to be a divine Messiah without also claiming to be a pre-existent one.

Certainly the way the gospels speak of the Son of Man is fully consonant with his pre-existence, and almost impossible to explain if it be denied. This is particularly true of two sayings which speak of the Son of Man's coming into the world: Mark 10:45 and Luke 19:10. The former tells us that Christ came, not to be served, but to serve and to give his life a ransom for many. The latter tells us that he came to seek and to save the lost. The point is not simply that the Son of Man is in the world because he came into it (presumably from somewhere else), but that these passages ascribe to him a deliberate intention in coming. He came because he wanted to serve. He came because he wanted to save the lost. Some of the sayings add a further dimension by suggesting, sometimes obliquely, the glory of the state from which he had come. Mark 10:45 itself does this by saying, '*even* the Son of Man'. There is something unexpected and incongruous in the fact that he, of all men, should serve. In fact, in the words attributed to him here, Jesus is making the same practical use of his pre-existent glory as Paul does in Philippians 2:5ff. and 2 Corinthians 8:9: his willingness to forego his own rights and privileges is a model for our Christian *kenōsis* and a rebuke to all our human pretensions.

A similar awareness of the incongruousness of his low earthly condition is reflected in Matthew 8:20 (parallel, Lk. 9:58): 'Foxes have holes and birds of the air have nests, but the Son of Man has nowhere to lay his head.' Again, what is remarkable is that he, of all people, should be homeless:

But thy couch was the sod,
O Thou Son of God
In the deserts of Galilee.[36]

Having said all this, there is a difficulty in relating Christ, in his first advent, to Daniel's vision of the Son of Man. This is that there is no 'coming with clouds'. All the allusions in the gospels relate these to the second coming (for example, Mk. 13:26; 14:62).

Two things may be said in response to this.

First, the nativity and the earthly ministry were not altogether without divine splendour. The nativity is set in the context of the mission of the Forerunner, the visit of the Magi (Mt. 2:1ff.) and the appearance of the angelic multitude (Lk. 2:8–13). The ministry itself receives repeated divine accreditation through the miracles and the Voice from heaven (Mk. 1:11; 9:7). Even on the basis of the synoptic accounts, John's comment would be fully justified: 'We have seen his glory, the glory of the One and Only, who came from the Father' (Jn. 1:14).

Secondly, it is perilous to carry back the distinction between the first and the second advent of Christ into the prophecy of Daniel. To the Old Testament the *parousia* is an undivided whole. It is only in the New Testament that the distinction is formulated, and even then only gradually. The implications of this for our present study are well expressed by Vos:

> If in the hands of our Lord the Messianic advent resolves itself into two instalments, a first and a second appearance, then the general signature of the undivided advent, such as the supernaturalness of the theophonic character and the celestial provenience of the coming, can be indiscriminately applied to either stage, which is not denying, of course, that the features Daniel seized upon may find a more realistic fulfilment in the second stage than in the first.[37]

In his first advent, no less than in his second, Jesus is the Son of Man: and as such a pre-existent heavenly being.

There remains a fourth consideration from the synoptic gospels: the clear assumptions of the parable of the tenants (recorded by all three: Mt. 21:33–46; Mk. 12:1–11; Lk. 20:9–19). Everything in this parable conspires to emphasize the greatness of the rejected Messiah: he is the last to be sent, he is a son not a servant, he is the beloved son, he is the only son and he is the heir. It is because of his greatness that the consequences of rejecting and murdering him are momentous. When Jesus asked, 'When the owner of the vineyard comes, what will he do to those tenants?' the Jews replied: 'He will bring those wretches to a wretched end, and he will rent the vineyard to other tenants, who will give him his share of the crop at harvest time' (Mt. 21:40–41). As Vos points out,[38]

> This answer assumed that nothing more radical would follow than a change of administration; that Caiaphas and his fellows, the Sanhedrists, would be destroyed, and other rulers put in their places, after which the theocracy might go on as before. Jesus corrects this facile assumption; to his mind this answer was utterly inadequate. They had not appreciated the full gravity of the rejection of the Son of God as entailing the complete overthrow of the theocracy, and the rearing from the foundation up of a new structure in which the Son, thus rejected, would receive full vindication and supreme honour: 'Therefore I tell you that the kingdom of God will be taken away from you and given to a people who will produce its fruit' (Mt. 21:43).

The greatness at issue here (the greatness which underlies the gravity of rejecting him) is not merely the greatness of Jesus' messiahship. The messiahship itself rests on something deeper: the sonship. He is Son before he is sent and he is sent because he is Son: 'They will respect my son' (Mt. 21:37). The ideas of pre-existence and sonship belong to the very essence of the story.

The meaning of pre-existence

The doctrine of the pre-existence seems secure enough, then, in its exegetical foundations. But what does it mean? Many scholars have subjected it to radical and reductionist re-interpretation. Foremost among these has been John A. T. Robinson.[39] Robinson begins with the unpromising statement that pre-existence, like messiahship or 'impersonal humanity', is a concept which may in modern times mean nothing. Having said that, however, it appears he is not sure what to do with the concept, because he proceeds to give no fewer than three interpretations of pre-existence.

First, he says the doctrine of pre-existence represents simply an upgrading of the idea of foreordination.[40] Christ pre-existed in the sense that his ministry was part of the deliberate will and plan of God. Robinson neither expounds nor defends this. It is surely obvious, however, that there can be no tension between foreordination and pre-existence. To establish the one is not to disprove the other. The two doctrines, in fact, are sometimes found in close connection in the New Testament. In 1 Peter 1:20, for example, we read that Christ 'was destined before the foundation of the world but was revealed at the end of the ages' (my translation). The safest conclusion with regard to this verse is that it neither affirms nor denies the pre-existence of Christ. So far as its connection with foreordination is concerned, it is clear that throughout the New Testament what is foreordained is not the existence of Christ but his manifestation (1 Pet. 1:20), his cosmic sovereignty (Eph. 1:9–10) and especially his sufferings (Mk. 8:31; Jn. 17:1; Acts 2:22ff.).

Secondly, Robinson offers what can only be called a biological definition of pre-existence. The one kind of pre-existence of which we can be sure, he writes, is that, 'Jesus must have been linked through his biological tissue to the origin of life in this planet and behind that to the whole inorganic process reaching back to the star dust and the hydrogen atom – as much part of "the seamless robe of nature" as any other living thing.'[41] So far as what this statement is *affirming* is concerned, it is perfectly acceptable. As Robinson himself points out, it is explicitly provided for in the New Testament itself, notably in the Lucan genealogy which traces the Lord's physical descent back to Adam. Robinson is saying no more than C. S. Lewis: 'Behind every spermatozoon lies the whole history of the universe: locked within it is no small part of the world's future.'[42] It is what Robinson is *denying* that causes problems. Is this really the *only* kind of pre-existence? As he himself recognizes, his language says nothing of the pre-existence of the individual as such. His sentiments correspond, at the opposite end of the chronological scale, to Shakespeare's words on the post-existence of Julius Caesar:

> *Imperious Caesar, dead, and turned to clay,*
> *Might stop a hole to keep the wind away.*[43]

Could we reduce the New Testament doctrine of the resurrection to that? No more can we reduce the doctrine of the pre-existence to the idea that Christ was present in the star-dust. Was it as a hydrogen-atom that he had glory with the Father before the world was (Jn. 17:5)?

The third approach[44] is more sophisticated. Robinson begins by noting that for us there is hopeless tension between pre-existence and the humanity of Christ. Why? Because of our presuppositions, especially our assumption that what pre-existed was a person. The writers of the New Testament, according to Robinson, felt no such tension, because they did not share our presuppositions. In their view, what became incarnate was not a person, but a life, power or activity which came to embodiment and expression in an individual human being. Christ was the incarnation of divine agency and divine presence and divine glory. But he was not the incarnation of a divine person.

One is tempted to respond to this by saying: This may be true, but it is not what is taught in the New Testament. In the New Testament, Jesus' existence as a man is a continuation of his previous or prior existence as a heavenly being. The Word who dwelt among us is the same as the Word who was with God. The Christ who is found in form as a man is the very one who previously existed in the form of God. The Christ who lives in poverty is the one who, previously, was rich. Besides, while we may properly distinguish between God and his word, power, activity and presence, there is no doubt that in the New Testament those are hypostasized in the persons of the Son and the Spirit. The Son is not only sent; he comes, by his own volition and as the expression of an incomparable altruism. The combination of the volitional and the altruistic surely adds up to the personal?

Anthony Tyrrell Hanson also wishes to reinterpret the doctrine of pre-existence, but his approach is different from Robinson's. In fact, Hanson is sharply critical of Robinson's approach to the New

Testament evidence: 'In each case it seems to me that he has simply failed to take into consideration the evidence that in fact these writers did believe that Christ was a pre-existent divine being.'[45] But although Hanson knows what Paul and John say, he does not feel bound to accept it: 'The evidence that convinced the New Testament writers of his existence does not convince us.'[46] What we must do, he argues, is to retain the intention that lay behind the doctrine of pre-existence, even if we cannot accept it in detail. The doctrine did not originate with Jesus but with the early church. Why did they invent it? To conserve and express the reality of Christ as the revelation of God! If God had revealed himself supremely in Christ, then (thought the early Christians) God must always have been as he is now known in Christ. Consequently, any revelation of God in pre-Christian times must have been a revelation of God-in-Christ. In effect (and in intention) Hanson is demythologizing the doctrine of pre-existence: it represents the prior existence of the self-giving love of God.

It is, of course, true and important that Christ is the revelation of God. But in the New Testament this 'revelational unity' rests on ontological unity. Jesus can say, 'Anyone who has seen me has seen the Father' (Jn. 14:9) only because he can also say, 'I and the Father are one' (Jn. 10:30). Otherwise, Christ reveals God only from the outside, as an observer, and is no more than the last of the prophets: a position which would contradict the point made in Hebrews 1:1, which tells us that God spoke his last word not through a prophet but through a Son. If the ontology is wrong (if the writer is giving a wrong answer to the question, Who is he?), then his whole theology of revelation is also wrong. The true relation of the doctrine of pre-existence to the work of revelation is well expressed by Pannenberg: 'Jesus' revelational unity with the God who is from eternity to eternity forces us conceptually to the thought that Jesus as the Son of God is pre-existent ... If God has revealed himself in Jesus, then Jesus' community with God, his sonship, belongs to eternity.'[47]

Other scholars resist the temptation to demythologize the pre-existence of Christ and instead reject it on theological grounds. Of these grounds, the most common is that it is inconsistent with the humanity of Christ. This is stated with particular force by John Knox: 'Belief in the pre-existence of Jesus is incom-patible with a belief in his genuine normal humanity ... We can have the humanity without the pre-existence and we can have the pre-existence without the humanity. There is absolutely no way of having both.'[48]

Three comments may be made on this.

First, Knox's use of the humanity of Christ as the regulative principle of Christology is unacceptable. For him, it is not enough to preserve the truth of the humanity. He must protect it from all strain and pressure: 'If we should find ourselves having to decide between the pre-existence and a fully authentic human life, there is no doubt what our choice should be.'[49] This is pure dogmatism. There is at least as much justification for making the deity the controlling principle and making a statement exactly opposite to Knox's: 'If we should find ourselves having to decide between the crucifixion and a fully authentic *divine existence*, there is no doubt what our choice should be.' It is surely a tribute to the stress which the early church placed on the Saviour's godhead that the first Christological heresy was denial of the flesh of Christ (Docetism). Knox, of course, knows this perfectly well and even accuses Paul of using the language of Docetism in Philippians 2:7–8 and Romans 8:2: 'We have to recognize the presence in Paul's thought, at least sometimes or in some connections, of a reservation, or misgiving, as to the full genuineness of the humanity of Jesus.'[50] Whether or not this is fair to Paul, it does at least concede that the early church was extremely sensitive with regard to the deity of Christ and far more concerned, at least on the face of things, to avoid straining *it* than to avoid straining the humanity. This is not a matter of mere words. It appears, too, in the practical attitude of the church to Christ. Rightly or wrongly, the early Christians worshipped him. Rightly or wrongly, they called him not *Brother* but *Lord*. These attitudes were utterly central to the church's existence and they reflect a consciousness which put a premium on the Saviour's deity. Against such a background there is no justification whatever for making the humanity the regulative Christological principle, to be protected from all strains and burdens and ruling out in principle every suggestion of transcendence.

Secondly, it is difficult to accept Knox's implicit assumption that there must be complete continuity between Christ's humanness and ours. Commenting on John 17:5 ('glorify me in your presence with the glory I had with you before the world began'), Knox asks, 'Can we imagine a true man's speaking in any such fashion?'[51] A *true* man in this connection presumably means a *mere* man. To which we may retort: Can we imagine a true man saying, 'Come to me, all you who are weary and burdened, and I will give you rest' (Mt. 11:28); or doing and saying any of the things recorded in the gospels? More radically still: Can we imagine the gospels being written about a *mere* man? In fact, even though Knox denies the virgin birth, the sinlessness and the pre-existence, his own Christ is very far from ordinary. 'The reality of the

Logos', he writes, 'was fully present in the Event of which the human life of Jesus was the centre and therefore pre-eminently in that human life itself.'[52] Is this, too, not the language of Docetism? It is certainly not usual to speak of a man's life as the centre of an Event (complete with capital E); and there is certainly nothing ordinary about a man in whom the reality of the *Logos* was fully and pre-eminently present. Knox's religion is putting an intolerable strain on his logic.

Thirdly, Knox's denial of the personal pre-existence of Christ is fatal to the doctrine of the Trinity. He himself would not accept this: 'If one is asked what happens, in such an understanding of the pre-existence, to the Church's doctrine of the Trinity, the answer should be clear: "Nothing at all".'[53] Knox's position is rather curious. He accepts that 'there are grounds for speaking of God the Father, God the Son and God the Holy Ghost as three personal modes or hypostases of the divine being'.[54] He also accepts that it was specifically God the Word who became incarnate in Christ. What he does not accept is that Jesus of Nazareth is identical with the *Logos*. The *Logos* was pre-eminently present in the human life of Christ, but 'without being simply identical with Jesus'. The nett effect of this is to pit the authority of John Knox against that of John the apostle, who explicitly identifies the two. It was the very *Logos* who was with God and who made all things, who, according to John, became flesh, wept at the grave of Lazarus and was crucified on the cross of Calvary. We cannot go half-way down the road with John, borrowing his terminology and a percentage of his teaching. If the Word became flesh, John's credit is secure. If the Word was only pre-eminently present in the human life of Jesus, John's credit is not secure; and if not, we should refrain from making any connection at all between the *Logos* and Jesus. Our 'true' man should be left to enjoy his role as a *mere* man in peace.

Knox even goes the length of saying that, 'If we are intending to speak with any precision at all, we cannot simply identify Jesus, for all his importance, with one of the "persons" of the Trinity.'[55] In the abstract, this may be true. But how the doctrine of the Trinity could survive such a truth it is impossible to conceive. To say that Jesus is not one of the *persons* of the Trinity is to say that he is not the Son of God: and if *he* is not, who is? In fact, it was the problem created by this very identification that made the doctrine of the Trinity necessary. If Jesus is not the Son, there is no evidence that God has any Son or that there is any plurality in the deity. If that is the case, the doctrine of the Trinity can safely be dispensed with.

The point which Knox is trying to make may, of course, be a different one: that the human nature of Jesus can no more be identified with the *Logos* in its totality than the *Logos* himself can be identified with the godhead (*theiotes*) in its totality. This is true. But what creates Knox's problem is his assumption that the human nature is a person. Because he denies the ancient doctrine that the human nature of Christ was either impersonal (*an-hypostatos*) or in-personal (*en-hypostatos*, finding its personal identity in the *Logos*) he has to distinguish between the historical Jesus and the *Logos*, regarding them as separate persons. In terms of classical theology, although the human nature of Christ cannot be identified with the *Logos*, the man Christ Jesus can. The historical Jesus is the *Logos* incarnate.

The most formidable barrage of theological objections, however, comes from G. W. H. Lampe.[56] At some points, unfortunately, it is extremely difficult to follow Lampe's logic. This is particularly true of the argument that belief in the pre-existence of Christ seriously affects the concept of mediation. What he appears to be saying is that as long as mediation is effected through the Spirit (conceived of as 'the outreach of God towards his creation'), it had real directness and immediacy: in contact with the Spirit, we were in contact with God himself. When mediation is through the pre-existent *Logos*, however, the effect is to distance us from God: 'Son suggests a being who is not God himself but who co-exists beside God and acts as God's agent.'[57] Surely, however, denying the pre-existence only makes the problem worse. It effectively reduces the kinship between Christ and God and limits the Son's knowledge of the eternal Father to what he was able to glean in the thirty or so years of a brief life. By contrast, in the New Testament (and in later orthodoxy) the sonship was so defined as to enhance the mediation. To be the Son is to be equal with God (Jn. 5:18). To be the Son means that if one has seen him, then one has seen the Father. To be the Son means that he and the Father are one. These were the statements that lay behind the later doctrine of the *homoousion*: Father and Son are one and the same in being. According to this construction, in Christ the Mediator we are already face to face with God. To appear before Christ's throne is to appear before the divine throne. He is at the heart of the divine monarchy. He even *is* the heart of the divine monarchy. We do not encounter the Word *in* him; we encounter him *as* the Word.

Lampe also argues that the doctrine of the pre-existence makes the Christian doctrine of God inescapably tri-theistic. The reason for this is that once the *Logos* became conceptualized in human terms as Jesus it became plausible to give *person* the full meaning it has in the definition of Boethius: 'an individual substance of a rational nature'. This, says Lampe, is quite incompatible with the unity of God. If the *Logos* is a person in this sense and the Father is a person in the same sense, we must abandon monotheism. Part of the answer to this must be that the identification of Jesus with the *Logos* is already made by the canonical writers (most notably by John) and that if Christian theology is going to sit in judgment on its own canon, then we have the death of Christian theology. Furthermore, the church has always recognized that the doctrine of one God in three persons involved an element of mystery and even of apparent contradiction.

God was one Being. God was three persons. The canon warranted both statements, but it gave no hint as to how they could be harmonized. The church had no right to deny either the one or the other for the sake of coherence, any more than it had the right to deny the divine love because it could not be harmonized with the existence of evil.

Besides, the church has always protested that it does not understand the tri-personalness of God in a way that contradicts his unity. John's personal, pre-existent *Logos* asserts his own deity only in strictly monotheistic terms: 'I and the Father are one' (Jn. 10:30). The Nicene theology does the same. The Father and the Son are not two beings (*ousiai*); they are one and the same being (*homoousios*). It was fundamental to this whole line of thought to draw a distinction between *person* and *essence*. There was a difference between the way God was *one* and the way that he was *three*: he was one in essence, three in persons. So long as that distinction was maintained there was no contradiction in affirming the three-in-one. Admittedly, the church knew that in struggling to express the distinction it was using the word *person* not in order to speak but in order not to be silent.[58] This need not lead, however, to an orgy of humility on the part of theologians. Other disciplines, including the exact sciences, face similar problems. In physics, no less than in theology, much is counter-intuitive. Paul Davies writes,

> Of course, physicists, like everybody else, carry around mental models of atoms, light waves, the expanding universe, electrons, and so on, but the images are often widely inaccurate or misleading. In fact, it may be logically impossible for anyone to be able to accurately visualise certain physical systems, such as atoms, because they contain features that simply do not exist in the world of our experience.[59]

Lampe also claims that pre-existence weakens belief in the

incarnation: it is then not God but his partner we encounter in Jesus. It is difficult to see the force of this. In fact, without pre-existence the idea of incarnation would be impossible. The Son could not *take* flesh if he did not exist. Nor could a nonentity *take* the form of a servant. The subject of the incarnation, whoever he was, must have been pre-existent. Nor is it at all fair to say that pre-existence weakens belief in the incarnation by removing all cultural and social conditioning from the life of our Lord. It is certainly true that Christ came into the world as a divine person with a well-defined personal character and identity. Yet we have no right to dismiss his human experience as of no significance for his personality. Nor can we agree with Lampe when he writes: 'It is a human nature which owes nothing essential to geographical circumstances; it corresponds to nothing in the actual concrete world; Jesus Christ has not, after all, "come in the flesh".'[60] Christ's human nature was not a mere metaphysical abstraction. It had a marked individuality which distinguished it sharply, for example, from that of Peter and John, Judas and Caiphas. It was *his*. Besides, this individuality was not merely given, once for all, in the mystery of his conception. It developed as a result of his experience. He developed his own distinctive vocabulary and teaching methods. He had his own distinct social circle. He had his own highly individual experiences. We have no right to confine these things to his human nature. The Person (the Son of God) is modified by the experiences of the earthly life. The Son of God learns obedience. The Son of God is tempted, suffers and dies. The Son of God learns compassion in the only way that anyone can learn compassion: by experience. In Christ, divine personality is caught up in the process of learning and becoming. We may even say that his experiences are taken up to be part of the meaning of godhead itself. Gethsemane is part of the memory of the triune God.

One further point may be extracted from Lampe's critique. He argues, although not quite in so many words, that the doctrine of pre-existence renders the incarnation virtually mythological: Jesus becomes 'a kind of invader from outer space'; he is seen essentially as 'a superman who voluntarily descends into the world of ordinary mortals'; he is 'an omnipotent spaceman fighting, as it were, with one hand voluntarily kept behind his back'.[61]

The reply to this must be that the New Testament doctrine of the incarnation really has no defence against the charge of appearing mythological. The very idea of being sent inevitably suggests a journey, and the idea of returning to the Father inevitably suggests a flight. The only way this can be avoided is by abandoning the whole idea of incarnation and calling Christianity back from the world of the flesh to the world of ideas. We would then have an ideal incarnation (an inspired man), an ideal atonement (in the heart of God) and an ideal resurrection (the survival of precious memories). Such ideas could not be mocked or caricatured. But then, neither would they constitute Christianity: at least not the Christianity of the New Testament. There, Christ came in the flesh, rose in the flesh and ascended before the gaze of his astonished disciples. Such a Christ can be no more invulnerable to profanity ('Now we have lift-off!') than he was to crucifixion.

But if there are theological objections to the doctrine of pre-existence there is also strong theological support for it. These came particularly from the two most basic affirmations of Christianity.

The first is the post-existence of Christ. According to every strand of the New Testament Christ rose from the dead and this doctrine is perceived by the apostles themselves as the very foundation of Christianity (1 Cor. 15:14f.). Without it, all else is vain and the Christian message is a monstrous falsehood. Furthermore, for the early Christians the risen Jesus had absolute significance. They lived by union with him. From him they derived grace and peace. Their lives were built on him and rooted in him. He was the source and even the content of their salvation. As C. F. D. Moule points out, 'They experienced Jesus himself as in a dimension transcending the human and the temporal.'[62] That being so, Moule has every right to ask: 'If the identity of Jesus of Nazareth is thus retained after his death, in a different dimension and in one to which it is difficult to deny the epithet *eternal*, what are we to say of him before his birth and conception? Can *eternal* personality existing after the incarnation be denied existence before it?'

The second is the deity of Christ. At first sight, the paucity of references to the pre-existence of Christ in the New Testament is remarkable. The same is true in later Christian reflection. But there is an obvious explanation. The pre-existence was not an independent doctrine. It was involved in the deity of Christ (and overshadowed by it). It was on the deity that Christian life and devotion were built, and it was upon the deity, naturally, that opponents concentrated their attacks. On this front, therefore, the church has had to marshal its forces, focusing on the main issue (the deity of Christ) and referring only incidentally to such matters as his pre-existence. Yet the greater truth surely included the lesser. A person who was divine could not but be pre-existent. His godhead proved that he could not have come into being in 4 BC.

3

CHRIST, THE SON OF GOD

The concept of the divine sonship eventually became the dominant one in orthodox Christology. This is probably a fair reflection of its importance in the New Testament itself, but there is considerable variety in the amount of attention devoted to it by individual writers. This will become apparent if we survey the respective contributions of the fourth gospel, the writer to the Hebrews, Paul and, finally, the synoptists.

The Son of God in John

As Oscar Cullmann points out, 'the reserve with which Jesus speaks of his sonship in the synoptics disappears in John'.[1] It is central to his whole purpose, as he himself acknowledges: 'these are written that you may believe that Jesus is the Christ, the Son of God' (Jn. 20:31).

The most distinctive feature of John's contribution is his use of the epithet *monogenēs*. He describes Jesus with this word on five occasions: John 1:14; 1:18; 3:16; 3:18 and 1 John 4:9. This precise usage is unique to John, but there are interesting parallels in the rest of the New Testament. As we shall see, the acknowledgment of Jesus as 'my beloved Son' in the synoptic accounts of the baptism and transfiguration probably echoes the description of Isaac in Genesis 22:2 as 'your only son'. Paul refers to Christ as 'his own Son' (*ton heautou hyion*, Rom. 8:3; *tou idiou hyiou*, Rom. 8:32). In Romans 8:29 and Colossians 1:15, 18 he speaks of him as the 'firstborn' (*prōtotokos*). Even more remarkable is the phrase 'the Son of his love' (my translation), which Paul uses in Colossians 1:13.

Clearly, then, although the phrase *monogenēs hyios* is unique to John, the concept it conveys is not.

But what is that concept? There is little doubt that *monogenēs* expresses the uniqueness of Jesus. He is the only one of his kind. The Old Latin used *unicus* to translate *monogenēs*; and *monogenēs* itself was originally introduced into the Septuagint to translate the Hebrew *yāḥîd*, the basic meaning of which is clearly indicated in, for example, Judges 11:34, where it is applied to the daughter of Jephthah: she was 'his only child'. It is also used in Psalm 25:16 of the solitary sufferer: 'Turn to me and be gracious to me, for I am lonely and afflicted.' Luke uses it of the widow of Nain's son (Lk. 7:12), Jairus' daughter (8:42) and the demoniac boy (9:38). It is also applied to Isaac in Hebrews 11:17: Abraham was ready to offer up 'his only son'. In these instances, *monogenēs* is at least equal to *monos* ('only'). In fact, it usually suggests not only that the person referred to had no brothers or sisters but that his parents never had but this one child.[2] It thus indicates not only ontological but ontogenetic uniqueness.[3]

Is it possible to put some content into this uniqueness? It certainly meant that Jesus was uniquely beloved. This idea is never far away from *monogenēs*. In some ways, indeed, it follows from the very fact of uniqueness. An only son would inevitably be the object of special affection. This is confirmed by the fact that in the Septuagint *monogenēs* is used interchangeably with *agapētos* to translate *yāḥîd*. The most significant instances of this are Genesis 22:2, 12, 16 which consistently describe Isaac as a 'beloved' son. So far as Christ is concerned this same idea is clearly suggested in the acknowledgments 'my beloved Son' and (in Colossians 1:13) 'the Son he loves'. Peter suggests the same idea when he speaks of Christ as 'chosen by God' (1 Pet. 2:4), an epithet which itself echoes Isaiah 42:1 ('my chosen one in whom I delight'). In the Lucan account of the Voice at the transfiguration, the participle *eklelegmenos* alternates with *agapētos* in the manuscript tradition (*cf.* RSV, 'This is my Son, my Chosen', Lk.

9:35). The best English rendering of *eklektos* in such contexts would probably be 'choice'.

This explains why, especially in John, the giving of the Son is seen as the outstanding proof of the love of the Father (Jn. 3:16; 1 Jn. 4:9; *cf.* Rom. 5:8; 8:32). There was a unique bond between the Father and the Son, arising from the fact that the Son was uniquely lovable and the Father was uniquely affectionate. God could not have made a greater sacrifice. His love is astonishing precisely because at this point he put the world before his Son. The statement, 'God gave the world for his Son' would evoke no wonder. The statement, 'God gave his Son for the world' borders on the incredible. Conversely, the Son could not have suffered a greater loss. To have 'lost' the Father, as he did in the dereliction (Mk. 15:34), was the greatest of all possible pains.

But is there a uniqueness more fundamental than that the Son is uniquely loved? Is he uniquely loved because there is something either in the origin of his existence or in the mode of his existence that is unique?

It is extremely doubtful whether *monogenēs* by itself refers to uniqueness of origin. The translations *unigenitus* in the Vulgate and *only begotten* in the KJV probably rest on a misapprehension. Etymologically, *monogenēs* is related not to *gennaō* ('beget') but to *ginomai* ('become') and Raymond Brown is fully justified in commenting that 'there is little Greek justification for the translation of *monogenēs* as "only-begotten"'.[4] This is confirmed by the fact that Isaac, although *yāḥîd*, was not Abraham's 'only-begotten'. Ishmael, too, was Abraham's natural son, others were born to him from his second wife, Keturah (Gn. 25:1), and yet others from his concubines (Gn. 25:6).

The problem, so far as Christology is concerned, lies in the use of the concept of origin itself. The Son is the *Logos* and the *Logos* has no origin. In the beginning, he was already in being. He is the eternal Son. Even when later, post-Nicene theology applied to him the idea of generation, it defined it as 'eternal' generation and poured little conceptual content into it, apart from drawing a sharp distinction between being 'begotten' and being 'made' or 'created'. This is probably as far as we can go. The Son is distinguished from the Spirit in that he is Son; and he is distinguished from other sons (angels and men) in that he alone is eternal and uncreated. Christ is Son by nature, human beings only by adoption. It is doubtful whether *begotten* adds anything to *Son*, apart from laying down that he is Son in a unique way. All the Father's nature is in him (what Paul calls the *plērōma* of godhead, Col.

2:9). Consequently, he is equal with God; which is why, in turn, he is the unique revelation of God. Precisely because he has the likeness of his Father, to see him is to see the Father (Jn. 14:9).

But can we speak of the Son as *monogenēs* from eternity? Or does the epithet apply to him only from the incarnation? Several factors bear on this question.

First, there is the description of Christ as *monogenēs theos* in John 1:18. If he is *monogenēs* as *theos* then, surely, he is *monogenēs* from eternity? This is true whether we render the phrase 'God only-begotten' or 'God the only Son'.

Secondly, there is the language of John 3:16 and its parallel, 1 John 4:9. According to these passages the sending of the Son is the sending of a *monogenēs* and as Geerhardus Vos points out, the idea 'is robbed of its force if the *monogenēs*-filial character is regarded as beginning with the incarnation'.[5]

Thirdly, there is the clear evidence for an eternal sonship afforded throughout John's Gospel. Admittedly, this is not something that Jesus himself habitually emphasized. He contented himself with declaring his present sonship without repeatedly saying, 'Of course, I was eternally Son!' Any such insistence would have been unnatural. Yet the evidence for an eternal sonship is clear enough. It is implied, for example, in John 3:16, where the greatness of God's love lies precisely in the fact that he gave his Son to incarnation, humiliation, pain and death. He was Son at the point of giving; that is, at the point of incarnation (sending). Calvary is the climax of the giving, not its commencement. Equally, the eternity of the sonship lies behind John 17:1, 5: 'Glorify your Son ... with the glory I had with you before the world began.' This clearly implies that his pre-existent glory was a glory he had as Son. John 6:46 speaks to similar effect: 'No-one has seen the Father except the one who is from God; only he has seen the Father.' It is difficult to believe that this refers to some vision enjoyed by Jesus after the incarnation. It is much more natural to take it as referring to something pre-temporal, especially in view of Jesus' description of himself a few verses later as 'the bread that comes down from heaven' (Jn. 6:50). He comes to earth both as the Son and as the bread of life.

The following conclusions, then, seem safe. First, *monogenēs* says nothing about origins because the Son is unoriginated. Secondly, it emphasizes the uniqueness of Jesus' sonship. Thirdly, this uniqueness consists in four things: he is an object of special love, he is the Father's equal, he is the Father's likeness and he is an eternal, not an adopted, Son.

Subordinate?

But does John also portray the Son as subordinate to the Father? Many scholars are convinced that he does. J. M. Creed, for example, writes: 'Even the Prologue to St John, which comes nearest to the Nicene Doctrine, must be read in the light of the pronounced subordinationism of the Gospel as a whole.'[6]

This allegedly subordinationist material is of several kinds. Some passages, for example, convey the impression that the Son possesses only a delegated authority. This is most explicit in John 8:28, 'I do nothing on my own but speak just what the Father has taught me.' Other passages strongly suggest his dependence on the Father. This is implicit in portrayals of him as praying to the Father. It becomes explicit in John 5:19: 'the Son can do nothing by himself'. This passage and its context also describe the Son as simply imitating the Father. The Son can do 'only what he sees his Father doing, because whatever the Father does the Son also does. For the Father loves the Son and shows him all he does.' John 10:18 carries this even further and represents the Son as under authority and acting on orders even in his death and resurrection: 'This command I received from my Father.' According to one interpretation of John 5:26 the Son's very life is a grant from the Father; and John 14:28 appears to make this subordinationism totally explicit when it says, 'the Father is greater than I'.

The first response to this must be that John's Gospel also contains a substantial body of material which points in the opposite direction and equalizes the Son with the Father. As C. H. Dodd points out, 'it is impossible to overstate the extent to which divine powers and prerogatives are exercised by the Son'.[7] This, despite Creed's comment cited above, is obviously clear in the Prologue, which asserts both the eternal pre-existence of the Son and his full participation in the divine being: 'the Word was God'. It also appears in the Epilogue when Thomas responds to the risen Christ with the words, 'My Lord and my God!' In between, we are told that he is equal with God (5:18), that he who has seen him has seen the Father (14:9), that we are to believe in him as we are to believe in God (14:1) and that he and the Father are one (10:30). We also encounter a series of prepositions which define his relationship to God in the most intimate way. He was with (*pros*) the Father, beside (*para*) the Father and even in (*en*) the Father (14:10). With regard to the latter, the indwelling is mutual: the Father is in the Son as surely as the Son is in the Father.

It is the presence of such material that justifies the kind of comment made by C. K. Barrett, namely, that John, more than any other New

Testament writer, lays the foundation for a doctrine of a co-equal Trinity.[8] The presence of subordinationist material should in fact be seen as a tribute to John's historical credibility. It embarrasses his main thesis (the divine grandeur of Christ), yet he resists the temptation to suppress it.

Secondly, although on the face of things such a passage as John 14:28 appeared to afford ammunition to Arians in their denial of the co-equal deity of Christ, Christian orthodoxy has been only too willing to allow a subordinationist strain to remain in its own confession, just beside the insistence on Jesus' deity. This arose from the general perception of the orthodox fathers that if the eternal relations within the trinity were to be described in terms of Father and Son, it was clear that the Son was from the Father rather than the Father from the Son. This led to the portrayal of the Father as the *fons et origo* (source and origin) of the deity, the *principium* (principle) and *archē* (beginning) of the godhead. Within such a vocabulary subordinationism flourished, and statements such as 'the Father is greater than I' caused no embarrassment. They were confidently assimilated into the doctrine of the co-equal deity on the basis that eternal generation implied derivation, and therefore some sort of subordination. Chrysostom, for example, allowed himself to say, 'If any one say that the Father is greater, inasmuch as he is the cause of the Son, we will not contradict this.'[9] This (what Westcott called 'the immanent pre-eminence of the Father')[10] was the general position of Patristic theology. It is reflected in Pearson: 'in the very name of Father there is something of eminence which is not in that of Son; and some kind of priority we must ascribe unto him whom we call the first, in respect of him whom we call the second Person.'[11]

Thirdly, some kind of functional subordination is clearly implied in the incarnation and mission of the Son. He could not be the *servant* of the Lord without becoming in some sense less than the Lord. The same principle is implied in other expressions. In 2 Corinthians 8:9, for example, Paul declares that Christ 'became poor'. It was in terms of such expressions that Augustine, for example, interpreted John 14:28: 'in the form of a servant which he took he is less than the Father; but in the form of God, in which he also was before he took the form of a servant, he is equal to the Father'.[12] We might even say that in some sense Christ made himself inferior to the disciples because he came to serve them. This surely implies a genuine altruism which put the interests of his people before his own.

Yet this state of dependence, accountability and subordination on the part of the incarnate Son is always contrasted with another state of the same Son. Before becoming Servant, he was equal with God; before becoming poor he was rich; before washing his disciples' feet he knew that he came from God and was returning to God (Jn. 13:3). This makes it precarious, to say the least, to read the subordination indicated in John's Gospel back into the pre-temporal relations between the Son and the Father. What the Jews themselves concluded from his claim to be God's Son was precisely that he saw himself as equal with God (Jn. 5:18).

Even the fact that he was *sent* by the Father need not point to any ontological subordination on the side of the Son, since it would be premature to reject the idea of a *pactum salutis* according to which the Son, as Mediator, acts by mutual agreement with the Father.[13] From the standpoint of this pact or covenant Witsius is able to say:

> If the mediator be considered in the state of humiliation, and the form of a servant, he is certainly inferior to the Father, and subordinate to him. It was not of his human nature only, but of himself in that state, that he himself said, *The Father is greater than I.* Nay, we may look upon the very mediatorial office in itself as imparting a certain economical inferiority or subordination; as being to be laid down, when all things shall be perfectly finished, and *God himself shall become all in all.*[14]

James Packer has endorsed this idea of a *pactum salutis* in his Introduction to a recent reprint of Witsius' classic:[15]

> Scripture is explicit, on the fact that from eternity, in light of human sin foreseen, a specific agreement existed between the Father and the Son that they would exalt each other ... the full reality of God and God's work are not adequately grasped till the Covenant of Redemption – the specific covenantal agreement between Father and Son on which the Covenant of Grace rests – occupies its proper place in our minds.

Packer also points out that it is the Gospel of John that contains the most explicit indications of this covenant. He cites, as examples, Jesus' references to his work as obedience to the Father's will, to his mission as a being sent into the world to perform a specific task and to his Father 'giving' him particular persons to save.

It is in terms of this covenant that the Son becomes servant: not by the Father's bare decree, but of his own volition and by mutual consent, his incarnation reflecting not only the Father's love for the church, but his own. From this point of view, New Testament subordinationism is federal, not ontological.

It is important, in the fourth place, to interpret the relation of the Son to the Father in a way that leaves room for the exaltation of Christ. The Son, on earth, is not only less than the Father but less than what he himself will one day be. There is a 'not yet glorified' (Jn. 7:39). This appears most closely in John 17:1ff., where the Son asks the Father to glorify him. The precise nature of this glory in question is indicated in verse 5: 'the glory I had with you before the world began'. This clearly implies not only that his glory was then less than the Father's, but that it was less than what his own used to be. The prayer finds its fulfilment precisely in the installation of the Mediator in the glory possessed by the Son in his pre-temporal condition. In this consists the Son's *hyper*-exaltation (Phil. 2:9). It is such an exaltation as could not be surpassed. The Mediator shares the Father's sovereignty, his resurrection body the Omega-point of the material creation, his soul suffused with the blessedness of God and his face radiant with the glory of the Eternal. None of that was true when he said, 'The Father is greater than I.' But it is all true now.

One last point may be made: we must pay attention to the purpose of these subordinationist passages. Jesus was vulnerable to the charge that he was concerned only with his own glory. He appeared to make himself equal with God; he performed miracles without any specific invocation of God; he legislated by saying simply, 'I say to you!' Hence the need to remind his contemporaries that he was in the world to reveal and glorify the Father and to do his will. But just there lay the paradox: to reveal the Father he had to reveal himself ('Anyone who has seen me has seen the Father', Jn. 14:9). Hence the two kinds of material: the material that reveals the Son, and the material that obscures him. There is no way of resolving the difficulty, if only because the Father is as determined to glorify the Son as the Son is to glorify the Father. This is why Jesus himself can say, 'Now is the Son of Man glorified and God is glorified in him' (Jn. 13:31). Hence, too, the portrayal of even the cross itself as a 'lifting up' (*hypsōsis*: Jn. 3:14; 12:32; 12:34).

The Son of God in Hebrews

The writer to the Hebrews refers regularly to the divine sonship of Jesus, beginning indeed with the opening sentence of the epistle: 'In the past. God spoke to our forefathers through the prophets at many times and in various ways, but in these last days he has spoken to us by his Son.' The form in the Greek, '*a* Son', is deliberate, the omission of the article serving to emphasize the uniqueness of Christ. In former days God spoke through men: in the end, he spoke through a Son.

The radiance of God's glory

The implications of this sonship are brought out in Hebrews 1:3: 'The Son is the radiance of God's glory and the exact representation of his being.'

The main problem raised by the first phrase is the precise meaning of *apaugasma*, which occurs only here in the New Testament. The noun *auge* means brightness; the verb *apaugazō* to radiate or reflect; and the ending *-ma* is passive, which, as Geerhardus Vos suggests, indicates that it refers to the product of *apaugazō*, not to the process itself: 'here we have the concrete product of the act, not the abstract act itself. The Son, therefore, is the product of an act of shining forth in God. He is the product of the radiation of God'.[16]

The question is, does *apaugasma* in this context mean *effulgence* or *refulgence*, *radiance* or *reflection*? There are several reasons for preferring *effulgence* or *radiance*.

First, the idea contained in *reflection* is set forth in the following phrase by means of the word *character*. If *apaugasma* means reflection then *character* is repetitive and superfluous.

Secondly, the balance of evidence from the use of *apaugasma* in Judaism favours effulgence. As we have seen, the word occurs in the Wisdom of Solomon 7:25ff. The Revised Version (1905) reads:

> For she [Wisdom] is a breath of the power of God,
> And a clear effluence of the glory of the Almighty;
> Therefore can nothing defiled find entrance into her.
> For she is an *effulgence* from everlasting light,
> And an image of his goodness.

The word *apaugasma* also occurs four times in Philo and of these only one requires the rendering *reflection.*[17]

Thirdly, the Greek fathers, virtually unanimously, preferred *effulgence*. Montefiore recognizes this, but then goes on to opt for *reflection* on the ground that the noun (ending in *-ma*) is passive in form. The Greek fathers (who, after all, spoke the language) were surely in a better position to evaluate such grammatical niceties. Gregory of Nyssa, for example, specifically understood the phrase by analogy with rays of light emanating from the sun:

> as the radiance of light sheds its brilliancy from the whole of the sun's disc (for in the disc one part is not radiant and the rest dim) so all that glory which the Father is, sheds its brilliancy from its whole extent by means of the brightness that comes from it, that is, by the true light; and as the ray is of the sun (for there would be no ray if the sun were not), yet the sun is never conceived as existing by itself without the ray of brightness that is shed from it, so the Apostle delivering to us the continuity and eternity of that existence which the Only-begotten has of the Father, calls the Son 'the brightness of his glory'.[18]

Chrysostom finds two interesting connections for the word *apaugasma*. On the one hand, he links it to the words of Jesus in John 8:12, 'I am the light of the world.' On the other, he links it to the Nicene Creed: 'Therefore, he uses the word "brightness", showing that this was said in the sense of "Light of Light".'[19] Behind the Nicene phrase (*phōs ek phōtos*) lies the statement in 1 John 1:5, 'God is light'. Christ is the Light from that Light, God's glory radiated and made accessible to men, so that they were able to see his glory: glory as of an only begotten from a father (Jn. 1:14). He is the glory made visible: not a different glory from the Father's but the same glory in another form. The Father is the glory hidden: the Son is the glory revealed. The Son is the Father repeated, but in a different way.

The phrase *charaktēr tēs hypostaseōs autou* has also provoked debate. The word *charaktēr* occurs only here in the New Testament. It appears again, however, in Clement's *Epistle to the Corinthians* (1:33): 'Above all, as the most excellent and exceeding great work of his intelligence, with his sacred and faultless hands he formed man in the impress of his own image [*tēs heautou eikonos charaktēra*].' The contrast with Hebrews is interesting. Man is the *charaktēr* of God's image; Christ is the *charaktēr* of his *hypostasis.*

Charaktēr (from *charassein*, 'to scratch') is an engraving. In the case of coins, for example, it is the exact reproduction of the image on the stamp. But of what is Christ the *charaktēr*? The obvious answer is, 'Of the *hypostasis* of God!' But unfortunately in a Christological context the word *hypostasis* bears two meanings. Calvin confidently asserted that in Hebrews 1:3 it means *person*: 'The word *hypostasis* which along with others I have translated a substance, denotes (in my opinion) not the *esse* or the essence of the Father, but the person. It would be absurd to say that the essence of God is impressed on Christ, since the one and the same is the essence of both.'[20]

Owen shared this view,[21] and Westcott acknowledges that 'many mediaeval and modern writers have taken *hypostasis* in the sense of "person" here'.[22] Calvin derives support from this fact, arguing that, 'The orthodox fathers also take *hypostasis* in this sense, as being threefold in God, the *ousia* being one. Hilary throughout takes the Latin word *substantia* as equivalent to person.'

There are two responses to this.

First, the position of the fathers is not as clear as Calvin suggests. One major difficulty is that the Greek and Latin fathers used *hypostasis* in different ways. The Greeks used it as equivalent to *person*: hence, three *hypostases* in God. The exact Latin translation of *hypostasis* was *substantia*, but the Latins equated *substantia* with essence and generally shrank from ascribing three *substantiae* to the deity. This confusion was, and is, the source of many problems. To the Eastern church, there were three *hypostases* in God; to the West, there was only one *substantia*. The situation was rendered even more complicated by the fact that individual fathers used the terms inconsistently.

Hilary, on whom Calvin relies so heavily, was particularly guilty in this respect. The overall impression conveyed by his treatment of Hebrews 1:3 is that he takes *hypostasis* to mean *nature.*[23] But this does not by itself enable us to ascertain how Hilary used the terms *person* and *substance*. R. P. C. Hanson[24] points out that Hilary was reluctant to use the word *persona* (supplied by Tertullian) to distinguish what God was as three from what he was as one. In the same way, when discussing what God was as one he preferred to use *natura* rather than *substantia*. Yet he sometimes used *persona*; and he sometimes used *substantia*. 'The great defect of Hilary's theological vocabulary', Hanson concludes, 'is that he uses *substantia* both to mean what God is as Three (*hypostasis* in the later Cappadocian sense) and for what God is as One (*ousia* in the Cappadocian sense), and in some contexts it is almost impossible to determine which sense he intends.'

There is no need at the moment to unravel the confusion. Suffice to point out that it exists, and that it makes it difficult to rely on Hilary as a guide to the meaning of *hypostasis* in Hebrews 1:3.[25]

The other, more serious, problem is that, as Westcott points out, the use of the word *hypostasis* in the sense of person 'is much later than the apostolic age'.[26] The Vulgate renders it *substantia* and the Syriac *essence*. The word occurs in four other instances in the New Testament and in none of these is the sense *person* remotely possible.

Etymologically *hypostasis* is 'that which stands under' and this passed naturally into *support* or *steadiness*, which in turn led to the meaning *confidence* or *assurance*. This last sense is required in 2 Corinthians 9:14; 11:17 and Hebrews 3:14 ('We have come to share in Christ if we hold firmly till the end the *confidence* we had at first'). The same rendering is almost certainly required in Hebrews 11:1 ('faith is the *hypostasis* of what we hoped for'). Hebrews 1:3 clearly requires a non-metaphorical meaning: 'an exact representation of his *real being*' (Arndt and Gingrich); 'the very stamp of his *nature*' (RSV); 'the exact representation of his *being*' (NIV).

'Behold', comments Chrysostom, 'how here also he goes on two paths, by the one leading us away from Sabellius, by the other from Arius.'[27] What he had in mind, of course, was that the phrase 'the radiance of his glory' indicated (against the Arians) that the Son was of the same nature as the Father ('Light from Light'); and that the phrase 'the exact image of his being' indicated (against Sabellianism) that the Son was in some sense distinct from the Father ('For the "express image" is something other than its Prototype: yet not Another in all respects, but as having real subsistence').[28]

The former idea (the consubstantiality of light and its radiance) is familiar enough. The latter idea is more difficult. In what sense is the Son the image of the Father's essence? We can still feel the force of Calvin's objection: 'It would be absurd to say that the essence of God is impressed on Christ, since the one and the same is the essence of both.'[29] However, when Chrysostom said that the 'express image' is something other than its Prototype, he did not mean that it was another being or had a separate existence. In fact, he specifically excluded this interpretation by adding, 'yet not Another in all respects, but as to having real subsistence'.[30] Certainly Hebrews 1:3 is incapable of a Sabellian interpretation. The Father cannot be the Son through whom he spoke and through whom he made the world. Neither is the Son the Father whose image he bears. Yet in this context the stress falls not on the distinction but on the correspondence and resemblance between the Father and the Son.[31] The primary idea is that the Son is the *charaktēr* of the Father and this is strengthened by introducing the word *hypostasis*. The Son is the exact impression of the very nature of God; of his real being. He is one and the same *hypostasis* repeated. It exists in one form in the Father, in another in the Son. From this point of view, if we take *hypostasis* in its later, Cappadocian sense (*person*) we cannot say that the person of the Son is the exact image of the person of the Father because (in Cappadocian terms) the Son is begotten/generate and the Father is not. What is duplicated exactly in the Son is the Father's nature or being; which is why he himself could say, 'Anyone who has seen me has seen the Father' (Jn. 14:9).

Adoptionist?

According to John A. T. Robinson, however, the writer to the Hebrews is a far from consistent witness to the eternal sonship of Christ. Much of his language is adoptionist: 'Nowhere, in fact, in the New Testament more than in Hebrews do we find such a wealth of expressions that would support what looks like an adoptionist Christology – of a Jesus who becomes the Christ.'[32] This wealth of adoptionist expressions includes (translating literally) '*made* heir' (Heb. 1:2), '*made* superior to the angels' (1:4), 'the title he has *inherited*' (1:4), '*made* to sit at God's right hand' (1:13) and a '*forerunner* on our behalf' (6:20).

Similar sentiments were expressed by J. D. G. Dunn: 'there is more adoptionist language in Hebrews than in any other New Testament document – that is, language which speaks of Jesus as becoming, or being begotten or being appointed to his status as the decisive intermediary between God and man during his life or in consequence of his death and resurrection'.[33]

The first point to be made in response to this is that even Robinson and Dunn have to concede that the epistle to the Hebrews quite unmistakably emphasizes the deity of Christ. Robinson acknowledges the author as one who 'stresses the eternal pre-existence (and of course post-existence) more than any other New Testament writer'.[34] Exactly the same point is made by Dunn: 'Hebrews describes Christ as God's Son in language which seems to denote pre-existence more clearly than anything we have met so far.'[35] In fact, there can be no doubt that this is the dominant note of the writer's Christology, sounded, as we have seen, in the very opening verses. When God spoke through Christ he spoke through one who was already a Son: a Son who was the shining of his glory, the express image of his being, his associate in the work of creation and a sharer in the worship offered to him by the angels. All this is unmistakable. The Christ of Hebrews is a divine being and we should require compelling reasons to interpret any of the epistle's statements in a way that contradicts this.

Secondly, the so-called adoptionist language can easily be interpreted in the light of the doctrine of the incarnation. Through the enfleshment, Christ became a creature, a dependent, a servant and a subordinate. As such he could be made heir; as such he could be exalted; and as such he could be the forerunner of his people.

The plausibility of Robinson's argument derives largely from the assumption that to prove Jesus' humanity is to disprove his deity. This assumption is allied to John Knox's famous claim (which Robinson endorses) that the assertion of Jesus' pre-existence places a strain upon his humanity which it cannot bear.[36] But this is pure *a priori* speculation, as E. L. Mascall pointed out:

> When Knox writes that it is 'impossible, by definition, that God should become a man', he is doing what theologians of his empiricist outlook profess to abhor, namely putting logical deduction in the place of the recognition of actual fact. Indeed, I would maintain that only God, the Creator, *can*, without losing his own identity, become a being of an order radically different from his own. A donkey cannot become man, nor can an angel; but God can.[37]

As Mascall also pointed out, the incarnation is an enhancement of human nature far beyond anything offered by adoptionism: 'if, as I believe, the eternal God has become man, then man is what the eternal God could become; and this gives human nature a vastly nobler status than it could have on any adoptionist or quasi-adoptionist view'.

The other problem facing Robinson is that from his point of view it is very difficult to explain the uniqueness of Christ. On adoptionist principles, nothing is left of the fundamental contrast indicated in Hebrews 1:1–2: 'God spoke to our forefathers through the prophets … in these last days he has spoken to us by his Son'. Robinson can allow no real discontinuity between Jesus and the prophets; or even between Jesus and ourselves. For example, referring to Hebrews 2:17 ('For this reason he had to be made like his brothers in every way'), he notes that according to the traditional interpretation the *Logos* had to be made man having been previously something else, namely, a heavenly, divine being. 'I believe,' he continues, 'that the whole context of his argument shows that our writer intended no such thing. Jesus was never anything but like his brothers. For it is essential that a consecrating priest and those whom he consecrates should be all "of one stock" (2:11).'[38] The full import of this becomes clear in Robinson's comment on an analogy used by Frank Weston: the king's son becoming one of his father's subjects.[39] Robinson comments: 'Our author seems to be working with exactly the opposite analogy, of the worker who is raised above his comrades (1:9) and is summoned to live as the king's son.'[40]

This is 'ordinary' with a vengeance! But if it is true, how can we account for the impact Jesus made, and for the subsequent development of Christianity? S. W. Sykes asks perceptively: 'But can Jesus *both* be ordinary *and* a climacteric? can we assert *both* that there is nothing remarkable about his history *and* yet that it points through to the absolute so that men could conclude that to have seen Jesus was to have seen the Father?'[41]

Within the epistle to the Hebrews the uniqueness of Christ is set forth in two ways.

First, in the descriptions of his humanity. This aspect of Jesus' life and personality were extremely important to the writer. This is the grain of truth in the charge that his language is adoptionist. But his references to Jesus' humanity are quite remarkable. It is almost as if the humanity, far from being self-evident, were a puzzle or widely denied or scarcely credible. He has to explain why Jesus was made a little lower than the angels (2:9); why he partook of the same nature as his children (2:14); and why he had to be made like his brothers in every way (2:17). He also has to insist that, although Jesus was sinless, he was tempted in the same way as ourselves and is therefore able to sympathize with us in our weaknesses. He even has to say that, though a Son, Jesus *learned* obedience (5:8). This kind of language is hardly consistent with ordinariness. An ordinary man does not deliberately take human nature or have to prove that he can understand human beings. All the indications are that the real danger in the circle addressed by the writer to the Hebrews was that they were so obsessed by the augustness of the Mediator that they tended to view him as a remote, untouchable figure, infinitely distanced from themselves. Some of the most sublime passages in the epistle (notably Heb. 4:14–16) are directed to this problem.

Sykes' conclusion, then, is fully warranted: 'Any account which does not distinguish him from the rest of humanity is not credible as Christology; and any account which does so distinguish him is clearly not merely "normal" or "empirical" humanity.'[42]

It was not only in his humanness that Christ was unique, however. He was also unique in his being more than human. He was the Son of God. This was what distinguished him from the prophets and set him above the angels. He performed the functions of God (creation and providence); he enjoyed the prerogatives of God ('Let all God's angels worship him'); he inherited the titles of God; and he was exclusively related to God as the shining of his glory and the very image of his being. He was, and is, *God* (1:8); which is why to commit apostasy is to commit a sin for which there is no forgiveness (6:6).

For the writer to the Hebrews, the significance of Jesus is absolute. He is Ultimate Reality. But he is Ultimate Reality in a form which is fully conversant with our human plight.

The Son of God in Paul

Paul uses the designation 'Son of God' (*hyios theou*) comparatively infrequently: fifteen times as against one hundred and eighty-four instances of *kyrios*. When he does use it, however, it is in passages of seminal importance for his theology: first, in descriptions of the redemptive initiative of God (Rom. 8:3; Gal. 4:4); secondly, in allusions to the sacrifice of Christ (Rom. 5:10; 8:32); and, thirdly, in relation to the exalted Christ (1 Cor. 15:24–28).

This last passage raises the idea that the reign of the Son is temporary and thus appears to contradict other passages which speak of his reign as eternal: for example Daniel 7:14 and 2 Peter 1:11. In the very nature of the case, however, redemptive work must have a terminus. When the last soul is redeemed, the last enemy destroyed and the cosmos regenerated, then the work assigned to the Mediator will be fully accomplished.

Yet there are good reasons for believing that the moment when Christ delivers up the kingdom to the Father is only the end of the beginning. The current phase of the kingdom is itself subsequent to the 'end' referred to in John 19:30, when Jesus cried, 'It is finished.' Even in the High Priestly prayer he is already claiming that he has finished the work (Jn.17:2). In effect, then, the work of Christ has already survived two termini: the close of the public ministry and the completion of the work of sin-bearing. Yet significant phases of the work continued after these; and in the same way it will continue beyond the terminus indicated in 1 Corinthians 15:24, 28. His activity as redeemer and conqueror will be at an end, but his work as both head of the church and the Last Adam will continue. In the former capacity he will continue to shepherd his people (Rev. 7:17). In the latter, he will resume the mandate forfeited by the First Adam (Gn. 1:28), subduing and colonizing the world to come (Heb. 2:8f.). Such work may, in turn, have its own termini. But none of them will be absolute. Each climax of achievement will be followed by a new phase of endeavour as man moves ever more deeply into the living knowledge of God and progresses ever further as conserver and developer of the universe.

But the words of 1 Corinthians 15:28 contain an even more formidable difficulty. They seem to teach blatant subordinationism: the

Son himself will be subject to the Father. Does this not place him very clearly on the side of creation rather than on the side of the Creator?

The first thing to be said in response to this is that the kingdom referred to in this passage is one which Christ holds not absolutely as Son of God but as Messiah. As the pre-existent Son he was already equal with God (Phil. 2:6) and shared his glory (Jn. 17:5). But there is another authority which is 'given' to him (Mt. 28:18; Jn. 17:2). According to Philippians 2:9 this eminence was conferred on him after his obedience and because of it. There is similar teaching in Revelation 5:9: the Lamb is worthy to open the scroll precisely because he purchased men by his blood. Indeed, it was that act of redemption which gave him a kingdom to rule. He *made* us a kingdom for God (Rev. 5:10). Furthermore, this sovereignty is given to him precisely in order to advance the interests of redemption. He is the head over all things 'for the church' (Eph. 1:22).

All this gives a fairly clear picture: a kingship which Christ exercises as Redeemer on the basis of the redemption he achieved on earth, and in the interests of that redemption. He reigns because of it and he reigns for it. It is this kingship which will one day achieve its goal; and when it does so it will be surrendered to the Father.

Secondly, this kingship inevitably implies subordination. The very fact of its being 'given' indicates this. But it stems from something more fundamental: the Mediator is Servant. He is the Last Adam. L. S. Thornton rightly comments: 'God is the only true king of the world which he has created. The dominion of Adam, therefore, is a delegated sovereignty, rightly exercised under obedience.'[43] So long as Christ remains human, and so long as he functions as Servant-Messiah and as head of the church, subordination is unavoidable. It was modified but not eliminated by his resurrection and ascension, and the passages which underline this are among the most moving in the New Testament. In John 17:1, for example, Jesus asks the Father to glorify the Son so that the Son will glorify him. Even his exaltation is not to be used for his own purposes. His new powers are to be used for the very same objects as the capacities of the earthly ministry, when his food and drink was to do the will of the One who sent him (Jn. 4:34). There is a similar point of view in Philippians 2:11. However splendid the exaltation of the Lord, it is only a point on the road to something greater. Every knee is to bow to the exalted Christ, and every tongue to confess him. But the final glory accrues to God the Father.

Thirdly, despite this element of subordination it would be a grave mistake to underestimate the current reign of Christ. As Paul explicitly states in this very context, the only one not subject to the sovereignty of Messiah is God the Father: 'when it says that "everything" has been put under him, it is clear that this does not include God himself' (1 Cor. 15:27). All else is at his command.

The full meaning of this is brought out in the Apocalypse: the Lamb sits in the very centre of the throne (Rev. 5:6), exactly where we would expect to see God the Father. He is the centre-piece, with whom every other form of existence is enthralled; the Lord of history, not only revealing but executing God's plan. And, equally with the Father, the slaughtered Lamb is the object of the great paeons of praise uttered by the ransomed church, by the angels and by the very universe itself. There is even a suggestion that if, in the economy of redemption, the Son is servant to the Father, so the Spirit is servant to the Son, who sends the seven spirits of God forth into all the earth (Rev. 5:6). This suggestion is abundantly confirmed elsewhere in the New Testament. In Acts 2:33, for example, the risen Jesus is already spoken of as the one who poured out the Spirit at Pentecost.

Yet we should not overlook the complexities of the situation. In the New Testament, service is greatness; and one may even ask (using the terms of later theology) whether the persons of the godhead do not seem to vie with one another for the privilege of serving. The gospels indicate not only a service performed by the Son for the Father but also a ministry (and even an extreme solicitude) on the part of the Father for the Son: 'I am not alone, for my Father is with me' (Jn. 16:32).

Fourthly, the New Testament does not always describe the *eschaton* in terms of the Son surrendering the kingdom to the Father. There are considerable variations on the theme and some of them should serve as warnings against building too confidently on 1 Corinthians 15 alone. For example, in Jude 24f. the Father is represented as presenting us faultless before his own glory. In Ephesians 5:26, the Son presents the church (his bride) to himself. In Revelation 21:2, 9ff., the church is again represented as a bride, 'the wife of the Lamb', but in this instance it is clearly implied that it is the Father who presents her to the Son. These passages should give us pause. The idea of the Father handing over the bride to Christ is as definitive as that of the Son handing over the kingdom to the Father. Neither concept implies complete renunciation or abdication by the other party. The bride of Christ remains the city of God. The kingdom of God remains the flock of Christ.

Finally, even in the current phase of the kingdom, when the Son clearly stands in the forefront, we should not minimize the involvement of the Father. In fact this appears very clearly in connection with both the title 'Son of God' and the concept of the kingdom in Colossians 1:12ff., where Paul urges the church to give thanks to the Father, who 'has rescued us from the dominion of darkness and brought us into the kingdom of the Son he loves'. Here is the Father fully engaged in the work of the kingdom even before it is handed over to him. If this is possible (and without any subordination of the Father to the Son), why should there not be kingdom involvement on the part of the Son after the Father becomes the primary focus? This is the kind of problem which made later trinitarian theology necessary. The monarchy of Father and Son is one monarchy, and however necessary it became to stress that the Father was not the Son nor the Son the Father, it became equally necessary to insist that they were not two separate kings. In the last analysis, the resolution of the problems implicit in 1 Corinthians 15:24ff. could be found only along the lines suggested by John 10:30: 'I and the Father are one.'

What of the clause, 'so that God may be all in all'? Calvin answers as follows: 'Then God will be governing heaven and earth by himself, without any intermediary, and then in that way he will be all.'[44] It is difficult to square this with other biblical passages which clearly indicate the supremacy of Christ over the world to come. The most important of these is Hebrews 2:5ff., which states categorically that the world (*oikoumenēn*) to come is to be subject to the enthroned Saviour. The writer bases his assertion on the role assigned to the Son of Man in Psalm 8, especially verse 6: 'You made him ruler over the works of your hands; you put everything under his feet.' The sentiments of the psalmist are themselves rooted in Genesis 1:28, which directs Adam to exercise dominion over the whole creation. This clearly indicates that the dominion of God over the primal creation was not immediate. It was exercised through the First Adam. In the same way, the sovereignty of God over the new creation will be exercised through Jesus, the Last Adam and the Son of Man, already clothed with glory and honour.

Did Jesus 'become' Son?

Many scholars claim to see in the Pauline writings clear evidence that the apostle's teaching was adoptionist: he did not believe that Jesus was the eternal, pre-existent son of God but held instead that he 'became' Son. Specifically, he became Son at the resurrection.

The strongest argument in favour of this is Romans 1:4: 'declared with power to be the Son of God, by his resurrection from the dead'. The position is complicated by the fact that some scholars distinguish between Paul's personal beliefs and the teaching of this passage, which they regard as a pre-Pauline Christian creed. James Dunn appears to take this view and links Romans 1:4 with Acts 13:32f.:

> What God promised our fathers he has fulfilled for us, their children, by raising up Jesus. As it is written in the second Psalm:
>
> 'You are my Son;
> today I have begotten you' (NIV margin).

From these passages Dunn concludes 'that the first Christians thought of Jesus' divine sonship principally as a role and status he had entered upon, been appointed to, at his resurrection'.[45] He writes later to the same effect: 'The language of the earliest post-Easter confession of Jesus' sonship and the earliest use of Ps. 2:7 certainly seem to have placed the decisive moment of "becoming" quite clearly in the resurrection of Jesus.'[46]

Other scholars share Dunn's point of view. According to John A. T. Robinson, for example, Romans 1:3 describes 'not a heavenly being who becomes human so much as a man who enters into the office of Son of God marked out for him from all eternity'.[47]

But the arguments against an adoptionist interpretation of Romans 1:3 are formidable.

First, there is the fact that the title 'Son of God' already appears in the earliest Pauline epistles without the slightest hint of his becoming Son only at the resurrection. In Galatians 4:4, for example, Paul speaks of God sending forth his own Son. The one who was already a Son became a slave in order that the slaves might become sons. Furthermore, it was his coming, not his resurrection, that marked the inauguration of the eschaton. He came 'in the fulness of the times': that is, his advent itself introduced the Last Days.

In First Thessalonians (another early epistle) Christ is referred to according to his earthly designation, Jesus, and yet described as 'his Son from heaven' (1 Thes. 1:10). God is indeed said to have raised him from the dead, but there is not the least hint that this had anything to do with making him Son of God. On the contrary, it was precisely as God's Son that he rescued us from the coming wrath.

These passages indicate that some twenty years before he wrote the letter to the Romans Paul was already describing Christ as the Son of God and doing so without a hint of adoptionism. It would be very strange if Romans 1:4 set forth a different doctrine; or even set the apostle's imprimatur on an earlier creed propounding a doctrine so much weaker than his own.

Secondly, there is the wider context in Romans itself. The title 'Son of God' occurs in three other notable passages in this epistle (Rom. 5:10; 8:3; 8:32) and in none of them is it related to the resurrection. On the contrary, all of them require the assumption that at the moment of his incarnation and sacrifice Christ was already the Son of God. This is why God's love was so astonishing. And this is why Christ's sacrifice was so definitive. The flesh in which sin was condemned was the flesh of God's own Son. Once we accept this, it is difficult to believe that Paul would endorse any formula which compromised the pre-existent sonship.

Thirdly, there is no reason to believe that the mere fact of resurrection would have been seen as proof of divine sonship or even of messiahship. As Martin Hengel points out, the exaltation of a martyr was not by any means taken as an indication of unique status.[48] Enoch and Elijah had not tasted death. Moses had died in unique circumstances. Lazarus (and the widow of Nain's son) had experienced resurrection. But none of these occurrences had been seen as any affirmation of messianic or divine status. It had not even led to their being specially venerated: Lazarus disappears from Christian history almost immediately. Besides, if mere resurrection meant exaltation to divine status, what of Jairus' daughter (Mk. 5:42)?

It is worth noting, too, that far from making the sonship rest on the resurrection, the New Testament characteristically makes the resurrection rest on the sonship. This is seen, for example, in Acts 2:24: 'God raised him from the dead ... because it was impossible for death to keep its hold on him.' He was raised because of what he was. He did not become Son by being raised: he was raised because he was Son.

Fourthly, so far as his contemporaries were concerned, the resurrection would not have been enough to remove the scandal of the cross. For one thing, the crucifixion had a finality about it that precluded all further discussion and development. To Jew and Greek alike it was the last word. A crucified God or Messiah was an absurdity. This attitude was surely embodied completely in Paul himself. He had probably had some contact with the earthly Jesus, was certainly familiar with the story of the resurrection and yet felt it his bounden duty to do all in his power to extinguish the new religion. Nor is this all. The resurrection itself was a stumbling-block; part of the problem rather than part of the solution. In fact, one suspects that many scholars who see the resurrection as the point which (biblically) establishes Jesus' sonship themselves dismiss the empty tomb as incredible. This was certainly the reaction of those to whom the apostles preached. When Paul preached the resurrection at Athens, for example, his hearers mocked (Acts 17:32). They were too intellectually sophisticated to believe that the hard fact of the cross could be cancelled by the 'myth' of the resurrection.

How, then, are we to interpret Romans 1:4? One possibility is to translate *horizein* as 'to declare'. This is the rendering preferred by KJV and it certainly solves the theological problem: the resurrection was not the point at which Jesus 'became' Son of God but the point at which he was 'declared' Son of God.

However, there are weighty objections to this. For example, if we take the synoptic history seriously, Christ had already been declared Son of God many times before the resurrection: for instance, at his birth, at his baptism and at his transfiguration; by the demons he exorcised; and by the miracles he performed. More important, the philological evidence makes the translation 'declared' impossible.[49] The primary meaning of *horizein* is 'delimit'. There is no example either before the New Testament or in the New Testament of the meaning 'declare'. In all other instances it means 'appoint, fix, determine'. We see this, for example, in Luke 22:22: 'The Son of Man goes as it has been *determined*' (RSV); and in Hebrews 4:7: 'God again *set* a certain day'. It would be quite arbitrary to impose a different meaning on *horisthentos* in Romans 1:4. Usage dictates that it be rendered 'appointed'.

But this does not necessitate an adoptionist interpretation (which, as we have seen runs counter to the whole thrust of Paul's Christology elsewhere). In all likelihood, the phrase *en dynamei* should be taken not with *horisthentos* but with *hyiou theou*: he was appointed Son of God 'with power'.[50] The contrast is not between a time when he was Son and a time when he was not Son, but between a time when he was Son in weakness and a time when he became Son with power. In his earthly life, he was the Son humiliated: to all outward appearance a mere man, homeless and friendless, without power or influence. Now he is transfigured, regnant and pre-eminent. The resurrection marks not his adoption but his investiture.

The Son of God in Hellenism

Some scholars, however, have accused Paul of more than adoptionism. They have argued that his use of the title 'Son of God' constitutes a radical breach with primitive Christianity; that the title does not go back to the original Aramaic-speaking church; and, more important, that it does not go back to Jesus himself. He, it is alleged, did not call himself 'the Son of God' and did not see himself as 'the Son of God'. It was in the later, Greek-speaking churches of the Pauline mission that the title originated; and its use represented a quantum-leap in Christology.

Often associated with this idea is another: that the title 'Son of God' emerged under the influence of Hellenistic and Gnostic ideas. Rudolf Bultmann, for example, argued this strongly.[51] The title, he claimed, would be understood primarily as an assertion of Jesus' divinity: a fact not to be wondered at since 'the figure of a Son of God was familiar to Hellenistic ways of thinking'. The church simply appropriated these Gentile traditions.

If this is true, then the Gentile churches, with or without the genius of Paul, effected a radical reconstruction of Christianity: 'basically a wholly new religion, in contrast to the original Palestinian Christianity'.[52] This is remarkably similar to the theory of Christian origins proposed by such Jewish scholars as Isidore Epstein: 'within a few decades the Christian church under the influence of Paul was altering its conception of Jesus in a way that meant that he was no longer thought of as merely human, and implied that he was in fact a second God – a belief which was a denial of the unity of God as Jews understood the term'.[53]

Bultmann's construction has been severely criticized by, among others, Martin Hengel. Hengel claims that 'Bultmann, his teachers Bousset and Heitmuller, and his followers repeated this argument *ad nauseam* without verifying it adequately by the ancient sources'.[54] He concludes: 'The constantly repeated view that the development of the Son of God christology is a typically Hellenistic phenomenon and represents a break in primitive Christianity hardly bears closer examination.'[55]

This conclusion is based on the following arguments.

First, serious students of Hellenistic religion are agreed that the mystery religions did not know of sons of God who died and rose again. Nor did the mystic himself become a child of the god. Hengel quotes M. P. Nilsson to this effect: 'As far as I know the initiate is never called a child of the god in any of the mystery religions.'[56]

Secondly, there is the problem of chronology. We have no idea how widespread the mystery religions were in Syria in the first half of the first century. Our evidence is from the third and fourth centuries, when there was probably a strong Christian influence on the mystery religions themselves.[57] This makes it very difficult to speak of the dependence of

Christianity on such cults between AD 30 and 50. The same difficulty applies to the Gnostic–Redeemer myth. Hengel is confident that 'in reality there is no gnostic redeemer myth in the sources which can be demonstrated chronologically to be pre-Christian'.[58]

Thirdly, so far as the notion of the divine man is concerned, it is surely fatal to Bultmann's thesis that 'never in the available evidence is the term *hyios theou* used for this concept in Hellenistic Judaism'.[59] Besides, it is not at all clear that such a concept was widespread in the first century. The Greeks were certainly familiar with the idea of heroes descended from the gods. But these heroes were not pre-existent. Nor were they sent into the world on missions of redemption.

Finally, the incarnation and shameful death of a divine figure represented not a point of contact between Christianity and Hellenism but a *skandalon*: a stumbling-block. 'For educated or noble men of antiquity,' writes Hengel, 'the crucified Jesus was only an expression of folly, shame and hatefulness.' He concludes with the telling comment: 'The "Hellenisation" of Christianity thus necessarily had to lead to docetism. The humanity and the death of Jesus were only tolerable as "show".'[60]

Does the title go back to Jesus?

But what of the other and more important question: does the title 'Son of God' go back to the early church and at last to Jesus himself? Or is it a later addition representing a radical breach with primitive Christianity?

The first point to be made in response to this is the very obvious one that the occurrence of the title in Paul is so early as to leave no time for the development of a separate Gentile theology. It occurs in both Galatians (4:4) and 1 Thessalonians (1:10). These epistles contest the distinction of being the earliest of the Pauline writings, taking us back to the period AD 40–50. At this stage Paul's influence was merely beginning, yet he refers to Christ as 'the Son of God' without betraying any sense of innovating. The use of the title is so natural as to suggest that the apostle is simply conforming to well-established usage. All the indications are that it was already naturalized in Christianity before Paul began his ministry.

Secondly, the title occurs in the early preaching in the book of Acts. One possible example of this is when the Ethiopian Chancellor declares, 'I believe that Jesus Christ is the Son of God' (Acts 8:37, NIV margin). Unfortunately, the passage is of doubtful authenticity and is regarded by most modern editors as a Western addition. The idea of

Jesus' divine sonship does appear, however, in Acts 13:32ff., where Paul quotes Psalm 2:7: 'You are my Son; today I have begotten you' (see NIV margin). This takes us back to the very beginning of Paul's ministry. In all likelihood, he found it already current, and already closely linked with a messianic interpretation of Psalm 2:7. It is, however, very doubtful that the early Christians were following Jewish precedent. As R. H. Fuller points out, 'While there is plenty of evidence in early Rabbinic tradition for the Messianic interpretation of most of the verses of Ps. 2, v. 7 is conspicuously lacking.'[61] Far from borrowing the notion of Christ as 'Son of God' from Psalm 2:7, then, the probability is that the early Christians first saw him as the divine Son and subsequently drew on the psalm for biblical proof and illustration.

Thirdly, according to the synoptic tradition the title 'Son of God' clearly goes back to Jesus himself. To that tradition we now turn.

The Son of God in the synoptics

It is remarkable how often the gospels portray Jesus as calling God, 'Father'. As Joachim Jeremias[62] has demonstrated, this was totally original: '*We do not have a single example* of God being addressed as *Abba* [an Aramaic term for "father"] in Judaism, but Jesus always addressed God in this way in his prayers. The only exception is the cry from the cross.'[63]

Jeremias points out further that Jesus' calling God 'Father' appears in all strata of the gospel tradition: in Mark, in the material common to Matthew and Luke, in the material peculiar to each of them and, of course, in the Gospel of John. This unanimity establishes beyond all doubt that Jesus' invocation of God as 'Father' was a central element in the tradition. And within this distribution Jeremias detected another pattern: there is a notable increase in the use of the designation 'Father' in the Gospel of Matthew (31 times against Mark's 3); and in the Gospel of John (where it occurs 100 times) it has become 'almost a synonym for God'.[64] Jeremias concludes from this that 'there existed an increasing tendency to introduce the designation of God as Father into the sayings of Jesus'.[65] But the true explanation may lie in another phenomenon noted by Jeremias, namely, that Jesus employed the name 'Father' only on special occasions.[66] The very fact that 'Abba' is an individual invocation of God means of necessity that it could be used only in situations of relative privacy. If the Gospel of Mark (at one extreme) is concerned mainly with the public ministry of Jesus, while the Gospel of John (at the other extreme) gives disproportionate attention to the more private, this will naturally be reflected in a much more frequent occurrence of 'Abba' in the latter.

This is dependent on Jeremias' conclusion that, although the gospel writers usually recorded it in the Greek as *patēr*, when Jesus called God 'Father' he habitually used the Aramaic 'Abba'. While conceding that this precise form of the invocation is handed down only in Mark's account of the prayer in the Garden (Mk. 14:36), he holds it to be virtually certain that Jesus used it in his other prayers as well. The reason for this certainty is not merely that the corresponding Greek word *patēr* occurs in virtually all of Jesus' recorded prayers. There is also the fact that the grammatical form of *patēr* in these prayers shows remarkable variations. The evangelists record Jesus as saying *ho patēr*, *patēr*, and *ho patēr mou*. The interesting thing here is the use of the nominative *patēr* as a vocative. This represents a literal translation of *Abba*, which did not inflect and could not distinguish between a nominative and a vocative. Even more important is the occurrence in the Pauline epistles of the prayer, '*Abba, ho patēr*' (Rom. 8:15, Gal. 4:6). It is very difficult to conceive of the early church inventing such an invocation of God. Its existence as a liturgical formula can be explained only on the supposition that the early believers took their cue from Jesus, adopting his form of address to the Almighty.

While such scholars as James Barr have expressed well-founded reservations about some of the details of Jeremias' argument,[67] the central conclusion remains unshaken: Jesus did call God 'Father' and his doing so was revolutionary. The significance of his practice can be gleaned only from an examination of the relevant passages in the gospels. So far as Jesus' inner consciousness is concerned, the most important is Matthew 11:25–30 (*cf.* Lk. 10:21–24):

> I praise you, Father, Lord of heaven and earth, because you have hidden these things from the wise and learned, and revealed them to little children. Yes, Father, for this was your good pleasure. All things have been committed to me by my Father. No-one knows the Son except the Father, and no-one knows the Father except the Son and those to whom the Son chooses to reveal him. Come to me, all you who are weary and burdened, and I will give you rest. Take my yoke upon you and learn from me, for I am gentle and humble in heart, and you will find rest for your souls. For my yoke is easy and my burden is light.

Here is a clear window into Jesus' soul. Not even in the Gospel of

John is there a stronger reflection of the divine self-consciousness of Jesus. It was this that led Karl von Hase, Professor of Church history at Jena, to make the oft-quoted comment that here was 'a meteor from the Johannine sky'.[68]

It is hardly surprising, considering the importance of the passage, that it has become a battlefield of critical scholarship. Its authenticity has been strenuously denied. Fuller, for instance, 'cannot accept the "thunderbolt" as directly from Jesus'. He regards it as 'a church-formation representing a bridge between the synoptic Jesus and the Jesus of the fourth gospel'.[69]

The main objection, inevitably, is the Johannine character of the passage. Jesus, we are told, could not possibly have said this; and this is borne out (allegedly) by the fact that the language of Matthew 11:25ff. is without parallel in the synoptics.

But is its Johannine character a fatal objection? 'Is it a legitimate canon of criticism,' asks David Hill, 'that any Synoptic saying which has a parallel in John must *ipso facto* be spurious?'[70] A similar point is made by Jeremias: 'without such points of departure in the synoptic tradition it would be a complete puzzle how Johannine theology could have originated at all'.[71] Furthermore, the Johannine elements of this passage (particularly verse 27) are frequently exaggerated. All its main features have clear parallels in the synoptics. For example, Jesus' claim to possession of a unique knowledge of God is clearly reflected in the Sermon on the Mount, where he unequivocally set himself above 'the ancients' (Mt. 5:21), refrained from appealing to any higher authority and said simply, 'I say to you.' In keeping with this, there is, he says, *one* small gate and *one* narrow road (Mt. 7:14): language clearly reminiscent of John's, 'I am the way, the truth and the life' (Jn. 14:6). Besides, there is nothing in John bolder than the closing words of the Sermon: 'everyone who hears these words of mine and does not put them into practice is like a foolish man who built his house on sand' (Mt. 7:26). In addition to these general considerations Jeremias highlights significant differences of detail between the Johannine vocabulary and the language used in Matthew.[72] For example, neither *epiginōskein* ('know') nor *apokalyptein* ('reveal') are Johannine words; and *paradidōmai* ('hand over') is never used by John with God as subject.

It is equally difficult to argue that the relationship between Jesus and God indicated by this passage is uncharacteristic of the synoptics. As we have seen, the tradition that Jesus called God 'Father' is clearly attested by Matthew, Mark and Luke. On the other hand, the supplementary phrase, 'Lord of heaven and earth', is not found in John. Clearly, again, although the designation 'Son of God' is not found as frequently in the synoptics as it is in John, it *is* found. What is more, it is traceable, ultimately, to himself. In a few instances it is found on Jesus' own lips (*e.g.* Mk. 13:32); in others, it is implied by him (Mk. 12:6); in yet others it is accepted by him (Mt. 16:16). In fact, it was precisely because he refused to deny that he was the Son of God that, according to the synoptics, he was crucified (Mt. 26:63). He was making a claim which, supposing he was not divine, was blasphemous.

It may even be argued that we need precisely such a claim and such a self-consciousness on the part of Jesus to make any sense of the gospels and of the history of the church. He was deemed to have risen. He was worshipped. He came to be seen as the only way to God. He was reported as making absolute, categorical, claims on men. Without some such personal claim as is reflected in Matthew 11:27ff. – and some such self-consciousness – it is impossible to understand how people came to believe as they did and to act (and suffer) as they did. Above all, if believers today are justified in calling him God and worshipping him as Lord it is simply incredible that he never understood or projected himself as such. If he *was* God's Son he could have spoken as Matthew says he did. If he did not sometimes speak as Matthew says he did, what warrant have we to believe that he was either uniquely Revealer or uniquely Son? We then have no right to worship him or to regard him as other than a blasphemer. It is double-talk to describe as 'valuable' any tradition which portrays a man as God. Such arguments may leave us free to admire Jesus as the Omega-point of human religiosity. But they sound the death-knell for the Christian community conceived of as gathered for worship at the feet of incarnate God.

What we face here is a problem of methodolgy.

First, there is the prejudice that Jesus could not have claimed to be Son. Why not? Are we saying that the idea of God incarnate is impossible? Or are we saying that although he was God incarnate he could not have known it, and in fact later generations of Christians understood him better than he understood himself?

Secondly, there is the dubious procedure of isolating one statement from the gospels, detaching it from its total context and challenging someone to prove that Jesus uttered it. What kind of proof would suffice? We cannot write to Christ himself for confirmation. Nor can we call up the Seventy. What we can do is remind ourselves that the saying occurs in both Matthew and Luke; that from the very beginning the church accepted their testimony as reliable; that Luke in particular was a self-consciously critical historian (see Lk. 1:1–4); that these gospels convey a powerful sense of authenticity ('attesting themselves to be the Word of God', to use the language of later theology); that the whole tone of John's Gospel is testimony that it was precisely in this kind of saying that he, the last living apostle, saw the very heart of Jesus' message; and that down through the centuries this very passage, taken as the *ipsissima vox* of Jesus, has been the saving power of God to countless thousands.

What insight, then, do these words afford us into the mind of Christ? First, they express a breath-taking sense of divine sonship. Jesus addresses God as 'Father'; he refers to him as 'my Father'; and even describes him as 'the Father' absolutely and himself as 'the Son'. As we have seen, all this is utterly without precedent in either the Old Testament or Rabbinic Judaism. Yet Jesus does not argue or prove the relationship. His words contain not a hint of aggression or defensiveness. The sonship is simply assumed. Besides, he is Son in a unique sense. He is *the* Son. John A. T. Robinson's argument[73] that the definite article here is generic and that verse 27 means, 'only a father knows a son' is surely untenable. A mother and sister, presumably, also know a son. For Jesus, *the Son of God* is not only a relationship. It is a proper name, appropriate to himself alone. The *my* Father never becomes *our* Father.

Secondly, Jesus possesses a unique knowledge of God: 'no one knows the Father except the Son' (Mt. 11:27). This unique knowledge clearly rests on the unique relationship. He knows because he is Son (*cf.* Jn. 1:18: 'No-one has ever seen God, but the only begotten of God, *who is at the Father's side*, he has made him known' [my translation]). Yet on the face of things the claim is absurd. Many people apart from Christ have some knowledge of God. Is he not revealed through creation (Rom. 1:20)? Is he not revealed in the Old Testament? How then can it be said that God is not known except where Jesus reveals him?

It is not enough to say that Jesus reveals him more fully, more clearly or more finally. What is claimed in Matthew's *logion* is that Jesus is the source of all knowledge of God and although this theme is not developed in Matthew 11:27ff. it is fully supported by the New Testament's teaching elsewhere. For example, the knowledge of God given through 'what has been made' (Rom. 1:20) is closely related to Christ's role in creation. All things were created through him and all things hold together in him (Col. 1:16ff.); through him God made the ages (Heb. 1:2); and without him nothing came into being (Jn. 1:3). Creation is revelatory because it is the work of Christ, the Exegete of

God. Similarly, the Old Testament proceeds from Christ. It was his Spirit who spoke in the prophets (1 Pet. 1:11). In the same way the apostles were emphatic that the tradition they were handing down came from the risen Christ: 'I did not receive it from any man, nor was I taught it; rather, I received it by revelation from Jesus Christ' (Gal. 1:12).

None of this means that there is no truth in other religions. It means that such truth as there is derives from Christ.

Thirdly, the Son's own nature and identity are known only to God the Father: 'No-one knows the Son except the Father'. Luke's form of this saying is more specific: 'No-one knows who the Son is except the Father' (Lk.10:22). Jesus made exactly the same point in response to Peter's confession at Caesarea Philippi: 'Blessed are you, Simon son of Jonah, for this was not revealed to you by man, but by my Father in heaven' (Mt. 16:17). What is emphasized here is not merely the historical fact that no-one recognized Jesus as God's Son, but the theological truth that no-one *can* recognize him. His identity is a mystery known only to God: his glory a depth penetrable only to omniscience. The Son is a being of such complexity that God alone can fathom and understand him. This means, in effect, that the Son, no less than the Father, is *deus absconditus*. Those who knew him only 'after the flesh' did not know him at all. They heard his teaching and recognized its authority. They saw his miracles and were filled with wonder. They saw his crucifixion and were disillusioned. Only the Father knew; and only the Father could make him known.

Fourthly, the Son is able to bear the burdens of the whole world: 'Come to me, all you who are weary and burdened, and I will give you rest.' It is easy to be so preoccupied with the problems involved in the Father–Son relationship that we overlook the astonishing nature of these words. The assumptions behind them, the promise they hold forth and the claim they propound are startling. An alleged parallel is found in the Prayer of Jesus, Son of Sirach, at the close of Ecclesiasticus (51:23–30), and there are indeed some verbal similarities: 'Draw near to me, ye unlearned ... Put your neck under the yoke.' The Son of Sirach, however, is inviting people to Wisdom, not to himself; his language is largely derived from Isaiah 55:1ff. and the book of Proverbs; and there is nothing in his words corresponding to 'Take *my* yoke ... *my* yoke is easy ... *I* will give you rest.' All that this passage in Ecclesiasticus proves is the absurdity of arguing on linguistic grounds that Matthew 11:27ff. comes from Hellenistic and Gnostic sources. In its underlying assumptions, Jesus' invitation, as Vos[74] points out, is reminiscent of some of the greatest words spoken by Yahweh in the Old Testament, most notably Isaiah 45:22. He is extending the same invitation and making the same promise as God himself: 'Turn to me and be saved, all you ends of the earth.' Such a commitment requires the highest possible Christology: 'for I am God, and there is no other' (Is. 45:22).

The transfiguration of Jesus

The idea of the divine sonship is also central to three of the great crises in Jesus' life: the baptism, the temptation and the transfiguration. The fact that the story of the transfiguration occurs in all three synoptics has not prevented many scholars dismissing it as either a mystical experience on the part of the disciples, a free creation of the Christian imagination or an unusually elaborate resurrection story. But the evidence strongly supports its authenticity.

First, it occupies virtually the same chronological slot in all three synoptics. It follows Peter's confession at Caesarea Philippi, Jesus' prediction of his passion and the enigmatic saying about the kingdom ('some who are standing here will not taste death before they see the kingdom of God come with power', Mk. 9:1). In turn, the transfiguration is followed by the descent into the community below and the encounter with the demoniac boy. If the story were anything other than historical, it would be difficult to account for this chronological fixity.

Secondly, the story has a precision of description which strongly suggests a historical episode. For example, there is the reference to 'after six days' (Mt.17:1; Mk. 9:2. Luke has the equivalent phrase, 'about eight days after', Lk. 9:28). There is the use of the homely word *gnapheus* ('fuller') to describe the whiteness of Jesus' garments; Luke's observation that Jesus was praying; and Peter's outburst, 'Let's put up three shelters!' This proposal reflects little credit on the apostle and it is difficult to conceive of the community inventing it. But in its given historical context it is exactly right. Peter was terrified. This would not override his natural impulsiveness, but it would mean that when he did speak he spoke nonsense.

Another recurring detail is Jesus' injunction to silence. According to all three synpotists Jesus forbade the disciples to disclose 'in those days' what they had seen. Again, dramatically this is exactly right. It accords ill, however, with the notion that the experience was merely visionary. Such injunctions to silence normally followed the performance of miracles (Mk. 1:44; 5:43; 7:36). They would be quite inappropriate to something inward and subjective. The fact that Jesus insisted on silence strongly suggests that the transfiguration had the same objective, wonder-evoking character as, say, the healing miracles. The disciples were forbidden to tell what they had *seen.*

Thirdly, the writer of 2 Peter clearly regarded the transfiguration as a historical event of considerable significance (see 2 Pet. 1:16–18). As J. B. Mayor[75] points out, what Peter (assuming him to be the author) is seeking to establish here is the ground of belief, particularly belief in the second coming of Christ. This is why he refers to the transfiguration: 'We did not follow cleverly invented stories when we told you about the power and coming [*parousia*] of our Lord Jesus Christ, but we were eye-witnesses of his majesty.' The usual procedure in the New Testament is to ground the hope of the *parousia* in the fact of the resurrection. Nothing in 2 Peter 1:16ff. contradicts this. In fact, the same essential emphasis on personal testimony remains, only this time it refers to the transfiguration. They saw him receive 'honour and glory'; and they heard a voice address him from the Majestic Glory. None of that was a myth or a fable, Peter insists. It was as real as the resurrection appearances; it confirmed the word of prophecy; and it gave the community a basis for faith in the *parousia.* It is with the latter that Peter is particularly concerned. The *parousia* could be no greater wonder than what they had already seen, which was, after all, a vision of the kingdom of God (Mk. 9:1). Besides, it was only to be expected that one so majestic as the Christ of the transfiguration should receive final honour and glory on the scale envisaged in the *parousia.* The important thing, however, is Peter's logic. He argues to the hope of the *parousia* from the fact of the transfiguration, clearly implying that, whatever the nature of the event, it happened *before their eyes*, not in the depth of their imaginations.

Finally, the transfiguration is fully congruous with the portrait of Christ painted by the synoptics. This is the crucial issue. As A. M. Ramsey points out,[76] 'If the view of his person which was held by the evangelists and the apostolic church in general is true, then a frankly supernatural occurrence in the course of his earthly ministry will be credible.' In its own setting, the transfiguration is entirely 'natural', because it refers to one to whom God was *Abba*, to whom disease, death and demons yielded, and to whom at last the grave itself surrendered. To those who believe such things, the transfiguration presents no difficulty. On the other hand, for those to whom such a view of Jesus is incredible, the transfiguration will be incredible. This brings us back to the basic assumptions of Christology. The issue is the same as the one posed by Peter in John 13:8: 'You shall never wash my feet.' Peter's problem was that he did not see how one who was his Lord could wash his feet. The problem of the modern critic is that he cannot see how one who washes feet can be his Lord. From both directions, the conclusion is the same: there can be no incarnation of the divine. It is along this road that the general argument against the transfiguration proceeds. Christ is human, therefore he cannot be divine and therefore events such as the transfiguration must be mythical.

Accepting the historicity of the event, however, what does it mean? For our present purpose the crucial thing is the Voice from heaven: 'This is my Son, whom I love. Listen to him!' (Mk. 9:7). Matthew's version adds the words, 'with him I am well pleased'. Luke substitutes 'chosen/choice' (*eklelegmenos*) for 'beloved' (*agapētos*). None of these variations makes any substantial difference to the sense.

The words serve, first of all, to confirm Peter's confession of Christ at Caesarea Philippi: 'You are the Christ, the Son of the living God' (Mt. 16:16). As we have seen, the two incidents are placed in close proximity in all three synoptics. There was obviously some danger of the impression made by Peter's confession receding. As a matter of supernatural insight (Mt. 16:17) it was something which even Peter himself might not be able to sustain. The narrative of the transfiguration is certainly at pains to stress that the incident was directed mainly at the disciples. He was transfigured before *them*; there apeared unto *them* Elijah with Moses; there came a cloud and overshadowed *them*. Even the Voice strikes the same note: 'listen to him'. Considered on its divine side, Peter's confession (or, more precisely, the revelation which lay behind it) was intended to strengthen the disciples for the ordeal which lay before them. They were to see the Passion in the light of the Glory. The transfiguration has the same function, the only difference being that in this case the procedure is more vivid. The transfiguration itself was memorable, imparting to Jesus' 'form' an unsurpassable majesty. The presence of Moses and Elijah talking with Jesus underlined the augustness of his native sphere and the exaltedness of his office. The cloud, reminiscent of the Shekinah, spoke of the divine presence residing upon Jesus. Above all, the Voice gave an unforgettable endorsement of his sonship: 'This is my Son, whom I love'; adding (according to Luke) that he is elect and precious; and adding further that he, the promised prophet like Moses (Dt. 18:15; Acts 3:22), is the only voice they are to listen to.

In the immediate historical outworking, of course, the transfiguration failed of its purpose. The disciples did not, in the event, see the passion in the light of the transfiguration. Instead, they deserted him (Mk. 14:50). But this is no proof that the incident itself was not fitted to strengthen and encourage. In fact, if we were to judge Jesus by the short-term progress of his disciples we would have to conclude that he was a very poor teacher. When we take a longer view, however, the picture is different. The lesson, 'Listen to him!' was taken to heart. Furthermore, it is clear from 2 Peter 1:16ff. that the fundamental Christological message, too, went home, and that the disciples continued to derive support from it to the very end of their lives. They never forgot the 'majesty' they had seen. Nor did they ever forget the honour and glory he received from the Father. This, as Peter indicates, made them confident of his power and *parousia*, his lordship and his divine sonship.

But the message was not only for the original disciples. True, unlike the identical words spoken at the baptism, the Voice at the transfiguration was oriented specifically to the three apostles. But it was undoubtedly heard by Jesus as well. This is brought out clearly in Peter's account: *he* received from God the Father honour and glory. The Voice was borne to him by the Majestic Glory. These details make it plain that the Son, too, was to see the passion in the light of the transfiguration. He was to take the cup as one encouraged by the knowledge of his own identity, reassured as to his Father's on-going love and fortified by heaven's endorsement ('I am well pleased'). 'What the Baptism is to the public ministry of Jesus,' wrote A. M. Ramsey, 'the Transfiguration is to the passion.'[77] The cross stands between the transfiguration on the one side and the resurrection on the other.

Yet the transfiguration is more than a confirmation of the glory of Christ. It also reinforces the prediction of the passion. To the consternation of the disciples, Jesus had responded to Peter's confession at Caesarea Philippi by declaring that 'the Son of Man must suffer many things' (Mk. 8:31). These words were hard to take. The disciples did not want to hear such nonsense (Mk. 8:33). They certainly did not want to talk about it. Yet in Luke's account of the transfiguration the suffering of Jesus is precisely what the heavenly visitors, Moses and Elijah, do want to talk about. They discussed with Jesus the 'departure' he was to accomplish at Jerusalem (Lk. 9:31).

Whether or not Peter wrote 2 Peter (including the reference to the transfiguration, 1:16–18), it is interesting that in 1 Peter 1:12 the apostle refers to the angels' interest in the sufferings of Christ: 'angels long to look into these things'. The lesson on the Mount had been well learned: the cross was the talk of heaven. It would be fascinating to know what aspects of it Moses and Elijah discussed. They would certainly have expressed gratitude and assured him of the interest (and indeed the astonishment) of heaven. Nor is it inherently impossible that Moses and Elijah were able to enhance Jesus' understanding of the 'departure'. They had been prophets and now they enjoyed the insights of glorified humanity. Just as they had earlier ministered to Jesus through their written words, so, now, they probably ministered to him face to face. Such a ministry of encouragement on their part poses no more theological problems than the ministry of the angel who comforted him in Gethsemane (Lk. 22:43).

Yet there is no doubt that in the encounter with Moses and Elijah the passion, too, is transfigured. The very word 'departure' suggests this. So does the word 'accomplish' (*plēroun*). The cross is to be no mere passion, and Jesus no helpless victim. Calvary is to be an achievement, a mighty redemptive act, securing deliverance and salvation. The cross is to be the instrument of that Exodus which calls into being the New Israel.

But even this is not all. The transfiguration also represents the fulfilment of the words of Mark 9:1: 'some who are standing here will not taste death before they see the kingdom of God come with power'. All three synoptic accounts are prefaced by some such words, linking the incident to a special manifestation of the kingdom of God.

One possible interpretation of this is to link the transfiguration with the resurrection. From this point of view, the glory on the Mount is proleptic: a pre-vision of the Lord's resurrection body. But there are difficulties with this. One is the injunction to silence (Mk. 9:9). By the time of the transfiguration, the resurrection was no longer part of the Messianic Secret: Jesus had referred to it openly at Caesarea Philippi (Mk. 8:31). Another difficulty is that the resurrection did not, by itself, lead directly to such a transformation of Jesus' body as is indicated here. The risen Christ could be mistaken for a gardener (Jn. 20:15) or for an ordinary traveller (Lk. 24:16ff.). It is better to say that the transfiguration is proleptic of the entire exaltation of Jesus, including resurrection, ascension and heavenly session; and including also the *parousia*. Taken together, these constitute the glory which was to follow the sufferings of Christ. From this point of view, what the disciples saw on the Mount corresponds with what Paul saw on the Damascus Road (Acts 9:3) and John saw on the Isle of Patmos (Rev. 1:12ff.). They saw Jesus as he is (1 Jn. 3:2). The *parousia* does not, as such, add anything to the glory already possessed by Jesus. It is a revelation (*apokalypsis*) or appearing (*epiphaneia*) of the glory; it makes it present (the root meaning of *parousia*), but it does not enhance it. In effect, the church on the Mount was given a foretaste of the glory which, for Jesus, lay on the far side of his sufferings.

It is no contradiction of this to go on to say that what happened in the transfiguration was also a momentary unveiling of the underlying divine splendour of Jesus. In the words of Calvin:

> Christ clothed himself with heavenly glory for a short time ... in the brightness of an unusual form his Godhead became visible ... his transfiguration did not altogether enable his disciples to see Christ as he now is in heaven, but gave them a taste of his boundless glory, such as they were able to comprehend ... this was not a complete exhibition of the heavenly glory of Christ, but, under symbols which were adapted to the capacity of the flesh, he enabled them to taste in part what could not be fully comprehended.[78]

The background to this is that Jesus, the pre-existent Son of God, lived in this world under conditions of *krypsis*. His glory was veiled by his ordinary human appearance; by poverty, homelessness, hunger, thirst, weariness, powerlessness, friendlessness, pain and sorrow; and, at last, by death. But in the transfiguration, for a moment, the veil is drawn aside. He is given a form which corresponds to his true identity. He is attested by heaven. He is overshadowed by the Shekinah. Of course, as Calvin said, these are not the glory. But they are the insignia of it, just as, formerly, Yahweh had appeared on Sinai in the accoutrements of splendour; and just as, in the *parousia*, Jesus finally will come in the paraphernalia of greatness. Had there been no *krypsis* Jesus would have moved all his days amid such attestations of majesty.

The reason that the transfiguration can be simultaneously both a pre-vision of the exalted humanity and a revelation of the underlying divine glory is made clear in the Gospel of John. The exaltation of Jesus consists precisely in the elevation of his total person to share in the pre-existent glory of the *Logos* (Jn. 17:5). For Jesus, glorification is a return to the Father: a resumption of a previous state. This is why we cannot drive a wedge between the glory of the exalted humanity and the glory of the divine nature. Even when he comes in the *parousia* he will come in the glory of his Father (Mt. 16:27).

If we relate this to its psychological horizon in the experience of Christ, it means that on the very threshold of the passion he is fortified with both the Father's acknowledgment and the Father's promise. He is

God's Son; and beyond the cross there lies transfiguration and glory. But there are other psychological horizons, too: the disciples, soon to be devastated; and the church down the ages. In the short term, as we have seen, the transfiguration did little for the disciples, but when God restored their hope (1 Pet. 1:3) the transfiguration came into its own, as we see in 2 Peter 1:16ff. From this point of view, it has an on-going ministry. For Jesus, the trauma is past: he has entered into his rest. For us, it is not past. We are still struggling and suffering. To that situation the transfiguration still speaks, because it discloses not only the glory eternally possessed by the Lord, and not only the glory for which, as incarnate Mediator, he was destined, but also the glory of his people. Anselm expressed it aphoristically: *suam suorumque glorificationem praemonstravit* ('He gave a pre-view of his own glory and of the glory of his own').[79] The transfiguration showed not only what *he* would become but what *we* would become. The New Testament makes this connection explicitly. We are to be where he is (Jn. 17:24). Our bodies are to be conformed exactly to his (Phil. 3:21). We, in him, are to become sharers in the divine nature (2 Pet. 1:4). For Jesus on the Mount, this vision of what lay beyond the cross, not only for himself but for his people, would have been an immeasurable encouragement.

A. M. Ramsey relates this to the twin concepts, *opsis* and *theiosis*. *Opsis* is the spiritual vision which beholds the glory of the Lord. *Theiosis* is the transfiguring process which results: we are changed into the same image (2 Cor. 3:18), transformed by the renewing of our minds (Rom. 12:2), and one day we shall be like him, because we shall see him as he is (1 Jn. 3:2). This goes back to the core of God's own redemptive determination: to conform all his people to the image of his Son (Rom. 8:29). Yet, as the sequel to the transfiguration shows, neither *opsis* nor *theiosis* goes on in ideal circumstances. We have to go down from the Mount to the demon-possessed valley. It is there that we must practise *opsis*; and only there that we can experience *theiosis*.

4

THE JESUS OF HISTORY

Across what Lessing called 'the broad, ugly ditch of history' we seem to be in secure possession of two remarkable facts.

First, that the early church believed Jesus Christ to be divine. It applied to him the highest conceivable designations (Son of God, Son of Man, Lord, God); it saw him as possessing the full range of divine attributes, performing the full range of divine functions and enjoying the full range of divine prerogatives; it worshipped him and prayed to him and broke out in doxology at the mere mention of his name. These early Christians did not simply catch the faith *of* Jesus: they had faith *in* Jesus.

The extraordinary thing is that there is no trace of any controversy on this issue in the early church. There was fierce argument over many things, notably Gentile mission, the nature of justification and the place of the law in the Christian life. There was obviously also fierce debate between the church and the outside world as to the identity of Christ. But within the church itself there was no such debate.

Considering the implications of belief in the deity of Christ, this unembarrassed, un-selfconscious, unhesitating belief is quite remarkable. They believed God to be invisible, yet worshipped one they had seen, heard and embraced. They believed in a God of almost absolute transcendence, yet worshipped a man. They believed God to be one, yet worshipped him *and* his Son. *A priori*, all such developments were inconceivable. Yet the evidence that this is what actually happened is overwhelming. The same kind of argument as establishes that Muslims regard Muhammad as The Prophet establishes that the early Christians worshipped Christ as divine.

So we come to the second remarkable fact: Jesus saw himself as divine; at least, the only Jesus accessible to us in our historical sources (the gospels) saw and projected himself as divine.

Precisely, here, however, we run into the most serious problem facing Christology today: the problem of historical scepticism. Many scholars believe that the gospels convey an entirely false impression. They are legendary creations of the early church and as such have no historical credibility, least of all when they speak of a divine Messiah. 'The Jesus of history' was a more or less typical, unpretentious Rabbi. It was the church itself which invented 'the Christ of faith'.

At its most radical, this historical scepticism is associated with the name of Rudolf Bultmann. Many have seen Bultmann as an incorrigible reductionist, but it is a tribute to the complexity of his thought that the American translators of one of his most influential books, *Jesus and the Word*, felt bound to enter the disclaimer, '(T)he book is no mere return to theological traditionalism'.[1] His plea for demythologization was made in *Jesus Christ and Mythology* and 'The New Testament and Mythology'.[2] He was careful to point out that what he was calling for was not the elimination of myth. That was the way of Literalism, which sought to remove all mythology on the mistaken assumption that one was then left with a core of values idealized in Jesus. What Bultmann sought was the reinterpretation of myth. By the time he has carried through his programme, however, little of the New Testament is left. In one of his most famous statements he declared, 'it is impossible to use electric light and the wireless and to avail ourselves of modern medical and surgical discoveries, and at the same time to believe in the New Testament world of spirits and miracles'.[3] The list of items to be discarded is formidable: heaven, hell, angels, demons, miracles, resurrection and judgment, to mention but a few.

What is much more serious, however, is Bultmann's view that the New Testament clothes the Christ-event itself in the language of mythology, all of which has to be stripped away. Here again the process is a drastic one. The pre-existence, eternal sonship and incarnation of Christ must go. And so, too, of course, must the virgin birth; and the idea of the cross as a sacrifice; and the resurrection, ascension and heavenly session; and the *parousia*; and the mission of the Comforter; and the whole corpus of mythical eschatology, including such ideas as immortality, personal resurrection and eternal conscious existence in a state of glory.

Even so, the process of elimination is not complete. Virtually all the biographical material in the gospels has to be discarded because it cannot be verified by rigorous critical scholarship. Hence the famous conclusion: 'we can now know almost nothing concerning the life and personality of Jesus, since the early Christian sources show no interest in either, are moreover fragmentary and often legendary; and other sources about Jesus do not exist'.[4]

The list of legends, like the list of myths, is a long one, the prime casualties being the great turning-points in the gospel story: the baptism, the confession at Caesarea Philippi, the transfiguration, the last supper and the empty tomb. Even more important, anything that suggests that Jesus thought of himself as divine is to be rejected. He did not believe himself to be the Messiah. Nor did he regard himself as Lord or as the Son of God. These titles arose much later, in the Greek-speaking churches resulting from the Pauline missions. Indeed, it was these churches that invented the *kerygma*, if we are to understand by that 'a *kerygma* proclaiming Jesus Christ'. From this point of view, '*The message of Jesus* is a presupposition for the theology of the New Testament rather than a part of that theology itself.'[5]

Response

The first response to be made to this is that Bultmann appears to assume that the people of the first century were credulous to the point of universal stupidity. This is not the impression we receive from the New Testament. The dominical and apostolic miracles filled the onlookers with wonder precisely because they did not fit into the prevailing worldview. It was no more common in the first century than in the twentieth for a mere word to still a storm or a mixture of clay and spittle to restore sight to the blind; and when Paul preached the resurrection at the University of Athens, the result was exactly the same as it would have been at Marburg in 1930. The dead stayed dead in the first century with the same monotonous regularity as they do in the twentieth. Early

Christian belief in the resurrection cannot be explained as due to mere ignorance of the facts of death.

Secondly, Bultmann is guilty of chronological snobbery, dismissing the cosmology of the first century as puerile and defining that of the 1930s as definitive. Late twentieth century man uses not only electric light, wireless and modern medicine, but nuclear energy and micro-computers, both of which resulted from paradigm-shifts in physics. We have already left Bultmann's world far behind; and we know that our own world will soon give way to another. Yet we continue to consult horoscopes, admire eastern mysticism, practise transcendental meditation and (like the ancient Canaanites) look for God in the high places. If our concern is to adjust to the spirit of the age, perhaps the more mystical and irrational our Christianity the better.

Thirdly, Bultmann's historical scepticism is incoherent. The gospel writers were well placed to bear witness to the life and ministry of Christ. They were contemporaries, companions and (often) eye-witnesses. They shared his language and culture. They revered him as a Rabbi, hanging on his every word and inevitably jealous of any attempt to attribute to him sentiments he never expressed. In some cases (notably Luke) they were self-conscious historians, carefully checking earlier records and consulting eye-witnesses.

All this raises an important issue of critical methodolgy. The fact that we today cannot be absolutely certain that an event occurred does not mean that another historian in another time and place could not be certain.[6] St Luke, having checked the earliest written accounts and spoken to eye-witnesses was absolutely certain that the transfiguration had occurred. Bultmann was certain that it is a legend. But his scepticism rested on two slender foundations: first, he was not prepared to take Luke's word for it; and secondly, he was not in a position (as Luke was) to check it for himself.

The effect of such scepticism is to make all historical scholarship impossible. Indeed, as Carnley points out, 'if the conception of truth is dissolved the conception of falsity dissolves with it. Thus, Bultmann is unable to say that it is certainly true that any of the statements in the nineteenth-century lives of Jesus were false!'[7] In practice, Bultmann is totally inconsistent. Although on the one hand we can know nothing of the life and personality of Jesus, on the other we can know that he did not regard himself as Messiah or accept the designations 'Lord' or 'Son of God'. We can also know that there is radical discontinuity between the teaching of Jesus and the *kerygma* of the early church; that the Matthaean form of the saying, 'Be perfect, as your heavenly Father is perfect' is older than the Lucan;[8] and that Jesus never thought of a mission to the Gentiles.[9] How, on Bultmann's principles, can we leap across the broad, ugly ditch of history towards certainty on such questions? Without impugning the great scholar's motives, it is difficult to avoid the conclusion that, albeit occasionally, he knew a good deal about the life and personality of Jesus. He was certain about what he wanted to be certain about.

But, not only does the kind of scepticism found in Bultmann make historical scholarship impossible, it would also make it impossible to verify any scientific law. Lessing stated his famous principle thus: 'If no historical truth can be demonstrated, then nothing can be demonstrated by means of historical truths. That is: *accidental truths of history can never become the proof of necessary truths of reason*.'[10] This poses as serious a threat to physics as it does to Christology. All scientific laws have to be verified by experiment and each experiment is an historical event. These experiments range from Galileo's dropping objects of different weights from the leaning tower of Pisa to highly complex modern research on the behaviour of sub-atomic particles under extreme conditions. However different the experiments, the end result is the same: the great paradigm shifts of science ('eternal truths of reason') depend for verification on a small number of events ('experiments') each one of which by itself can yield only accidental truths of history. If this is so, we cannot rule out in principle the possibility that such events as the empty tomb and the resurrection appearances may also prove eternal truths of reason.

The basic difficulty is that Bultmann is guilty of 'fallibilism': every witness is fallible and every compiler of every account is fallible and consequently all the records are unreliable. To put it otherwise: since we cannot secure complete verification we cannot be certain of anything.[11] If this criterion were applied to everyday life, human society would collapse. The world's stock-markets would crash, news agencies would go bankrupt and football fans would go mad because news of their teams' victories would always be 'unconfirmed'.

The creativity of the early church

It has to be said, too, that Bultmann's reliance on the creativity and inventiveness of the early church places a serious strain on our credulity. It ignores, for example, the powerful disincentives to divinizing Jesus which operated in the cultural milieu in which the gospels were born. The early believers were Jews and the apostles were

Jews, and nothing was more basic to their ideology than a horror of idolatry and polytheism. For James suddenly to decide to worship his brother or Saul of Tarsus to pray to a crucified Messianic pretender or John to place another beside God as his equal borders on the inexplicable. Some overwhelming force of evidence or some irresistible spiritual power might sweep such men along to such a faith, but they certainly had no predisposition to it. On the contrary their every instinct protested against it. As Hoskyns and Davey point out, 'The gospel was as much a scandal to the first century as it is to the twentieth.'[12]

To ascribe the gospel portrait of Jesus to the inventiveness of the early church also ignores the horrendous disadvantages under which Jesus laboured as a candidate for deification. Suppose that the monotheist prejudices of first-century Jews had been overcome and that they were open to some extension of their notion of deity; suppose they were even willing to entertain the idea that a man might, in some sense, be God; would they have turned to a crucified man, one whose weakness was only too palpable and whose sinful, criminal status had been highlighted so dramatically? It surely required the impulse of more than ordinary human loyalty to divinize a man crucified for blasphemy and Messianic delusions. Even in a Hellenistic milieu such a movement would have been totally unlikely, as Martin Hengel points out: 'The incarnation of a divine figure and still more his shameful death on the cross was not a "point of contact" but a "scandal" and a "stumbling block".' Men like Pliny regarded the worship of Jesus as 'depraved folly' and 'for educated or noble men of antiquity the crucified Jesus was only an expression of folly, shame and hatefulness'.[13] Logically, then, increased contact with Greek thought should have meant either a playing down of Jesus' divinity or a rapid descent into Docetism. Whatever the dynamics of the development of early Christian doctrine it certainly cannot be explained as an attempt to conciliate its intellectual environment. Instead, the Pauline gospel recklessly insisted on two blatantly incompatible truths: the lordship of Jesus and the primacy of the cross (Gal. 6:14).

There remains the fact that any attempt to explain 'the Christ of faith' as a creation of the early church still leaves the question, How do we account for the early church? What can explain the emergence in first-century Palestine of a rapidly expanding community of men and women who, ten years after Jesus' crucifixion, worshipped him as divine, preached his divinity with astonishing fervour and stood ready to lay down their lives for the belief that he was Lord of creation? The Christ of the New Testament tradition could account for such a phenomenon.

He saw himself as the Son of God, spoke like the Son of God and acted like the Son of God. In vindication of his deity, he was raised from the dead. In accordance with his promise and in pursuance of his ministry he poured out the Holy Spirit. Such a Christ explains the other facts such as the faith of the church and the expansion of Christianity. He also accounts for the New Testament itself. Indeed, if the Jesus of history was not the Christ of faith, the very existence of the New Testament becomes virtually inexplicable. Is the Christ of the epistle of James the work of the apostle's imagination? Is the Jesus of the synoptics the product of a syndicate? Is the *Logos* of John an invention of genius? And who was Peter kidding when he wrote, 'Though you have not seen him, you love him' (1 Pet. 1:8)? Had *he* seen the Christ of faith? 'The attempt to throw upon the evangelists the responsibility of having manipulated the earlier tradition in the interests of a remarkable Christology does not survive a rigidly critical examination,' write Hoskyns and Davey.[14] 'Their records have a clear and conscious purpose. That is obvious. But they extracted their purpose from the traditions they received: they did not impose it roughly upon a material unable to bear it.'

The gospels and scholarship

Christianity has nothing to fear from rigorous scholarship. On the contrary, the application of stringent historical criteria serves only to confirm our confidence in the gospels. This is true if we apply, for example, Bultmann's own principle of *dissimilarity* (which gives a higher credibility-rating to material for which there is no obvious context in the life of the early church). There is nothing in what we know of the first Christians to explain, for instance, Jesus' remarkable use of the title 'the Son of Man' (the early church never used it); nor the central role of the 'kingdom of God' in reports of the preaching of Jesus; nor Jesus' frequent involvement in disputes over the Sabbath. The only explanation for the prominence of such material is that it accurately reflects the specific interests and usages of Jesus.

The same conclusion follows if we apply the criterion of *non-intentionality*. This assumes that the intention behind the early Christian preaching was to build up a picture not of the Jesus of history but of the Christ of faith (pre-existent, almighty and divine). On such an assumption, any material which runs counter to this intention gains high marks for plausibility, even from the most radical critic. A considerable body of synoptic material falls into this category, notably Jesus' confession of ignorance, his inability to perform miracles because of people's unbelief and his manifest proneness to weakness and exhaustion. We might even argue that the prominence given to the passion in all the gospels renders Bultmann's assumption as to the church's motivation totally implausible. If the overriding concern of the early disciples was to aggrandize their Master, why does Mark devote seven chapters to the passion and only a few verses to the resurrection? Besides, the gospels contain not only a large amount of material which detracts from the greatness of Jesus, but an even larger amount which must have been embarrassing to the most prominent members of the church itself. None of the Twelve emerges from the synoptics with credit. They are portrayed as men of little comprehension and even less faith, frequently earning their Lord's rebuke, sometimes doing Satan's work, fleeing in Jesus' hour of peril, denying him in order to save their own skins and receiving news of his resurrection with incredulity. Why would such material have been invented?

The gospels stand up equally well to the criterion of *multiple attestation*. The witness to the Christ of faith is not confined to any one author or period or stratum or *genre* of the New Testament. It is all-pervasive. Open the New Testament where we will, we find not some benign Galilean primitive, but one who regards himself as uniquely and exclusively the bearer of the revelation of God: a revelation which summons all who encounter it to instant and urgent decision.[15] Whether we look at the synoptics or at John, at Mark or at L, M and Q, at Paul or at the writer to the Hebrews, at James or at Peter, at Jerusalem or at Antioch, at the Aramaic milieu or at the Greek, the portrait is the same: a Christ who is King, Lord and Son of God, risen from the dead, living in his people and saving the world.

The same conclusion follows if we apply the principle of *coherence*. Taken by itself and isolated from its context, no fact of the synoptic tradition is intelligible, and to a large extent the policy of radical criticism has been to divide and conquer. But in their total context the details make perfect sense. The attenuated Christ of recent Christian scepticism could not have built a mouse-trap, let alone a church. We need a Jesus who can explain the Christ of faith: one big enough to account for Jewish hostility and Roman fear; one big enough to explain why he became the subject of such a book as the Gospel of John: one who made such an impression that people easily believed that he had risen from the dead; such a colossus that within a few years of his death those who had known him best were identifying him with Yahweh and laying down their lives rather than refrain from worshipping him; a figure of such universality that his church has had a multi-ethnic, multicultural appeal without precedent in the history of religion.

What manner of man was he: able to overcome the scandal of his crucifixion and exert such an influence on human history that to this day scholars eagerly discuss his impact not only on religion but on art and science, politics and literature? Is it credible that one so insignificant that nobody had any interest in his life and personality (certainly not enough interest to give an accurate account of them) could have made such an impact on human affairs? The synoptic Jesus renders Christianity explicable. Take away the synoptic Jesus, replace him with a demythologized one, and Christianity becomes an insoluble historical enigma.

There is no doubt that Christianity, as a religion, depends on the deity of Christ as it does on no other single doctrine. If that doctrine had its origin only in the minds of the disciples, then Christianity is an unprecedented exercise in self-delusion and one would expect its early history to be fraught with the symptoms of incoherence and psychosis. Instead, it quickly became the most dynamic force in the Empire, winning a decisive victory in the intellectual battle and transforming society by sheer force of character. To ask us to base such a history on collective self-delusion is to task our credulity to breaking-point. On the other hand, to build it on the self-understanding and self-disclosure of Jesus is to relate it coherently to objective testimony and psychological reality. The Christ of faith explains the belief in the resurrection, the martyrdom of Peter and Paul, the Gospel of John, the conversion of Constantine and the massive credal statements of Nicea and Chalcedon.

Scholarship and faith

Where Bultmann is right, of course, is in his insistence that historical scholarship by itself cannot produce faith. But this has always been recognized. Christian faith is never a matter of pure reason. It is indeed rational in the very important sense that it is always based on evidence. But it cannot be engendered by the force of evidence alone. The apostles certainly never imagined that either their own eloquence or the persuasiveness of their arguments could account for the faith of their converts. Something else happened, without which faith would have been impossible. What that was is indicated in 1 Peter 1:12: 'those who have preached the gospel ... *by the Holy Spirit sent from heaven*'. This is exactly what Jesus had promised: the Paraclete would bear witness to him (Jn. 15:26).

This principle cannot be dismissed as a novelty introduced by recent Christian theology to explain the collapse of faith in the twentieth century. It is a central emphasis of the historical Christian tradition. According to John Calvin, for example,

> the testimony of the Spirit is more excellent than all reason. For as God alone is a fit witness of himself in his own Word, so also the Word will not find acceptance in men's hearts before it is sealed by the inward testimony of the Spirit. The same Spirit, therefore, who has spoken through the mouths of the prophets must penetrate into our hearts to persuade us that they faithfully proclaimed what had been divinely commanded.[16]

Two dangers, however, lie precisely here.

First, that we shall allow ourselves to ask, But how do we know that the Holy Spirit is correct? This is to flee again to rationalism, as if science or archaeology or historical scholarship could stand above the Spirit's testimony and vindicate it. This is impossible. The Spirit's witness is ultimate, often enabling faith to survive and flourish in the face of what it neither knows nor understands. Scholarship can give a substantial vindication of the facts, but it cannot enable us to see compelling beauty in the face of Jesus. That is possible only when God the Father, through the Holy Spirit, shares with us his own view of his Son.

The second danger is that because the sources of both belief and unbelief are ultimately spiritual we shall lose sight of the gravity of the latter. On one level, unbelief is due to the fact that 'the god of this age has blinded the minds of unbelievers' (2 Cor. 4:4). But on another, it is a wilful rejection of evidence. The bottom line here is that Jesus of Nazareth saw himself as the Son of God. Whatever we do afterwards, we must first of all decide what to do with this. If he was correct, we must fall down and worship him. If he was not correct, we must crucify him.

What we cannot do is to conclude that he was wrong and then add, 'But he was a great and good man nevertheless, and we love and revere him!' We could do that if Harnack were correct in his claim that Jesus pointed only to the Father and away from himself.[17] But that claim is historically unsustainable. We could do it, too, if Mackey were correct in portraying Jesus as one who merely called us to a faith like his own (a faith in which we meet the reality of God).[18] But that, too, is unsustainable. The historical Jesus portrayed himself not as the model of faith but as its object. Again, we could do it if Jesus was as Schweitzer portrayed him in the most famous passage of his *Quest of the Historical Jesus*:

> The Baptist appears and cries: 'Repent, for the Kingdom of heaven is at hand.' Soon after that comes Jesus, and in the knowledge that he is the coming Son of Man lays hold of the wheel of the world to set it moving on that last revolution which is to bring all ordinary history to a close. It refuses to turn, and he throws himself upon it. Then it does turn; and crushes him. Instead of bringing in the eschatological conditions, he has destroyed them. The wheel rolls onward, and the mangled body of the one immeasurably great Man, who was strong enough to think of himself as the spiritual ruler of mankind and to bend history to his purpose, is hanging upon it still. That is his victory and his reign.[19]

But this, too, is historically false. The consistent eschatology of Schweitzer is closer to the truth than the Liberalism of Harnack, but it discounts the resurrection, it discounts the centrality of the cross in post-Easter faith and it discounts the faith of the disciples. In their case we confront the same dilemma as we do in the case of their Lord: either he was God or they were not good. If their Christology was wrong, their whole credibility is destroyed and it is simple dishonesty to pretend otherwise.

The central feature of Christianity is (and always has been) the worship of Jesus. Any credible account of its origins must explain the rise of such worship. Where can that be found except in Jesus' understanding of himself as divine? To reject that is not only to deprive Christian worship of its legitimacy but to convict the church of self-deception and duplicity. In Christianity, the Sermon on the Mount is set in the framework of the virgin birth on the one side and the empty tomb on the other. Take away the framework and neither Christianity nor the Sermon on the Mount can survive. The 'I say unto you' statements of the Sermon are as imperious as the 'I am' statements of John.

The theological world has altered almost beyond recognition since the era of Victorian certainty. Yet the Christological *trilemma* posed by John Duncan in his *Colloquia Peripatetica*[20] remains as pointed as ever: 'Christ either deceived mankind by conscious fraud, or he was himself deluded and self-deceived, or he was Divine. There is no getting out of this trilemma. It is inexorable.' It would be far more creditable for

Christian theology to face this trilemma honestly than to engage in blatant denial of the deity of Christ while simultaneously contriving not only to admire his sanity and integrity, but to invoke his name in prayer and adoration. If the apostles manufactured him they were frauds (and geniuses); if he manufactured himself, he was a fraud (and a maniac); if he was what he (and they) said he was, then in him we meet ultimate reality: God in human form and man as the revelation of God.

5

THE CHRIST OF FAITH: "VERY GOD OF VERY GOD"

The early Christian church, we have seen, worshipped Christ as God. But the statement, 'Jesus Christ is God' (or any statement linking such a subject and such a predicate) raises momentous questions. In the first four centuries after the apostles, these questions were raised in an acute form and debated by a long series of theologians of outstanding ability. Their conclusions were encapsulated in a succession of credal statements, at once precise and pregnant, which serve as both boundary-markers and starting-points for Christological reflection today.

The single most important statement was the declaration of the Council of Nicea (325) that Christ, as the Son of God, was *homoousios* (consubstantial) with the Father. This patristic term is embodied in all the great Protestant creeds. The first of the *Articles of Religion* (1562) of the Church of England declares that 'in the unity of this Godhead there be three Persons, *of one substance*, power and eternity'. The language of the Westminster Confession is virtually identical: 'In the unity of the Godhead there be three persons *of one substance*, power and eternity' (II.III).[1]

The idea of consubstantiality was introduced into Christian theology in response to the Arian heresy. Recent scholarship has been much less confident than that of the past as to what Arianism actually was. According to Rowan Williams,[2] for example, 'The time has probably come to relegate the term "Arianism" at best to inverted commas, and preferably oblivion – with all its refinements of early, late, neo or semi (which last does appear to have vanished from serious scholarly discussion).'

Williams is doubtless right about the refinements, but it seems premature to conclude that the Nicene Council, Athanasius and the great Cappadocian theologians were tilting at windmills. However difficult it may be at our point in history to secure clarity on the details (particularly with regard to the *homoian-* or *semi*-Arians), the main points of Arius' own teaching can be stated with some confidence; and the fourth-century fathers certainly thought that Arianism was an identifiable phenomenon.[3]

First of all, Arius denied the self-existence and eternity of the Son. 'The Son', he wrote, 'has an origin, but God is unoriginated.' This did not preclude pre-existence: the Son was begotten timelessly, before aeons. Yet, 'There was when he was not'; and 'before he was begotten, or created or determined or established he did not exist'. He owed his existence to the Father's will, 'having received life and being from the Father and various kinds of glory, since he gave him existence alongside himself'.[4]

Secondly, Arius denied that the Son is equal with God. The Son was a creature, the Father was Creator and consequently they were totally unlike in substance. This was the gravamen of a letter written in 319 by Alexander, Bishop of Alexandria, to explain why he had excommunicated Arius. Arius, he alleged, held the Son to be a creature (*ktisma*) and a product (*poiēma*). He was not 'like the Father in substance' (*homoios kat' ousian*): on the contrary, he would not have come into existence had the Father not made him; and, like all creatures, he was mutable (*treptos*) and alterable (*alloiotos*). Yet the blatant impiety of worshipping a creature was obscured by the fact that to Arius the Son was no *ordinary* creature. He was a special creature, 'made for our sake, in order that God should create us through him as an instrument'.[5] Qualifications of this kind naturally had the effect of confusing the faithful and prolonging the controversy. After all, it could be said, Arius' Christ was a magnificent being; and the role Arius ascribed to him in creation could even claim the support of Scripture: 'through whom he made the universe' (Heb. 1:2). In the last analysis, however, the idea of the Son as a mediating creature is redolent only of Gnosticism, as if it were beneath the dignity of the true God to meddle with matter in the dirty business of creating.

Nicea: the response to Arianism

It was to combat Arianism that the Council of Nicea was convened in 325. The anti-Arian party, led during the Council by Alexander, Bishop of Alexandria, and afterwards by his successor, Athanasius, was driven by fundamentally religious concerns, whatever other, baser factors may have contributed to their motivation. In their judgment, the future of Christianity as a religion was at stake. If Christ were not God, he could not be the revelation of God. If Christ were not God, men had not been redeemed by God. If Christ were not God, believers were not united to God. Above all, if Christ were not God, Christians had no right to worship him. Indeed, if they did so, they were reverting to pagan superstition and idolatry.

These concerns are particularly clear in Athanasius. In the *Second Oration against the Arians* he refers specifically to the soteriological impact of Arianism: 'if the Son were a creature, man had remained mortal as before, not being joined to God; for a creature had not joined creatures to God ... nor would a portion of the creation have been the creation's salvation, as needing salvation itself' (69). Athanasius made the point all the more strongly because he tended to understand salvation in terms of *theiosis* ('deification') and the idea that Christ was a mere creature was absolutely fatal to this: 'man had not been deified if joined to a creature, or unless the Son were very God ... For therefore the union was of this kind, that He might unite what is man by nature to Him who is in the nature of the Godhead, and his salvation and deification might be sure'.[6]

There can be no doubt that Athanasius and his colleagues were correct in their perception that Arianism threatened Christianity at its very heart. If Christ were a creature, no matter how exalted, or even a kind of inferior deity (god, but less than the Absolute God) worship of him would be entirely illegitimate. This is why the term *homoousios* ('the same in essence'), incorporated by the Council in its final communiqué, was so important. It safeguarded not merely a theological dogma but the very core of the piety and worship of the church.

A distinct person

But what does the church actually affirm when it speaks of the Son as consubstantial with the Father?

It affirms, first, that the Son is a distinct person. The word *person* entered trinitarian theology at least as early as Tertullian, the occasion for its introduction being the monarchian denial of any real distinctions in the godhead. Tertullian's direct opponent, Praxeas, held that one cannot believe in One Only God in any other way than by saying that the Father, the Son and the Holy Spirit are the very selfsame Person.[7] The same person both sent forth and was sent forth.[8] Accordingly, it was the Father himself who was born of the Virgin and suffered on the cross, hence the term *Patripassianism.*[9] Thus Praxeas (who also strongly opposed Tertullian's Montanist views on prophecy) did a twofold service for the devil at Rome, according to Tertullian: he drove away prophecy, and he brought in heresy; he put to flight the Paraclete and he crucified the Father.[10]

Sabellius, who flourished early in the third century, propounded a more sophisticated form of the same generic heresy, holding that the Father, the Son and the Spirit were only different modes or aspects of the one undifferentiated God.[11] As creator, he was called the Father; as redeemer, he was called the Son; and as sanctifier, he was called the Spirit. Paul of Samosata, condemned by the Synod of Antioch in 268, represented yet another variant on the same monarchian theme, arguing that the *Logos* was not a person but only an attribute of God; and adding that Jesus was the Son of God only in the sense that this attribute (the divine speech) rested on him more fully than it did on other men.[12]

On the face of things, the term *homoousios* seemed to give countenance to monarchianism; so much so, in fact, that Sabellius himself had used it, to the severe embarrassment of its defenders at a later date. To make matters worse, the Council of Antioch (265/266) in condemning Paul of Samosata had explicitly rejected the word *homoousion*, on the ground that to attribute this title to God was to portray him as single and undifferentiated, at once Father and Son to himself.

Basil, however, stood this argument on its head. He wrote:

> This term also corrects the error of Sabellius, for it removes the identity of the hypostases, and introduces in perfection the idea of the Persons. For nothing can be of one substance with itself, but one thing is of one substance with another. The word has

therefore an excellent and orthodox use, defining as it does both the proper character of the hypostases, and setting forth the invariability of the nature.[13]

According to the Nicene theologians, then, the distinction between the Father and the Son was fundamental to the idea of the *homoousion*. Indeed, it is made crystal clear in the Nicene Creed itself, which, before declaring the Son to be *homoousios* with the Father, describes him as begotten *of* the Father, God *of* God, light *of* light and true God *of* true God. Such phrases are totally incompatible with Sabellianism.

Latin theology, as represented by Tertullian, expressed the distinction between the Father, the Son and the Spirit by means of the word *person*. God was one in essence, three in persons.[14] Unfortunately, the background to Tertullian's use of the word *person* is not entirely clear and the position is further complicated by the fact that the theologians of the Eastern church lacked a precise equivalent. Under the influence of the Cappadocian fathers the formula that eventually came to prevail in the East was that God was one in *ousia*, three in *hypostases*. But the Nicene Creed sowed the seeds of confusion when, in anathematizing the Arian formula of *another hypostasis* or *ousia*, it used *ousia* and *hypostasis* as synonyms. To muddy the waters still further, the Greek *hypostasis* was the exact etymological equivalent of the Latin *substantia*, yet Greek orthodoxy spoke of God as three *hypostases* while Latin spoke of him as one *substance*. It is not surprising, against such a background, that theologians have always bemoaned the inadequacy of the term *person* to distinguish the sense in which God is three from the sense in which he is one. Many have shared Augustine's famous lament: 'When the question is asked, What three? human language labours altogether under great poverty of speech. The answer, however, is given, "three persons", not that it might be spoken, but that it might not be left unspoken.'[15]

Laying aside the question of the original meaning of *persona* and the motives behind its introduction, the question that concerns us is, What kind of distinction does it point to? Karl Rahner reminds us that the word *person* has continued to have a history ever since it was introduced into theology and we must be extremely cautious about allowing these later notions (particularly modern notions of personality) to colour our thinking. Rahner is particularly anxious to avoid the idea that the three persons represent three centres of consciousness and activity, describing this as a heretical misunderstanding of the dogma.[16]

Karl Barth shared Rahner's concern, arguing that the idea of a threefold individuality is scarcely possible without tritheism.[17]

But the position is not as clear-cut as Rahner and Barth suggest. There can be little doubt, if we take Scripture as our guide, that the distinctions within the godhead are analogous to those which obtain between individual human beings. The Father, the Son and the Spirit act not only *with* each other but *on* each other. Each is both conscious and self-conscious, and each plays a distinctive and unique role in redemption. That at least is the impression we gain from the New Testament, particularly from the synoptic gospels, and no one has argued more persuasively than Rahner himself that the economic trinity is the immanent trinity. We must not let an *a priori* fear of tritheism come between us and the biblical data.

In the birth narratives of Matthew and Luke, for example, the Father, the Son and the Spirit surely come very close to being three centres of consciousness and activity. Neither the Father nor the Spirit is born of the Virgin, while both the Father and the Spirit perform activities which cannot be predicated of the Son. Similar conclusions can be drawn from the narratives of the baptism and the transfiguration, both of which highlight the distinctive roles of the divine persons. The story of the passion underlines this. The Father gives, the Son is given, the Holy Spirit upholds. All the data point in the same direction. Christ is conscious of himself as Son and of the Father as Abba. He prays to him, receives commandments from him, glorifies him, comes from him and returns to him. The more reflective and didactic passages of the New Testament are of similar import. The Word was with God (Jn. 1:1). He, and not the Father or the Holy Spirit, is the one who, being in the form of God, made himself nothing (Phil. 2:7); and he is the one whom the Father hyper-exalted (Phil. 2:9). Similarly, he is the one who, when his work is completed, hands over the kingdom to the Father (1 Cor. 15:24).

Such terms do not allow us to conceive of the distinction between the Father and the Son in abstract, sub-personal terms. We do not exhaust their force by speaking of Christ as Light from Light, or by distinguishing him as Speech from the Father as Speaker; or even by referring to him (with Emil Brunner)[18] as that which God has to say to us. The Father loves the Son, and the Son loves the Father, each looking into the other's eyes with wonder and adoration. Is it possible to describe this as less than an I–Thou relationship? Each says 'Thou' with his whole being. Each is addressed, and each answers.[19]

Surely what we have here is not something less than person-to-person and even agent-to-agent, but more? Even the meticulous and magisterial Daniel Waterland took the risk of saying, 'Each Divine Person is an individual intelligent Agent', although he went on to add, 'but, as subsisting in one undivided substance, they are all together, in that respect, but one undivided intelligent Agent'.[20]

Eternal sonship?

Granting, however, that there is a real personal distinction between the Father and the Son, is the sonship eternal? As Waterland points out, the ante-Nicene writers are 'more sparing than those that came after, in speaking of the first, the eternal generation; sparing, I mean, as to the term, or phrase; not as to the thing itself'.[21] It was the rise of Arianism that forced the issue into prominence, because it called in question not so much the sonship of Christ as his eternal pre-existence, arguing that the very fact that he was Son meant that he came into being *after* the Father; and arguing further that he was a creature made in time, and made out of nothing: 'There was when he was not.' Over against this the Nicene Creed insisted that the Son was begotten, not made; that he was begotten of the very essence of the Father; that he was the only begotten; and that he was begotten before all ages. The Nicene fathers also anathematized the distinctive Arian formulas. In particular they anathematized the statement that the Son was begotten of another *hypostasis* or *ousia*; and the statement that 'he was not before he was begotten'. After Nicea the idea of the eternal sonship became the received doctrine of the church, and it pervades the writings of Athanasius, Basil, Gregory of Nazianzen, Gregory of Nyssa and Augustine.

There have, however, been theologians who, while believing firmly in the eternal deity of the *Logos*, have questioned whether he was eternal as Son. This was the position of, for example, Professor Moses Stuart of Andover, whose strenuous denials of the eternal sonship led Richard Treffrey to publish his *Inquiry into the Doctrine of the Eternal Sonship of our Lord Jesus Christ* in 1837. There was also a debate on the issue among English Baptists in the middle of the nineteenth century, calling forth, among other things, a useful contribution from J. C. Philpott, entitled *The True, Proper and Eternal Sonship of the Lord Jesus Christ, the Only Begotten Son of God* (1861). More recently, John MacArthur has taken the view that although Christ was always God, he was not always Son. He became Son:

> Eternally he is God, but only from his incarnation has he been

> Son ... [H]e is no eternal Son always subservient to God, always less than God, always under God. Sonship is an analogy to help us understand Christ's essential relationship and willing submission to the Father for the sake of our redemption ... [H]is sonship began in a point of time, not in eternity. His life as Son began in this world.[22]

MacArthur's position must be kept in perspective. He believes passionately in the pre-existence, eternity and deity of Christ and his motive for taking the position he does is entirely laudable. He wishes to cut the ground from under those (such as Jehovah's Witnesses) who argue that because he was Son, Christ was eternally inferior and subordinate to the Father. The solution is drastic, but, on its own terms, effective: as eternal he is not Son, but Lord.

Besides, while MacArthur's position diverges from that of traditional orthodoxy, it has to be conceded that there has always been a certain hesitancy and confusion in the church's utterances on the eternal sonship. Apart from all else, the idea of the generation of the Son was used by the fathers in three different ways: of the procession of the *Logos* from the Father to undertake the work of creation; of his birth from the Virgin Mary; and of his eternal generation.[23]

It was against this background that Waterland argued that we should not make an issue of the eternal sonship, provided we secure the eternal deity: 'an explicit profession of eternal generation might have been dispensed with; provided only that the eternal existence of the Logos, as a real subsisting person, in and of the Father, which comes to the same thing, might be secured'.[24]

This may be true, but the issues raised by the eternal sonship are serious enough.

First, without it we lose our measure of the divine love. The force of a passage such as John 3:16 derives from Christ's unique relationship with the Father. He did not become God's Son by being given: he was given as God's Son. He was sent out from God's presence as his Son (Gal. 4:4). He became an atoning sacrifice as God's Son (1 Jn. 2:2). No doubt, as Waterland suggests, the statement, 'God gave his Logos!' is preferable to any Arian alternative. But it still falls far short of

> *... God his Son not sparing*
> *Gave him to die.*

Secondly, without the eternal sonship it becomes more difficult to understand and defend the *homoousion*. To the Nicene fathers, they were corollaries. Christ shared the Father's nature because he was the Father's Son and he was the Father's Son because he shared his nature. Athanasius, for example, specifically links sonship and consubstantiality: 'whoso considers the Son an offspring, rightly considers him as coessential'.[25] Gregory of Nazianzen spoke to similar effect: 'he is called Son because he is identical with the Father in essence'.[26] In the same way, it is the eternal sonship that excludes the possibility that the Son is a creature: 'If he is Offspring, how call ye him creature? for no one says that he begets what he creates, nor calls his proper offspring creatures'.[27]

In fact, without the eternal sonship we should have to abandon the phrase, *begotten, not made*, altogether. On MacArthur's construction, for example (taking the sonship to derive from the virgin birth), we should have to insist he was made, not begotten. This is surely perilous. We can speak of God creating the humanness of the Son from the substance of the Virgin, but we dare not speak of his begetting the Son from the substance of the Virgin. That would take us right back to the pagan notion of intercourse between the gods and the daughters of men.

Thirdly, without the eternal sonship the Trinity becomes inaccessible and incomprehensible. The main reason for this is that we lose the distinctive property by which we distinguish one person from another. As the Cappadocians repeatedly insisted, the Son is exactly like the Father in all respects except that he is Son:

> in these hypostatic or personal properties alone do the three holy subsistences differ from each other ... the Father alone is ingenerate, no other subsistence having given him being. And the Son alone is generate, for he was begotten of the Father's essence without beginning and without time. And only the Holy Spirit proceedeth from the Father's essence, not having been generated but simply proceeding.[28]

The Son is differentiated by being begotten. If not begotten, how is he differentiated?

But alongside this there is a further difficulty, connected with the fact that the nature of God's love is such that it excludes 'the possibility of Him wanting to remain alone'.[29] One of the great merits of the doctrine of the trinity is that it provides a foundation and framework for the fact that God is love (and does not merely *become* love when he creates an object for his affection). The eternal plurality within the deity provides a *with-ness* which ensures that God is never alone. Within himself there is both the subject and the object of love: the lover and the loved. The perception of Christ as eternal *Logos*, everlastingly with God, provides a logical plurality. But it does not provide an affective plurality. Does a person love his word as he loves his son? The Son is the Father's equal: his very nature. A son smiles back. It is not enough to say that the emotional distinction between *Logos* and Son is only a matter of human language. That language itself arises out of the deepest structures of human ontology and relationships; and these are in the image of God. Our human need for relationships is rooted in that image. That is why we produce not merely offspring, but sons and daughters capable of I–Thou relationships; and that is why we love our sons and daughters as we can never love our words. A God-alone-with-his-*Logos* is solitary in a way that a God-alone-with-his-Son is not. Hence the importance of Barth's comment that the only-begotten is the object of the Father's love before he becomes the object of our faith.[30]

But the decisive consideration in favour of the eternal sonship is the factor highlighted so effectively by Karl Rahner: the unity of the immanent and the economic trinity. The economic trinity is emphatically one of Father, Son and Holy Spirit, but if there is no eternal sonship, this economic trinity does not correspond to any real and ultimate truth about God; and if the trinity is not revealed in the economy (the administration of redemption), it is not revealed at all. For Christian theology to accept this would be to swallow Socrates' cup. The revelation would be one thing; the reality another. The sonship would become a device adopted for the purposes of revelation rather than an essential part of the revelation itself. We would have to say that God is not really Abba, that the *Logos* is not really Son, that the Spirit is not really the Spirit of the Son and that God does not come to us as himself. Then the knowledge with which Christ comes is not the knowledge he learned as a Son in the bosom of his Father, his glory is not the glory he had as Son beside the Father and the love that he demonstrated cannot be expressed in terms of a willingness to exchange the privileges of sonship for the rigours of servitude (Gal. 4:4). Neither can what he suffered be expressed in terms of his being prepared to lose the fellowship of a Father with whom he had had unbroken communion from eternity. The discontinuity between economic and immanent trinity thus becomes complete. The economic trinity reveals a God of the deepest affection, eternally loving his Son and yet sacrificing that Son for the salvation of a world which he made through his Son and which he loves with his Son. The immanent trinity, by contrast, remains undisclosed: a remote reality consisting of God, his Word and his Breath. Without the eternal sonship we are left with a redemption which is not a revelation. We have lost the core of the doctrine of the Trinity, namely, that the one Lordship is disclosed as the Father, the Son and the Holy Spirit.

Eternal generation

The idea of eternal generation is an inevitable corollary of the eternal sonship and figures prominently in the statements of the Nicene fathers and their successors. But it is far from clear what content, if any, we can impart to the concept. It is revealed, but it is revealed as a mystery, and the writings of the fathers abound with protestations of inevitable ignorance on the matter. Athanasius, for example, writes:

> nor again is it right to seek … how God begets, and what is the manner of his begetting. For a man must be beside himself to venture on such points; since a thing ineffable and proper to God's nature, and known to him alone and the Son, this he demands to be explained in words … [I]t is better in perplexity to be silent and believe, than to disbelieve on account of perplexity.[31]

Gregory of Nazianzen spoke in similar terms:

> But the manner of his generation we will not admit that even angels can conceive, much less you. Shall I tell you how it was? It was in a manner known to the Father who begat, and to the Son who was begotten. Anything more than this is hidden by a cloud, and escapes your dim sight.[32]

This does not mean, however, that the church has had nothing at all to say on the matter, even though it often proceeded only by way of negatives.

First of all, it insisted that divine generation cannot be understood in terms of human generation. Here, again, Athanasius set the tone for subsequent theology: 'As then men create not as God creates, as their being is not such as God's being, so man's generation is in one way, and the Son is from the Father in another'.[33] One point of difference was that whereas human generation was an act of passion, divine generation was not: 'the generation was impassible, and eternal, and worthy of God'.[34] More important, whereas in human generation a father always exists prior to a son, in divine generation this is not so. Athanasius writes:

> Nor, as man from man has the Son been begotten, so as to be later than his Father's existence, but he is God's offspring, and, as being proper Son of God, who is ever, he exists eternally. For, whereas it is proper to men to beget in time, from the imperfection of their nature, God's offspring is eternal, for his nature is ever perfect.[35]

The main thrust of the argument here was that the Father and the Son are correlatives and therefore to assign a beginning to the Son involves assigning a beginning to the Father.[36] The very notion of precedence traps the Father, as well as the Son, in time. If he existed before the Son, how long before? One can answer that only by positing a temporal origin of the Father and measuring the (finite) time between them; or by making the Father eternal and the Son temporal, thereby positing infinite time between them and introducing radical asymmetry and discontinuity between the Father and the Son. Instead, insisted Gregory of Nyssa, 'as the Son is Light from Light, Life from Life, Good from Good, so most certainly is he Eternal from Eternal.'[37]

Athanasius made one other point in this connection (and he made it very forcefully): if the Father is prior to the Son then the generation of the Son introduces radical change into the being of God. He writes:

> If the Word is not with the Father from everlasting, the Triad is not everlasting; but a Monad was first, and afterwards by addition it became a Triad ... What sort of a religion then is this, which is not even like itself, but is in process of completion as time goes on, and is now not thus, and then again thus?[38]

Closely related to this was a second negative: to beget does not mean to originate. In human generation, of course, it does, but in divine generation it does not. This was closely linked to the fundamentally important distinction between *agenētos* and *agennētos*. The Son was not *agennētos* (Ingenerate or Unbegotten). But he was *agenētos*, Unoriginate. The Father was both *agenētos* and *agennētos*: Unoriginate and Unbegotten.[39] This implies a clear distinction between being begotten and being originated.

The positive truth corresponding to this is that the generation of the

Son is eternal. Time and again the same illustrations of this occur in the fathers. The fountain no sooner exists than the river exists; the sun no sooner exists than the beam exists.[40] But this idea, too, has its difficulties. Some take it to mean that the generation of the Son is a continuous, endless and successionless divine act: the Son is eternally being generated. There is a hint of this in John of Damascus: 'Accordingly the everlasting God generates his own Word which is perfect, without beginning and without end, that God, Whose nature and existence are above time, may not engender in time.'[41] It seems safer, however, to take eternal generation to mean that the generation of the Son was complete from eternity. The Father was not becoming Father nor the Son becoming Son. The Father simply is and the Son simply is, without any hint of becoming. In the words of Gregory of Nazianzen, the Son is 'the unoriginatedly begotten'.[42]

Thirdly, generation is to be sharply distinguished from procession. The former is peculiar to the Son, the latter to the Holy Spirit. However, clear as the fathers were as to the fact of this distinction they were very unclear as to its content, and sharply critical of those who pried into it. 'We have learned that there is a difference between generation and procession,' wrote John of Damascus, 'but the nature of that difference we in no wise understand'.[43] Gregory of Nazianzen put it more colourfully: 'What then is procession? Do you tell me what is the unbegottenness of the Father, and I will explain to you the physiology of the generation of the Son and the procession of the Spirit, and we shall both of us be frenzy-stricken for prying into the mystery of God.'[44] Important as this agnosticism is, however, we do have to remember that the distinction between generation and procession signalizes an important fact: God has only one Son, the one he delivered up for us on the cross of Calvary. No-one else stands in such a relationship to him, not even the Holy Spirit. This also reminds us that sonship cannot be understood simply as consubstantiality. The Spirit, no less than the Son, is *homoousios* with the Father: a point the Nicene theologians eventually made quite explicit. 'What then?' asked Gregory of Nazianzen, 'Is the Spirit God? Most certainly. Well, then, is he consubstantial? Yes, if he is God'.[45] Yet this *consubstantiality* does not constitute him a Son. He is *homoousios*, but it is in a way peculiar to and appropriate to himself: as Spirit, not as Son.

Fourthly, there is a clear distinction between being begotten and being made. What is begotten is a Son, what is made is a creature. This latter position was precisely what the Arians argued for: Christ was a creature, made out of nothing. Over against this the Nicene theologians argued that to be made would be fatal to his sonship; that all made things were in fact made by him; and that he was God's offspring, not his creature. 'He is not a creature or work,' wrote Athanasius, 'but an offspring proper to the Father's essence'.[46] The definitive position was laid down by John of Damascus: 'For generation means that the begetter produces out of his essence offspring similar in essence. But creation and making mean that the creator and maker produces from that which is external, and not out of his own essence, a creature of an absolutely dissimilar nature.'[47]

This brings us back to the link between sonship and the *homoousion*. What a man makes does not share in his nature: what he begets, does. 'But if you say that he that begat and that which is begotten are not the same, the statement is inaccurate,' wrote Gregory of Nazianzen: 'For it is in fact a necessary truth that they are the same. For the nature of the relation of father to child is this: that the offspring is of the same nature with the parent.'[48]

Three further points may be made with reference to the sonship.

First, although the Father is willingly Father the generation of the Son is not contingent upon the Father's will. This follows from the fact that Christ is begotten of the essence of the Father. The generation is not optional, as if it were for the Father to decide whether or not to have a Son. Quenstedt[49] put it admirably: 'The Father begat the Son *volens*, but not *quia voluit*: willingly, but not because he willed to.' The sonship is of the divine essence in the sense that the godhead never existed and can never exist without it. So far as creation goes, it was open to God to create or not to create as he chose. With regard to generation, however, the father did not enjoy this freedom. The Son was coeval with himself, a necessary subsistence in the being of God.

Secondly, although the Father and the Son exist in different modes (the One ingenerate and the Other generate) this does not imply that they possess different natures. To those who suggested that it did (arguing that a begotten god and an unbegotten god must be two radically different deities) Gregory of Nyssa offered an effective answer: Adam and Abel came into being in different ways, the former by creation, the latter by copulation, yet they possessed the same nature.

> If, then, the idea of humanity in Adam and Abel does not vary with the difference in their origin, neither the order nor the manner of their coming into existence making any difference to their nature, which is the same in both ... what necessity is there

> that against the divine nature we should admit this strange thought?[50]

The underlying truth here is that the properties *begotten* and *unbegotten* belong not to the essence but to the persons. The divine essence of the Son is one with that of the Father. *Generateness* defined his relationship, not his nature, as Augustine pointed out:

> But because the Father is not called the Father except in that he has a Son, and the Son is not called Son except in that he has a Father, these things are not said according to substance; because each of them is not so called in relation to himself, but the terms are used reciprocally and in relation each to the other.[51]

Thirdly, it is the divine sonship, not the human, which is archetypal. It is easy to lose sight of this, as if the divine sonship were only figurative and the human alone real. But the reverse is the case, as the proponents of orthodoxy have strenuously insisted. Karl Barth expressed it clearly:

> It is therefore not as if the Father-Son relationship were itself a reality originally and properly creaturely, as if God in some hidden source of his essence were nevertheless something other than Father and Son, and as if therefore these names were optional and ultimately meaningless symbols, symbols the original and proper, non-symbolic content of which consisted in the said creaturely reality. On the contrary, it is precisely in God that the Father-Son relationship, like all creaturely relationships, has its original and proper reality.[52]

This implies that we must take our concept of sonship from the divine, not the human, and that, for example, the priority of Father to Son is no more an essential of sonship than is generation by physical copulation. In fact, the priority of father to son is a defect in the human relationship, compared to the divine. Divine fatherhood is complete and perfect because it is eternal; and because here alone is there total consubstantiality, absolute equality and perfect correspondence. The fulness of the Father and the image of the Father exist in the divine Son in a way that is impossible in the human relationship; just as the bond between them surpasses in love, intimacy and interaction anything that men can attain to.

Identical in being

The first implication of the *homoousion,* then, is that the Father and the Son are distinct persons. The second is that the Son is identical in essence with the Father. This was the fundamental question raised by the Arian controversy: were the Father and the Son God in the same sense? The Nicene answer was an emphatic, 'Yes!' But it was not free from ambiguity.

At one level it affirmed the generic identity of the Son with the Father. They shared the same nature. This was underlined in the parallel phrases of the Nicene Creed: Christ was Light from Light and true God from true God. It was also, as we have seen, the import of the phrase, 'begotten, not made'. Just as a human son has exactly the same nature as his father so the divine Son shares fully in the nature of God. This was something Athanasius stressed repeatedly. He put it most strongly in his *Third Discourse Against the Arians*, 4:

> [H]e is the same as God; and he and the Father are one in propriety and peculiarity of nature, and in the identity of the one Godhead, as has been said. For as the radiance also is light, not second to the sun, nor a different light, nor from participation of it, but a whole and proper offspring of it ... So also the Godhead of the Son is the Father's.[53]

Augustine deemed the idea of generic identity to be implicit in the words of John 10:30, 'I and the Father are one': 'For "we are one" means, what he is, that am I also; according to essence, not according to relation.'[54] He put it more graphically later: 'the Father begat the Word equal to himself in all things; for he would not have uttered himself wholly and perfectly, if there were in his Word anything more or less than in himself.'[55]

So far as our perception goes, this means that the nature of the Son is as divine as the Father's and equal to it in every way.[56] Christ possesses all that constitutes the image or the form or the likeness or even the glory of God. Every distinctive divine attribute is found in him.[57] He is infinite, eternal and unchangeable; omniscient, omnipotent and omnipresent; unalterable and self-existent.

But this fact of generic identity immediately poses a problem: if the Son has the exact nature and essence of the Father and is like him in all respects, how can we distinguish the one person from the other? Christian theology has not found it easy to answer this question; or, more precisely, it has not found it easy to explain what it means by its answers. The answer is that the Son is distinguished from the Father by the fact that he is Son; or (which is the same thing) by *generateness* or *begottenness*. This was the position laid down by the Cappadocian theologians as represented by, for example, Gregory of Nazianzen: 'Now these names are common to the Godhead but the proper name of the unoriginate is Father, and that of the unoriginately begotten is Son, and that of the unbegottenly proceeding is the Holy Ghost.'[58] It was taken up by Augustine, who, as we saw, spoke of the Father and the Son as identical in essence but not in relation. But as with so much else connected with the doctrine of the Trinity, the fine tuning was done by John of Damascus:

> For the Father is without cause and unborn: for he is derived from nothing, but derives from himself his being, nor does he derive a single quality from another ... But the Son is derived from the Father after the manner of generation, and the Holy Spirit likewise is derived from the Father, yet not after the manner of generation, but after that of procession ... For in these hypostatic or personal properties alone do the three holy subsistences differ from each other, being indivisibly divided not by essence but by the distinguishing mark of their proper and peculiar subsistence.[59]

The problem, as we have seen, is that although we know that the Son is distinguished by the fact that he is begotten, we know little or nothing of what divine begottenness is. It carries us little beyond, 'Is the Son of'. Barth has restated the position with some originality of phraseology. He writes, for example, that God is 'the same in unimpaired variety thrice in a different way';[60] and again, that '*Deus verus* and *Deus verus* do not confront each other as independent essences, but they exist in two different ways in the same independent essence.'[61] This may well be true. But what does it mean? In what way are the three who co-exist in unimpaired variety different? How is *Deus verus* (God the Father) to be distinguished from *Deus verus* (God the Son)? Even if we focus on the narrow issue, What is meant by Christ being the Son?, we make little progress. We can say, It means that whatever the Father is, the Son is. This, again, is true. But in what respect, then, is the Son different from the Holy Spirit, who is also *homoousios*? How does generation differ from procession? As we have seen, that question drove Gregory of

Nazianzen almost to apoplexy. The truth is, we are lost. We know that the Son is distinguished by the fact that he is begotten, but we do not know what *begotten* is.

Does this mean that Christian faith and worship have only a vague and dim apprehension of the Son as Son? Surely not! The *persona* of Christ is defined for faith by his exploits in redemption. He is the one who was born in Bethlehem, baptized in the Jordan, tempted in the desert and crucified on Calvary. He is the divine person who took flesh, carried our sins and defined himself as the friend of Mary, Martha and Lazarus. He is God in that form which did not insist on his rights, but made himself nothing and rendered an obedience which was to death, and therefore beyond reason (Phil. 2:6ff.). In Rahner's terms, he is the 'free self-communication of the divine reality ... as the "absolute bringer of salvation"'.[62] The Father, by contrast (though no less endearingly) is the one who sent him, encouraged him and sacrificed him; just as the Spirit is the one who represents him and thus encourages and empowers us. These, rather than the nature of generation and procession, are the facts revealed to us.

But is this not functionalism: identifying the Son by what he does rather than by what he is? The answer, surely, is that the ontological and the functional are not mutually exclusive. If asked, Who is Jesus Christ? it cannot be enough to answer, 'The eternal Son of God!', both because such an answer omits the most important facts we know about him and because it savours of ingratitude. The real answer is, He is 'the Son of God, who loved me and gave himself for me' (Gal. 2:20). In the last analysis, form and colour are given to the only begotten by the fact that, as the Son, he did things, and suffered things, which were not done or suffered by God the Father; and, further, that I have a relationship with him which I do not have with God the Father. As Karl Rahner points out, 'each one of the three persons communicates himself to man in gratuitous grace in his own personal particularity and diversity ... these three self-communications are the self-communication of the one God in the three relative ways in which God subsists'.[63] The Father is our Father. The Son is not our Father, but we share in his sonship and in his inheritance and in his Spirit and in his worship and obedience and love and even in his lordship over creation (Heb. 2:8–9). He is our Priest and our Sacrifice, our Leader and our Teacher. It is in such terms – in terms of his peculiar role in redemption and in terms of our peculiar relationship with him – that the Son's unique personality is defined for Christian faith and experience.

Numerical identity

It cannot be enough, however, to affirm a merely generic identity between the Father and the Son. *Homoousios* also points to numerical identity: the Father and the Son are one and the same in *ousia*. There is room for debate as to whether this is what it meant to the Nicene fathers, not least because Athanasius' terminology did not allow him to express clearly the distinction between the way in which God is one and the way in which he is three. Later theologians spoke of God as three *prosopa* or three *hypostaseis* (the word finally preferred by the Cappadocians). But Athanasius never used the word *prosopon* in a trinitarian context; and he tended to use *hypostasis* as synonymous with *ousia*.[64] But once *ousia* is sharply distinguished from *hypostasis*, as it was in later trinitarian thought, and identified with the Latin *essentia* as distinct from *persona*, it becomes imperative to insist that God is one *ousia*. The Father and the Son are not two beings linked by a generic identity, but one being and one God. Within this one being there are three subsistences, or three modes of being, or three forms of relatedness; and these are such that the divine essence is fully present in the Father and in the Son and in the Holy Spirit. But the Father and the Son and the Holy Spirit do not add up to three. They add up to one God. Basil wrote:

> We proclaim each of the hypostases singly,' wrote Basil, 'and, when count we must, we do not let an ignorant arithmetic carry us away to the idea of a plurality of Gods … For we do not count by way of addition, gradually making increase from unity to multitude, and saying, one, two, and three – nor yet first, second, and third.[65]

From this point of view, *homoousios* means that the Father, the Son and the Holy Spirit share one mutual existence, just as the word *homonumos* means sharing a common name.[66]

The only logical alternative is that there are three *ousiai*, and hence three beings and three gods: an alternative which the fathers vehemently rejected.[67] Modern defenders of the *homoousion* have been equally forthright. Jean Galot, for example, comments, 'If the substance of the Son resembles the substance of the Father in every respect, then the Father and the Son are identically one and the same substance.'[68] Karl Barth argued that the very purpose of the *homoousion* was to provide a safeguard against the multiplication of the essence of God:

> it forces us really to regard the Persons as modes of existence, i.e. not as two subjects, but as the same subject twice ... The really one essence in really two modes of existence is God himself and God alone. He himself, he alone is also Father and Son, Speaker and Word, light and light, original and copy.[69]

It was for this reason that the doctrine of the eternal generation of the Son had to be formulated with such care. The Son was begotten of the essence, but this does not mean that another essence was produced. God exists as triune; indeed, can only exist as triune. Yet his triuneness does not make him three. 'Wherefore neither is the Son another God,' wrote Athanasius, 'for if the Son be other, as an Offspring, still he is the same as God; and he and the Father are one in propriety and peculiarity of nature, and in the identity of the one Godhead ... they are one, and the Godhead itself one.'[70] Gregory of Nyssa spoke to similar effect: 'We who are initiated into the mystery of godliness do not see between the Father and the Son a partnership of Godhead, but unity.'[71]

Perichoresis

As Rahner points out,[72] however, this immediately leads to a paradox. The one essence, God, is given to us in the Father and in the Son and in the Holy Spirit; this means that each person is identical with the essence; yet the persons are not identical with each other – they are distinguished by in-generateness, generateness and procession.

How is such a numerical identity between three distinct persons possible? The church has always been conscious that this is in the highest sense a mystery. It is with respect to this very problem that Basil, for example, warns us 'not to feel distressed at points of doctrine whenever we meet with questions difficult of solution, and when at the thought of accepting what is proposed to us, our brains begin to reel'.[73] Yet it is not a mystery on which the church has remained altogether silent. Taking its cue from John 14:11 ('I am in the Father and the Father is in me') it formulated the idea of co-inherence (Greek *enperichoresis*, Latin *circumincessio* or *circuminsessio*). This was an attempt to combine both the unity of the essence and the distinction of the persons in an intelligible synthesis. Within the one godhead the three persons co-inhere in each other and interpenetrate each other.

It was John of Damascus who gave the idea of *perichoresis* explicit and classic formulation:

> The subsistences dwell and are established firmly in one other. For they are inseparable and cannot part from one another, but keep to their separate course within one another, without coalescing or mingling, but cleaving to each other. For the Son is in the Father and the Spirit: and the Spirit in the Father and the Son: and the Father in the Son and the Spirit, but there is no coalescence or commingling or confusion. And there is one and the same motion: for there is one impulse and one motion of the three subsistences, which is not to be observed in any created nature.[74]

There is little to add to this definition. Taken temporally, *perichoresis* means that the Father, the Son and the Holy Spirit occupy and fill the same time (or the same eternity). Each is unoriginated (*agenētos*), endless and eternal. Taken spatially, it means that each person and all the persons together occupy and fill the same space. Each is omnipresent while remaining unconfused with the others. Each fills immensity. Beyond that, each contains the other; each dwells in the other; each penetrates the other; and each conditions the mode of existence of the other.[75] None, not even the Father, would be what he is without the others.

What the idea of *perichoresis* really attempts is to explain a special kind and intensity of inter-personal unity to which there is no analogy in human experience. The one hint we are given is in Paul's reference to the mystery of marriage in Ephesians 5:32. Not only do man and wife constitute one flesh: Christ and his church constitute one flesh. Jesus himself makes a similar comparison in John 17:21ff.: 'that all of them may be one, Father, just as you are in me and I am in you ... I in them and you in me. May they be brought to complete unity ...' Christ fills every member of his spiritual body, while at the same time remaining personally distinct from them. However, the relationship is not (as it is in the case of the Trinity) mutual. Neither the Christian nor the church fills Christ, whereas the Father fills the Son as surely as the Son fills the Father.

The appropriateness of the marriage metaphor stems from the fact that marriage is a real confluence of two distinct lives; and that, at its most intense moments, it points to a deep human striving towards a degree of appropriation, penetration and mutuality which remains unattainable and yet always beckons. In the divine existence, there are neither physical nor mental barriers to complete co-inherence. The mutual understanding is complete; the experience of love is complete; the sharing of common purposes is complete; the co-operative involvement in creation and redemption is complete.

So far as our human experience goes, God comes towards us as one. Yet the one in whom he comes is the Father, the Son and the Holy Spirit. The coming is such that in the one the three come; and that in each the other comes. Yet we have an experience of each which is different from our experience of the other. There is an 'Abba, Father!'; a 'Lord Jesus!'; and a 'Come, Holy Spirit!' The three co-inhere in a single being so that there is no relation with the being apart from a relationship with the persons; no action of one person which does not also involve the action of the others; and yet no action of a person which does not have his own distinct mark upon it. The external acts of the triune God (the *opera ad extra*) are indeed common to all three persons, but that does not mean that each acts in the same way. The triune God creates; but the Father creates as Father, the Son as Son (or *Logos*) and the Spirit as Spirit. Each works in his own proper way.[76]

The Son and the Spirit: *Filioque*

The term *homoousios* focused primarily on the Son's relation to the Father. But what is his relation to the Holy Spirit? The original Nicene Creed had nothing to say on the Spirit beyond the bare statement, '[We believe] in the Holy Spirit.' After the Council, however, discussion was forced on the church by the emergence of various groups who held the same views with regard to the Spirit as the Arians had held with regard to the Son. As a result of these debates, the statement on the Holy Spirit in the Nicaeno-Constantinopolitan Creed of 381 is much fuller than that in the original document of 325: 'And [I believe] in the Holy Ghost, the Lord and Giver of Life; who proceedeth from the Father; who with the Father and the Son together is worshipped and glorified; who spake by the prophets.'

For our present purpose, the most important feature of this expanded statement is its reference to the procession of the Spirit: 'who proceedeth from the Father'. The striking thing here is that what is affirmed is a *single* procession, from the Father only. This is still the form of the Creed accepted by the Eastern church, which subsequently treated the subject of the procession with what H. B. Swete calls 'cautious reserve'.[77] The only significant development was that after John of Damascus (who died around 750) it became common to speak of the Spirit proceeding from the Father *through* the Son: 'we speak also of the Spirit of the Son, not as though proceeding from him, but as proceeding through him from the Father. For the Father alone is cause.'[78]

In the West, developments took a very different course. Ambrose tentatively, and Augustine emphatically, began to speak of a double procession of the Holy Spirit from the Father *and* the Son (Latin, *filioque*): 'Neither can we say that the Holy Spirit does not also proceed from the Son, for the same Spirit is not without reason said to be the Spirit both of the Father and of the Son ... the Holy Spirit proceeds from the Father and from the Son.'[79] This gradually became the accepted belief of the Western church. It was first given conciliar sanction by the Third Council of Toledo in 589, but this was only a local council and its pronouncements did not carry sufficient weight to lead to an alteration in the language of the Creed itself. Inevitably, however, the word *filioque* (or its equivalent, *et a filio*) crept into local liturgies and thence into local versions of the Creed, particularly in Spain, France and North Africa.[80] It was incorporated into the so-called Athanasian Creed, a compendium of Augustinian theology which first appeared in Southern Gaul around 500, but is known in its full form only from the eighth century[81] and which declared explicitly, 'the Holy Ghost is of the Father and of the Son'. The papacy, however, refused to sanction any change in the wording of the Creed, despite pressure from such potentates as Charlemagne and despite the fact that the outstanding pope of the period, Gregory the Great (590–604), personally believed in the *filioque*. By the beginning of the ninth century the doctrine of the double procession prevailed throughout the Western church and was firmly enshrined in the local creeds of Spain, France, Germany and even North Italy. The precise date at which the papacy sanctioned a change in the authorized text of the Creed is unclear. The best guess is that the decision was taken by Pope Benedict VIII in 1044. The Eastern church broke off relations with the West ten years later.

The *filioque* clearly had profound implications for the doctrine of the Holy Spirit, affirming that the Spirit *proceeds* from the Son, and thus implicitly denying that he was *created* by him. But what is the import of the *filioque* for Christology? Is the Son fully equal with the Father? On the Eastern understanding of the procession it is very difficult to maintain that he is. Either he has no role at all ('the Holy Spirit who proceedeth from the Father') or his role is a subordinate one ('who proceedeth from the Father through the Son'). But behind this lies something even more fundamental. Clear as the Greek theologians were that the Son was *homoousios* with the Father, and clear as they also were that the three subsistences were one being, when it came to describing the generation of the Son and the procession of the Spirit they enmeshed themselves hopelessly in the language of causality. John of Damascus, for example, explicitly speaks of the Father as the *producer* (*probaleia*) of the Holy Spirit, describes him as the origin of the Son and as greater than the Son and then goes on to say:

> For the Father is without cause and unborn; for he is derived from nothing, but derives from himself his being, nor does he derive a single quality from another. Rather he is himself the beginning and cause of the existence of all things in a definite and natural manner. But the Son is derived from the Father after the manner of generation, and the Holy Spirit likewise is derived from the Father, yet not after the manner of generation, but after that of procession.... All then that the Son and the Spirit have is from the Father, even their very being: and unless the Father is, neither the Son nor the Spirit is.

Such language is fatal to the co-equal deity of the Son. He derives his being from the Father. The ground of his being is in the Father. The cause of his being is in the Father. Furthermore, on this understanding it cannot be said that the Son has all that the Father has. He is excluded from being, with the Father, the *principium* of the Holy Spirit, which means that the Spirit is not the Spirit of the Son in the same sense as he is the Spirit of the Father. The Son is, at best, the instrumental cause of a procession in which the Father alone is agent.

But even this is not all. In the view of the Eastern theologians the doctrine of the dual procession is fatal to the unity of God because it implies that in the deity there are two *principia*: two fountains or springs from which the divine essence flows. In the Eastern tradition, the foundation of the divine unity was God the Father, conceived of as the sole *principium* of the godhead. From him the divine essence was communicated or emanated or proceeded to the Son and the Holy Spirit. According to the more careful statements of this point of view, he was not the cause of their *essence*, because their essence was one and the same as his own. But they had it from him. He was the cause of their subsistences in a way that neither of them was the cause of his.

The result was a totally asymmetrical trinity in which the Father held the essence underived, while the Son and the Spirit held it as derived from him. The Father alone was a principle without a principle; and any movement towards greater equality (as represented by, for example, the *filioque*) savoured of tritheism.

Curiously, even the Western theologians retained this language of causality. Augustine, for example, wrote, 'the Father is the beginning (*principium*) of the whole divinity';[82] and again, 'it must be admitted that the Father and the Son are a beginning (*principium*) of the Holy Spirit, not two beginnings'.[83] The difference (and it is obviously an important one) is that Augustine described the Son, as well as the Father, as a *principium* (hence the dual procession). He also went on to defend this position against the charge that it posited two *principia* and thus destroyed the divine unity. Not at all! said Augustine. If the Son is with the Father, he cannot be a second *principium*. He is one and the same in being with the Father: 'as the Father and Son are one God, and one Creator, and one Lord relatively to the creature, so are they one Beginning relatively to the Holy Spirit'. The position Augustine is adopting here is that just as the *opera ad extra* are common to all three persons, so the procession of the Spirit is common to the Father and the Son. However, Augustine complicated his position by reading his subordinationism back into the *homoousion* itself. The Son was the *principium* of the Holy Spirit along with the Father: but not a fully equal *principium*. Even in the dual procession there was asymmetry. The Father has it in himself that the Holy Spirit should proceed from him, but the Son has it by gift from the Father: his proceeding also from the Son is a property derived by the Son from the Father.[84]

The remarkable thing is that theologians who were so manifestly (and so commendably) reticent as to the nature of generation and procession were prepared to speak so freely about the *principia* which lay behind them. The truth is that the legacy of Origen's subordinationism clung to Christian theology long after Nicea and the *filioque*. But surely the whole framework of causality must be called in question in such a context? No matter how firmly we insist on the consubstantiality and co-eternity of the persons, that insistence is instantly jeopardized by our speaking of the Father as the First Cause, the Fountain and the Beginning; and even more seriously jeopardized by our speaking of derivation and origination. Those who use this terminology always introduce such disclaimers as that the Father is not before the Son in time nor greater than the Son in nature. But he *is* greater in that he is *principium*. He is the Source, Cause and Origin to whom the Son and the Spirit owe what they are, if not indeed *that* they are.

The response to this must be that if the Son and the Spirit are God then they are unoriginate (*agenētos*), that neither generation nor procession can mean origination and hence that all talk of derivation and causation are inappropriate. Neither the begetting of the Son nor the procession of the Spirit is to be understood in a way that discriminates between the persons. If it is true that each owes it to the others that he is what he is then just as the Son is not the Son without the Father so the Father is not the Father without the Son.

But how does all this relate to the data of Scripture? There are several points to bear in mind.

First, the relationship Father–Son is not sacrosanct as a framework for discussion of the Trinity. In some key passages the Second Person is described as the Word. In others he is described as Lord (*Kyrios*). This is particularly noteworthy in the case of the apostolic benediction in 2 Corinthians 13:14: 'May the grace of the Lord Jesus Christ, and the love of God, and the fellowship of the Holy Spirit be with you all.' The important point here is that we should not give exclusive sanction to one of these above the others. In particular, we should not read off from the designation 'Son' ideas of derivation and subordination which would be entirely inappropriate to the equally valid designation 'Lord'.

Secondly, in the explicitly trinitarian passages of the New Testament the order 'Father, Son, Spirit' is not sacrosanct. Again, this is most notable in the case of 2 Corinthians 13:14, where the order is *Lord, God, Spirit*, but similar variations can be observed in other passages, too. In Luke 1:35, for example, the Spirit is mentioned first: 'The Holy Spirit will come upon you, and the power of the Most High will overshadow you. So the holy one to be born will be called the Son of God.' Yet another order appears in 1 Corinthians 12:4–6: 'There are different kinds of gifts, but the same Spirit. There are different kinds of service, but the same Lord. There are different kinds of working, but the same God works all of them in all men.' The sequence in 1 Peter 1:2 is different again: 'chosen according to the foreknowledge of God the Father, through the sanctifying work of the Spirit, for obedience to Jesus Christ and sprinkling by his blood.' B. B. Warfield comments:

> The question naturally suggests itself whether the order Father, Son, Spirit was especially significant to Paul and his fellow-writers of the New Testament. If in their conviction the very essence of the doctrine of the Trinity was embodied in this order, should we not anticipate that there should appear in their numerous allusions to the Trinity some suggestion of this conviction?[85]

Thirdly, there is no doubt that in the economical trinity the Spirit proceeds from the Son as well as from the Father. He is the Spirit of

Christ (Rom. 8:9) in the same sense as he is the Spirit of him who raised Jesus from the dead (Rom. 8:11). Likewise, he is the Spirit of the Son (Gal. 4:6) and the Spirit of Jesus Christ (Phil. 1:19). In accordance with this, the Son, equally with the Father, can be said to send the Paraclete (Jn. 15:26; 16:17), to baptise in the Holy Spirit (Mt. 3:11), and to pour out the Spirit of promise (Acts 2:33). The point need not be laboured. As Barth points out, 'Even supporters of the Eastern doctrine do not dispute that the Holy Spirit in the *opus ad extra*, and so in revelation (and from there, looking backwards, in creation) is to be regarded as the Spirit of the Father and of the Son.'[86] The question is whether we have a right to extrapolate from the economical trinity to the immanent, ontological trinity. The procedure certainly requires care. For example, although God appears in the flesh we cannot deduce from this that flesh is immanent to the Trinity. Yet in general the principle is sound: God reveals himself in redemption and that revelation corresponds to what he is. If the heavens declare the glory of God (Ps. 19:1), so, even more luminously, does redemption, and this means that the divine modes of existence cannot be different in reality from what they are in revelation. If this is so, the relation of the Son to the Holy Spirit must be as it appears in the work of redemption, where the Spirit proceeds from the Son equally with the Father. The temporal procession presupposes an eternal. This is why the presence of the Spirit is the presence of the Son (Jn. 14:18) as surely as it is the presence of the Father (1 Cor. 3:16). In fact, this simply brings us back to the *perichoresis*: 'I am in the Father and the Father is in me' (Jn. 14:10). It is inconceivable that within such a relationship the Father should breathe his Spirit except in fellowship with his Word. As surely as he elects in Christ (Eph. 1:4) he breathes his Spirit in Christ. The procession as well as the election bears the impress of his Son. But it is *his* impress. Just as it is the Father (not the essence) who begets, so the procession is from the Father and the Son, not from the essence. Yet within the procession itself there is a difference (which we can indicate but cannot describe) between the contribution of God-begotten and the contribution of God-unbegotten.

The remaining question is whether it is at all appropriate to speak of some kind of 'procession' of the Son from the Father and the Spirit.[87] Otherwise, are we not guilty of blatant subordinationism with reference to the Third Person? He proceeds from the Father and the Son, but neither of them proceeds from him.

If we accept that the three persons of the trinity are *homoousioi* and therefore identical in nature, one and the same in being and equal in power and glory, there is nothing inherently shocking about this question. There is no doubt that the sonship of the adoptive children of God is closely linked to the ministry of the Spirit. They are born of the Spirit (Jn. 3:5f.), the very Spirit of Christ. Is it not possible that this is 'fitting' (Heb. 2:10) precisely because there is some such relationship between the Spirit and the Firstborn? Furthermore, there are clear biblical links between the Spirit and the incarnate sonship. Christ was conceived by the power of the Spirit; at his baptism he was the subject not only of the ministry of the Father (the Voice from heaven) but of the ministry of the Spirit (descending in the form of a dove); and throughout his life he was the object of the Spirit's solicitude as surely as he was the object of the Father's. The Spirit led him; through the Spirit he performed miracles; and through the Spirit he offered himself without spot to God (Heb. 9:14). Thus the economical trinity points clearly to a dynamic role for the Spirit in the life of the Son.

But the most suggestive statement of all is that of John 16:14, 'He will bring glory to me.' In the context, this refers, of course, only to relations within the economical trinity. But who is to deny that here, too, the economical trinity is a revelation of the immanent trinity? If the Father begets the Son, and if from the Father and the Son together there proceeds the Holy Spirit, why may we not introduce as the third movement 'the Spirit glorifies the Father and the Son'? This brings symmetry into trinitarian relations. Without that, we have one person (the Holy Spirit) who is always a recipient and never a donor.

It may be said, however, that the concept of *glorifying* does not meet the exigencies of the case: that there is an asymmetry in the language itself, because to glorify is a service-concept, while to beget and to spirate imply some kind of superiority. But do they? To beget is clearly a function of love: *monogenēs*, as we saw, is closely related to *agapētos*, and Christ is the Son of the Father's love (Col. 1:13). This entitles us to say that in relation to the Son the Father's love manifests itself by begetting. Similarly, in relation to the Son the Spirit's love might manifest itself by glorifying. As for the idea being servile, there is good reason to believe that loving service is precisely what characterizes relations within the godhead. It is certainly what appears in the economical trinity, where the Father upholds the Son (Is. 42:1). This also explains why the one who was in the form of God could, without self-destruction, take the form of a servant; and why in the very context in which we are commanded to be imitators of God (Eph. 5:1) we are also commanded to 'submit to one another' (Eph. 5:21). If greatness in the kingdom of God consists of service (Mk. 10:43f.), is this not a reflection of the King?

Barth, having raised the issue in the first place, dismisses the idea of a procession of the Son from the Spirit on the ground that to achieve true equality between the persons we should have to go on to speak of 'an origin of the Father from the Son and from the Spirit',[88] and such a notion is self-evidently absurd. But is it? Only if we equate procession (and, of course, begetting) with origination, as Barth clearly does, at least here. But this is something we have no right to do. The essence of both the Son and the Spirit is unoriginate, being one and the same with that of God the Father; and the persons of the Son and the Spirit are, equally, unoriginate. Was this not the primary protest of the church against the Arians: 'There never was when the Son was not'? Later, this was exactly the insistence of the Athanasian Creed: 'none is before and none is after'. Begetting and proceeding are descriptions of relationships, not accounts of origins. The subsistences (distinctions within the essence) are as eternal as the essence itself. By the very necessity of his being, God is triune. He has never been, and can never be, except as triune. For him, to be is to be the Father, the Son and the Holy Spirit. Once we accept this, it is clear that the Father owes it to the Son and the Spirit that he is what he is (Father) as much as they owe to him and to each other that they are what they are (respectively Spirit and Son). Only thus can we say that *none* is greater and *none* is lesser.

The Father begets the Son. The Father and the Son breathe the Spirit. The Spirit glorifies the Father and the Son.

Autotheos: God in his own right

Subordinationism survived the introduction of the *filioque* as it had that of the *homoousion*, largely because the successors of the Nicene theologians were content to reproduce their language and sentiments uncritically. According to Pearson, for example, it is the Father alone who is not only eternally but originally God: 'in that perfect and absolute equality there is, notwithstanding, this disparity, that the Father hath the Godhead not from the Son, nor any other, whereas the Son hath it from the Father: Christ is the true God and eternal life; but that he is so, is from the Father'.[89] H. P. Liddon is even more explicit:

> The Subordination of the Everlasting Son to the Everlasting Father is strictly compatible with the Son's absolute divinity; it is abundantly implied in our Lord's language; and it is an integral element of the ancient doctrine which steadily represents

> the Father as Alone Unoriginate, the Font of Deity in the eternal Life of the Ever-blessed Trinity.[90]

In all probability, Pearson and Liddon were taking their cue from Bishop Bull, who devoted the whole of Book IV of his *Defence of the Nicene Creed* to 'the subordination of the Son to the Father, as to His origin and principle', defending the view that

> the divine nature and perfections belong to the Father and the Son not collaterally and coordinately, but subordinately ... the Son has indeed the same divine nature in common with the Father, but communicated by the Father; in such sense, that is, that the Father is the fountain, origin, and principle, of the Divinity which is in the Son.[91]

This stubborn residue of subordinationism provided the background to John Calvin's formulation of the doctrine of the Trinity in the first book of his *Institutes.*[92] Calvin's mastery of the patristic material is total. He can tell us, for example, that 'you will find more than a hundred times in Hilary that there are three "substances" in God'.[93] But while he is more than happy to endorse the *homoousion*, Calvin's emphasis in expounding it differs significantly from that of Bull, Pearson and Liddon. His whole concern is to maximize the equality between the Father and the Son, and he is ill at ease with any suggestion of subordinationism. While he retains some of the language of causality he denies that the Father is in any sense the *deificator* ('god-maker') of the Son. The Father gave the Son neither his being nor his divinity.

This general position, already laid down in the first edition of the *Institutes* in 1536,[94] was clarified in the second edition and retained throughout all subsequent editions.[95] But Calvin's exposition, and especially its apparent difference from the Nicene and post-Nicene theologians, was not allowed to pass unnoticed. In particular, Calvin drew the fire of Peter Caroli and Valentinus Gentilis. Caroli, a Doctor of the Sorbonne, took strong exception to Calvin's doctrine that Christ was Yahweh and as such 'of himself alone was always self-existent'.[96] Gentilis, described by Beza[97] as a tritheist deeply influenced by Servetus, denied that the Son was *autotheos*, regarded the Father alone as the supreme, self-existent God and set forth an obscure doctrine of essentiation, described by Beza as involving 'a propagation of essences, three in number, both as persons and as essences'. Amid the obscurity, the one thing that was clear was that the Son was *essentiated of* (that is, owed his being to) the Father.

Calvin responded vigorously to both Caroli and Gentilis. His *Defence against the Calumnies of Peter Caroli* was published in 1545, his *Exposition of the Impiety of Valentinus Gentilis* in 1561. As these dates indicate, this controversy dogged Calvin from the publication of the second edition of the *Institutes* to the very end of his life.

Calvin's position rested on a clear distinction between *person* (*hypostasis*) and *essence* (*ousia*). It was perfectly correct, according to Calvin, to describe Christ as 'God of God' (*theos ek theou*) if we were referring to the former. As Son he was from the Father: 'Since he is the Son, we say that he exists from the Father.'[98] Calvin had already made this plain in a letter to Simon Grynee as early as 1537: 'if the distinction between the Father and the Word be attentively considered, we shall say that the one is from the other'.[99] But the essence of the Son was not from the Father. Simply as essence it was ingenerate and unbegotten. It could not be subordinate to that of the Father for the simple reason that it was not only generically but numerically identical with that of the Father (and, of course, that of the Holy Spirit). This was clearly implied in the divinity of the Son. To say that Christ was divine was to say that he had the divine essence and nothing was more fundamental to that essence than that it was self-existent. Time and again Calvin asked, 'Is He Jehovah?' If he is, then he is self-existent God, 'of Himself alone always self-existent ... If the essential quality of the Word be considered, in so far as he is one God with the Father, whatever can be said concerning God may also be applied to him, the second person of the glorious trinity.'[100] The same note is sounded in the *Institutes*:

> Since the name of Jehovah is set forth everywhere, it follows that with respect to his deity his being is from himself ... it remains that the essence is wholly and perfectly common to Father and Son. If this is true, then there is indeed with respect to the essence no distinction of one from the other.[101]

The core, then, is clear: the essence of the Son and the Holy Spirit cannot be subordinate in any sense to the essence of the Father because it is one and the same essence, equally self-existent in each person. Consequently, such terms as 'begotten' and 'proceeding' apply only to the persons of the Son and the Spirit, not to their essence. Otherwise, we have three divine beings. From this point of view, subordinationism implies tritheism.

The remaining question is whether traces of the idea of causality cling to the doctrine of the Trinity even in the language used by Calvin and others to disavow subordinationism. When we say that Christ is *autotheos* or that he has his deity *a se ipso* ('from his very self') are we not saying that the Son is the cause of his own essence, or that his essence is derived from himself? The truth, surely, is that the divine being has neither ground nor cause nor source. There is nothing more ultimate than itself (which, of course, is *himself*) and any language which suggests that person (or a particular person, God the Father) comes before the essence is inappropriate. The Son, as Yahweh, is simply *ho ōn*, the Being One: the One who was, is and will be eternally, open-endedly and necessarily. He is God in his own right, but God only and always with the Father and the Holy Spirit.

Part Two

"VERY GOD, VERY MAN"— *To Chalcedon & Beyond*

6

THE INCARNATION

'We do better', wrote Melanchthon in the Preface to his *Loci Communes*, 'to adore the mysteries of deity than to investigate them.' Later, in an even more famous statement, he declared, 'To know Christ means to know his benefits, and not as they (the Scholastics) teach, to reflect upon his natures and the modes of his incarnation.'[1]

Christology is certainly beset by the danger of an arid intellectualism. A man may be an expert on the incarnation and yet be totally lacking in faith and love. Conversely, someone may have little knowledge of the great creeds and yet have a real, living faith in Christ. Evangelicalism has always recognized this. James Denney, for example, emphasized that there was a distinction between soundness in the faith and soundness in doctrine.[2] This explains why sometimes, even when it has been necessary to denounce a man's teaching as heretical, those taking this step have paid full tribute to his piety. One instance of this was the case of Edward Irving, deposed from the ministry of the Church of Scotland in 1833 for promulgating views inconsistent with the sinlessness of Christ. Whatever they might think of his doctrine, none questioned his love for Christ. David Brown, at one time Irving's assistant in London and later Principal of the Free Church College in Aberdeen, vividly recalled their last meeting: 'With his hand held to mine, and mine warmly grasping his, he left me, my feelings very acute, and his, I am sure, the same. And thus ended my connection with this grand man, whose name can never be uttered in my hearing without a feeling of mingled love and reverence arising within me.'[3]

None of this, however, justifies the conclusion that reverent reflection on the person of Christ is either inappropriate or irrelevant to the church. Apart from all else, we have a duty to collate all the information afforded to us by the New Testament and try to build it up into a coherent whole. The research becomes inappropriate only when it loses touch with historical reality and degenerates into vain speculation. The very adoration of which Melanchthon spoke gratefully gathers up every crumb of knowledge in its endeavour to build up a living picture of Christ. Besides, other things being equal, the intellectual quest is an avenue to spiritual knowledge. The Great Commission itself makes plain that, for good or ill, Christian evangelism places a premium on the intellect: we are to go and make *disciples* of all nations (Mt. 28:19). The form of Scripture itself emphasizes the same point. God has revealed himself in written prophetic utterance and written apostolic tradition precisely because he expects us to prepare our minds for action (1 Pet. 1:13). Only as we do so can we hope to find ourselves on that pinnacle of adoring wonder from which Paul poured forth his doxology in Romans 11:33-36:

> Oh, the depth of the riches of the wisdom and knowledge of
> God!
> How unsearchable his judgments,
> and his paths beyond tracing out! …
> To him be the glory for ever!

It was no mystical or aesthetic experience which prompted such an exclamation, but a rigorous examination, sustained through eleven magnificent chapters, of God's good news concerning his Son (Rom. 1:2).

In any case, Melanchthon's warning (whatever its intention) came too late. The church had already devoted a prodigious amount of effort to Christological reflection, eventually laying down boundaries which, even today, a wise man would hesitate to trespass. Indeed, the church had no option but to reflect. The objections of her enemies and the speculations of her professed friends placed in jeopardy beliefs which lay close to the heart of her devotion and forced her to think through the implications of her belief that Christ was true man as surely as he was true God.

The attack on the doctrine of the incarnation came from two directions.

Docetism

The first attack came from the Docetists. This label covers a group of sometimes bizarre speculations bound together by a refusal to accept that God could in any real sense become man. Its best known representatives were Cerinthus, Ebion, Marcion and Valentinus, whose ideas are recorded with painstaking thoroughness by Irenaeus (*Against Heresies*, especially Book III) and rebutted mercilessly by Tertullian (*On the Flesh of Christ* and *Against Marcion*, particularly Book III).

Docetism rested on two fundamental principles: matter is evil, and the divine can experience neither change nor suffering. These principles obviously required a denial of the most cherished Christian beliefs. The Son of God could not be born of a human mother, and certainly not linked to her by an umbilical cord; nor could he suffer and die; nor take an ordinary flesh-and-blood body. Impelled by these considerations, Cerinthus, for example, drew a sharp distinction between Christ and Jesus.[4] Jesus was an ordinary man, born of Mary in the usual way, possessing a fleshly body and crucified on the cross of Calvary. Christ, by contrast, was a heavenly being who came upon Jesus only at his baptism and left him before he was crucified. This meant that Christ, as such, derived nothing from Mary, had no personal connection with matter and experienced no physical pain.

Marcion, on the other hand, regarded the humanity of Christ as only a phantom. He had the appearance of a man, but this was a mere mask, an image without substance (hence *docetism*, from the Greek *dokeō*, 'I seem'). His flesh had no reality, with the result, in the words of Tertullian, that he 'was not what he appeared to be, and feigned himself to be what he was not – incarnate without being flesh, human without being man'.[5] Such speculations stirred the great North African father to the depths of his soul, not least because they nullified belief in both the cross and the resurrection:

> How will all this be true in Him, if He was not himself true – if He really had not in Himself that which might be crucified,

> might die, might be buried, and might rise again? [I mean] this flesh suffused with blood, built up with bones, interwoven with nerves, entwined with veins, [a flesh] which knew how to be born, and how to die, human without doubt, as born of a human being.[6]

Apollinarianism

The second threat to the doctrine of the incarnation came from Apollinarianism. Apollinaris himself was a man of blameless life, powerful intellect and deep spirituality and his condemnation as a heretic (by the Council of Constantinople in 381) was, as G. L. Prestige points out, one of the great tragedies in the history of theology.[7] Unfortunately, it is not easy to build up a coherent picture of his Christology. Most of his work survives only in fragments gleaned from quotations by his opponents[8] and the position is further complicated by the fact that some of his writings, published posthumously, appeared under false names (for example, two pseudo-Athanasian compositions, *Quod Unus Sit Deus* and *De Incarnatione Verbi Dei*, are now widely regarded as works of Apollinaris).[9]

Apollinaris had a well earned reputation as one of the outstanding champions of Nicene theology. Yet, paradoxically, his most distinctive tenet was one he shared with Arianism: the *Logos* as incarnate did not possess a human mind. The statement, 'The Word became flesh', meant only that he took a human body. He did not take a human *pneuma* ('spirit') or *nous* ('mind'). Instead, the *Logos* himself supplied both the animating principle and the rational principle, so that the incarnate Christ had neither a human intellect nor a human will. In taking this position, Apollinaris seems to have been driven by an aversion to the dualist (or duophysite) Christology of Antioch with its emphasis on the distinction between the two natures in the incarnate Lord. He insisted, over against this, that the union of the *Logos* and the human body constituted one nature (*physis*), just as, in a human being, body and spirit constitute one nature. The presence of two minds and two wills would have produced hopeless incoherence, said Apollinaris: 'Two separate principles of mind and will cannot dwell together without one striving against the other'; 'such a subject would be in a state of perpetual turmoil, distracted by the conflicting wishes of the elements of which it consists'.[10] Besides, the human mind is sinful, 'the prey of filthy thoughts', and it would have been impossible for Christ to take it.

Much can be said in mitigation of Apollinaris: that he was rightly suspicious of the tendency (associated with Paul of Samosata) to portray Christ as inspired man rather than as enfleshed God; that when he spoke of one *physis* he meant something very similar to what a later generation meant by one *person* or *hypostasis*; that the tendencies which he distrusted in Alexandrian theology were exactly those which soon afterwards manifested themselves in Nestorianism; that his view of the Lord's human nature resembled that which was later encapsulated in the notion of the impersonal humanity (*anhypostasia*); that he was able to do some justice to the full humanity of Christ by pioneering a kenotic view of the incarnation, according to which Christ on earth lived a life of deliberate divine self-limitation; and that even the great (if unscrupulous) champion of Christological orthodoxy, Cyril of Alexandria, drew heavily on the terminology of Apollinaris' pseudepigraphic works, mistakenly believing them to be from the pen of Athanasius.[11]

That still leaves the central problem, however: Apollinaris' Christ was a truncated Christ. 'He is not man,' he wrote, 'though like man; for He is not consubstantial with man in the most important element.'[12] At best, he is man only titularly, 'for He is divine spirit united to flesh'.[13] Indeed, according to some of Apollinaris' statements, Christ is neither God nor man but a *tertium quid*, 'a mean between God and man, neither wholly man nor wholly God, but a combination of God and man'.[14] On occasion, he speaks of the qualities of the two natures as being 'mixed' or 'commingled', but this always leaves the divine nature unaffected. There is no real incarnation, no assumption of humanity and no becoming man. There is only God assuming the conditions of human existence. In that existence the human body and the divine *Logos* formed one *ousia*, but there was no room for a human psychology.

These formulations provoked a strong reaction, particularly from the Cappadocian theologians. Indeed, this reaction is already articulated in Athanasius' *Letter to the Church of Antioch* (*circa* 362), even though it is highly unlikely that this is aimed at Apollinaris personally (the two men appear to have been life-long friends). Athanasius insisted that the human nature of Christ was complete, and did not consist only of a body:

> The Saviour had not a body without a soul, nor without sense or intelligence; for it was not possible, when the Lord had become man for us, that His body should be without intelligence: nor

> was the salvation effected in the Word Himself a salvation of body only, but of soul also ... For the Saviour had a body neither without soul, nor without sense, nor without intelligence.[15]

However, it was the Cappadocian fathers, particularly the two Gregories, who had to face up squarely to the points raised by Apollinaris. Whether they were always fair to their adversary is a moot point. They were certainly in no doubt as to the gravity of the issues. 'The most grievous item of all in the woes of the church', wrote Gregory of Nazianzen in his *Letter to Nectarius*,[16] 'is the boldness of the Apollinarians.' The main reason for this estimate was that Apollinarianism was fatal to the humanness of Christ:

> If he has a soul, and yet is without a mind, how is he man, for man is not a mindless animal? ... But, says such a one, the Godhead took the place of the human intellect. How does this touch me? For Godhead joined to flesh alone is not man, nor to soul alone, nor to both apart from intellect, which is the most essential part of man.[17]

In the opinion of the Cappadocians, such a denial of the Lord's humanity was fatal to the Christian doctrine of salvation. If Christ did not become human, he did not save humanity. Gregory of Nazianzen crystallized the issue in a famous statement in his *Letter to Cledonius*: 'If anyone has put his trust in him as a man without a human mind, he is wholly bereft of mind, and quite unworthy of salvation. *For that which he has not assumed he has not healed*; but that which is united to his Godhead is also saved' (italics mine). Gregory of Nyssa expressed himself equally memorably: the Good Shepherd carried the whole sheep, not just the skin!

> Now it was not the body merely, but the whole man, compacted of soul and body, that was lost: indeed, if we are to speak more exactly, the soul was lost sooner than the body ... He therefore Who came for this cause, that He might seek and save that which was lost, (that which the shepherd in the parable calls the sheep,) both finds that which is lost, and carries home on his shoulders the whole sheep, not its skin only, that he may make the man of God complete, united to the deity in body and in soul. And thus He was in all points tempted like as we are, yet without sin, left no part of our nature which He did not take upon Himself.[18]

A true body

It was against the background of the Docetic and Apollinarian heresies that the church developed its doctrine of the incarnation. This contained two basic emphases: Christ took a true human body and he took a reasonable human soul.

First, Christ took a true body. This scarcely requires argument. Paul states it explicitly in Colossians 2:9 ('in Christ all the fulness of the Deity lives in bodily form') as does John in 1 John 4:2 ('Every spirit that acknowledges that Jesus Christ has come in the flesh is from God'). John also points to it more dramatically when he records that at the crucifixion the soldier's spear brought 'a sudden flow of blood and water' (Jn. 19:34; *cf.* Jn. 5:7–8).

These assertions are backed up by a mass of incidental details. Jesus was born in the usual way. He grew up (Lk. 2:52). He hungered and thirsted. He slept and wept. He sweated and bled. He felt exhausted. He was beaten and flogged and wounded and nailed to a cross. He died, was wrapped in grave-clothes and buried. He rose, but even of that resurrection-body he could say, 'a ghost does not have flesh and bones, as you see I have' (Lk. 24:39).

Against such a background it is hardly surprising that Christian orthodoxy has asserted the physical humanity of Christ unambiguously and, on occasion, even colourfully. 'He did not flutter about like a spirit,' declared Luther in one of his *Sermons on the Gospel of St John*, 'but he dwelt among men. He had eyes, ears, mouth, nose, chest, stomach, hands, and feet, just as you and I do. He took the breast. His mother nursed Him as any other child is nursed.'[19]

The great nineteenth-century Scottish preacher, Alexander Stewart, was equally emphatic:

> ... as the tabernacle after all was as truly a tent as the humblest in the camp of Israel, so Christ is as truly man as the meanest of our race. The blood which flows in the veins of the Hottentot, or springs under the lash from the back of an American slave, is that 'one' same blood which flows in the veins of the Son of God.[20]

The Formula of Chalcedon (451) speaks of Christ as 'consubstantial with us according to the manhood'; the Athanasian Creed specifically links his manhood to the substance of his mother and the later, Protestant creeds do the same. The Westminster Confession (VIII.II), for example, speaks of him as 'conceived ... in the womb of the Virgin Mary, of her substance'. This underlines the fact that in all essential respects Christ's human body was identical with our own. It had the same anatomy, the same physiology, the same biochemistry, the same central nervous system and the same basic genetic code. But the derivation from the substance of the Virgin also means that she as mother contributed to him all that any human mother contributes to her child, sin excepted. Through the umbilical cord, he is this particular man, the son of this particular woman, the bearer of the whole previous genetic history of her people and the recipient of innumerable hereditary features. He was a unique genotype precisely because she contributed at least half his chromosomes (as any human mother would). How the rest were contributed remains a mystery. The one certainty is that Mary could not herself have contributed the sex-determining chromosome, Y, which is always provided by the biological father. This chromosome, at least, must have been provided miraculously; and it remains possible that all the chromosomes normally derived from the male parent were provided in this way, the divine act which fertilized the ovum simultaneously creating twenty-three chromosomes complementary to those derived from the mother.[21]

As the true biological son of his mother Jesus is particularized as a well-connected first-century Jew, born in humble circumstances and sharing the poverty and harassment of an oppressed under-class. He is also particularized as a *man*. This is only to say that he was a normal human being, which he could not have been without being either male or female. We have every right, in the light of modern genetics, to regard this maleness as absolute, determined by the presence of one Y chromosome (there is no Y chromosome in the female). We must also believe that for Jesus, as for every other human being, the whole of his existence was conditioned by his sexuality. Although he appears to endorse the view that some human beings are born with no interest in the opposite sex (at least, this is one possible interpretation of the words of Mt. 19:12, 'some are eunuchs because they were born that way'), there is no evidence that this applied to himself. On the contrary, throughout his life he moved easily in the company of women, commanding their respect and affection.

We must also allow this aspect of Jesus' life to stand under the rubric indicated in Hebrews 4:15: he was 'tempted in every way, just as we are'. Temptation came through his sexuality as surely as it came through his need for food and his fear of pain. But he was tempted without sinning, which means not only that he avoided physical unchastity but also that he was guiltless of the lust which he himself condemns in Matthew 5:28.

The fact that Jesus, the Word of God, was male does not entitle us to draw any conclusions as to gender in God. Sexuality is biological, applicable to a *nephesh* (a living soul or an animated body) but utterly alien to one who is pure spirit. Insofar as the incarnation has any bearing on honours between the sexes the most appropriate word is that of Mascall: 'In no woman has human nature been raised to the dignity which it possesses in Jesus of Nazareth, but to no male human person has there been given a dignity comparable to that which Mary enjoys as theotokos.'[22] On the other hand, we do have every right to put forward the example of Jesus against every argument to the effect that singleness represents only a truncated or frustrated human existence. Celibacy, whether voluntary or involuntary, requires no special justification.

Through his body the Lord is linked to the whole of the physical creation and in particular to the whole of suffering humanity. He knows how we are formed; 'he remembers that we are dust' (Ps. 103:14). But the body is not just a memory for the risen Christ. He still has a body: a body which, by definition, is material and which stands in direct organic succession to the one he had in the days of his humiliation. This is what prompted the eccentric nineteenth-century Scottish Orientalist, John Duncan, to exclaim, 'the dust of the earth is on the throne of the Majesty on High'.[23]

Yet that body is in a very different state to that which characterized it here on earth. Paul refers to it as 'his glorious body' (Phil. 3:21). The underlying truth there is that as God 'hyper-exalted' Christ (Phil. 2:9, my translation), his Servant, so he 'hyper-exalted' his body in particular. What this means in detail is not so clear. It would be hazardous to draw firm conclusions from the post-resurrection appearances. The pre-ascension body of Christ was in a temporary, transitional state and the appearances are extremely variable: a point which is made explicitly in the longer ending of Mark, which tells us that, 'Afterwards Jesus appeared in a different form to two of them while they were walking in the country' (Mk. 16:12). If this is so, then none of these 'forms' can be determinative for our view of the body of his glory. It is safer to argue from the transfiguration, where the body appears as pure light; from Saul's experience on the Damascus Road (a far cry from Mary's impression that he was 'the gardener', Jn. 20:15); from the description of the resurrection body of believers in 1 Corinthians 15:42–44; and from the suggestion in Revelation 5:6 that the Lamb still bears the marks of his suffering.

If we collate all these passages (bearing in mind that they are more suggestive than propositional) what emerges is that the resurrection body of Jesus is his earthly body in another state (*morphē*); that it still bears, at least to the eye of faith, the impress of its history and particularly of its suffering; that it is glorious and powerful, possessing properties in relation to visibility and movement (light and space) which are far beyond our current experience; that it is not subject to illness, senescence or the law of entropy; that it is in some special sense 'beside' God (Jn. 17:5); that the glory of God is seen in its face; that it is spiritual (1 Cor. 15:44) and as such eminently adapted to the leading and prompting of the Holy Spirit; that it is also ideally adapted to the role assigned to Christ as 'head over everything' (Eph. 1:22); that it is the model for the bodies which God will one day give to ourselves; and that it is the Omega-point of creation, into which God the Father, in adoring and wondering gratitude for the service rendered by his Son, has poured all his wisdom, power and creativity, striving to create something as beautiful in its own way as the obedience offered on Calvary.

A reasonable soul

The second element in the Catholic doctrine of the incarnation was that Christ took a reasonable human soul (*anima rationalis*). He had a human psychology as truly as he had a human body.

For example, he had a human mind, subject to the same laws of perception, memory, logic and development as our own. This is highlighted in two passages in the synoptics: Luke 2:52 and Mark 13:32. In the former of these the evangelist records that the child Jesus grew in wisdom just as he grew in physical stature. He observed and learned and remembered and applied. This would have been impossible if he had been born in possession of a complete body of wisdom and knowledge. Instead, he was born with the mental equipment of a normal child, experienced the usual stimuli and went through the ordinary processes of intellectual development.

In the second passage, Mark 13:32, Jesus freely admits, and even emphasizes, that there is something he does not know: 'No-one knows about that day or hour, not even the angels in heaven, nor the Son, but only the Father.' These words have always been a problem for the church. Luke omitted the saying altogether; and many manuscripts omit the words 'neither the Son' from the Matthaean parallel (for example, the version cited by Basil in his *Letter 236* did not contain these words).

Ambrose regarded the whole statement as an Arian interpolation, but this is no more credible than that they were an invention of the early Christian community, embarrassed by the delay in the *parousia.* Nothing in the history of Jesus is more certain than that he confessed ignorance with regard to the timing of the second advent. But what are we to make of it?

First, if we take seriously the deity of Christ we have no option but to believe that as the eternal *Logos* he knew all things, including the hour of the *parousia.* It is difficult to formulate any concept of incarnation which could eclipse such omniscience without involving a renunciation of deity. There is no doubt that patristic exegesis focused too exclusively on this aspect of the truth, but truth it was nonetheless. If Christ was consubstantial with the Father, if he was the one who made the ages, if he was upholding all things and if the Father had given all things into his hands, then he could not but be privy to the purpose of God with regard to the *parousia.* Hence, for example, the language of Athanasius: 'it is proper to the Word to know what was made, and not to be ignorant either of the beginning or of the end of these (for the works are His) and He knows how many things He wrought, and the limit of their consistence'.[24] Cyril of Alexandria spoke in similar terms, accusing the Arians of

> ... foolishly asserting that the Word, issuing from God the Father's substance, actually does not know either that hour or day, in order that he may be ranked alongside the angels and may be deemed to differ in no respect from his creatures ... If they suppose that Christ, in so far as He is viewed as God, was actually ignorant of something, they are going off course, careering over boulders and raising their horn against His glory.[25]

The Cappadocian theologians took the same position, with one subtle difference: they applied the concept of order within the trinity to the divine knowledge as they did to the divine relations. As the Son has his sonship from the Father, so he has his knowledge from the Father. The Father knows first and is the source or *principium* of the Son's knowledge. For Basil, this is the key to Mark 13:32. The statement that the Son does not know means 'does not know as the Father knows, but knows only from the Father': 'Thus also', he writes, 'we understand "No man knoweth" to refer to the Father the first knowledge of things, both present and to be, and generally to exhibit to men the first cause.'[26]

Gregory of Nazianzen took virtually the same position, arguing that Wisdom could not be ignorant of anything, but also insisting that his knowledge must be referred to the Father as its cause: the Son knows otherwise than the Father does.[27]

This Cappadocian interpretation is an evasion rather than an interpretation; and in any case it rests on what we have already seen to be an unacceptable view of order within the Trinity. But it contains the germ of an important truth: the incarnate Lord, the Mediator, derives all his knowledge from the Father.

The Jesus of the gospels clearly possessed supernatural knowledge. This is already hinted at in the story of his visit to the temple at the age of twelve: 'Everyone who heard him was amazed at his understanding and his answers' (Lk. 2:47). It is true, of course, that observers were equally astounded by the young Mozart and we must be careful not to confuse the precocious with the miraculous. But later incidents confirm Jesus' extraordinary insight. For example, he knew the character of Nathanael before he met him (Jn. 1:47). He knew that the woman of Samaria had had five husbands (Jn. 4:18). He knew, long before he reached his dwelling, that Lazarus was dead (Jn. 11:14). He knew that inside the mouth of a fish there would be a coin sufficient to pay the temple tax (Mt. 17:27); that there was a shoal of fish beside a boat which had toiled all night and caught nothing (Lk. 5:4–6); and that when his disciples went to look for a room in which to hold the Passover they would be met by a man carrying a jar of water (Mk. 14:13).

These facts are impressive in themselves, but we must distinguish between supernatural knowledge and infinite knowledge. Not for nothing did the Syrians complain (2 Ki. 6:12) that the prophet Elisha told the king of Israel the very words spoken by their own king in his bedroom! But this did not mean that Elisha or any of the host of prophets who had similar experiences were omniscient. It meant only that they were the recipients of special divine revelation. Similarly, in the case of Jesus, no weight of evidence that his knowledge was extraordinary can amount to proof that it was infinite.

Jesus came by his knowledge of God in the only way that such knowledge is possible for man: by revelation. For him, as for us, the initiative in such knowing lies with God himself. He would know as much as God chose to reveal to him. True, his own capacity for such knowledge would differ significantly from that of ordinary men. But it would not differ in kind or in principle. He knew the will of the Father because the Father revealed it to him. For example, in Christ, as in other men, there was what Calvin calls the *sensus deitatis*, the awareness of God;[28] and what the same theologian calls the *notitia Dei insita* (the implanted knowledge of God). Through 'what has been made' he clearly perceived the power and god-ness of God (Rom. 1:19–20); from the Old Testament he learned of the great promises of the covenant; and from his mother, in all probability, he received the first intimations of his own unique identity and destiny.

In all these respects his experience was parallel to our own. Where it differed was, first of all, in his sinlessness, which meant that his intellect was perfectly attuned to the divine; and, secondly, in the unique intimacy of his relationship with God. He conversed with God as his Son; and he thought as his Son. We may even say that he lived in a thought-world of pure revelation so that to an extent that we cannot fathom God disclosed himself not only to his thinking but *in* his thinking. In this respect, revelation, in the case of Christ, was concurrent with his own thought-processes.

Yet, the incarnation inevitably involved some mode of ignorance. Humanness cannot be omniscient. Even when they were warning most vociferously against Arianism, the fathers were aware of this, stressing that the assumption of flesh inevitably meant the assumption of ignorance. Athanasius wrote:

> This is not the Word's deficiency, but of that human nature whose property it is to be ignorant ... since He was made man, He is not ashamed, because of the flesh which is ignorant, to say 'I know not,' that He may show that knowing as God, He is but ignorant according to the flesh.[29]

Cyril is equally explicit:

> We ought to touch on the divine plan and remark that God's only-begotten Word took on along with humanity all its attributes save sin alone. Ignorance of future events properly belongs to the limitations of humanity and so, in so far as he is viewed as God, he knows all the Father knows; in so far, though, as the same Son is man, he does not repudiate the appearance of ignorance because it is an attribute of humanity. Just as he who is personally the Life and Power of all took bodily nourishment out of respect for the measure of his self-emptying and is recorded as having slept and been weary, so, though knowing all things, he is not ashamed to allot himself the ignorance which

belongs to humanity; because his were all the attributes of humanity save sin alone.[30]

For Cyril, clearly, the ignorance was as real as the sleep and the weariness and reflected the same fact: the *Logos* had taken flesh. Gregory of Nazianzen took exactly the same position: 'we are to understand the ignorance in the most reverent sense, by attributing it to the manhood, and not to the Godhead.'[31] Calvin, working in a different theological context, is less anxious to hedge his language with qualifications, but otherwise simply echoes the patristic position: 'surely that man must be singularly mad, who would hesitate to submit to the ignorance which even the Son of God himself did not hesitate to endure on our account ... there would be no impropriety in saying that Christ, who knew all things, was ignorant of something in respect of his perception as a man.'[32]

But is it at all possible to integrate these two emphases? How does the omniscience of the *Logos* relate to the ignorance of the Mediator? Two things may be said.

First, that as Mediator he was never ignorant of anything that he ought to have known. John Duncan drew a distinction between ignorance and nescience, declaring: 'Christ was nescient, but not ignorant.'[33] The distinction Duncan had in mind was that *nescience* was simply that state of limited knowledge from which man, as a creature, cannot escape, whereas *ignorance* was the morally culpable condition of not knowing what one could have known and ought to have known. Admittedly the two words themselves were never intended to reflect this distinction, but it is a real one nevertheless. As a finite creature there was much that Christ did not know, but as Mediator he knew all that he needed to know; or, more precisely, all that his church needed to know. This cannot mean that the Father had told him everything about physics and chemistry and history and biology or even (in the light of Mk. 13:32) about eschatology. What it means is that the Father shared with him as much about the mystery of redemption as he needed to know. He received this knowledge in his capacity as the Great Prophet; he received it from the Father through the Spirit; and he received it not all at once but gradually, the progress of the revelation being determined by his own developing capacities and by the exigencies of the hour. It would be hazardous to believe, for example, that although Christ knew from the very beginning that he was to die a violent death (Mk. 2:20) he also knew the precise details of his arrest, trial and crucifixion; or even that in the Garden of Gethsemane he had an exhaustive understanding of what the cross was going to entail. It is clear from Mark 13:32 that the time of the *parousia* was not revealed to Christ; and it is virtually certain that the reason why it was not revealed was that this was not something his people needed to know. It either had no bearing on Christian life and devotion, or the divine judgment was that such life and devotion would be better served by uncertainty on this issue than by precise information.

The other line of integration between the omniscience of the divine nature and the ignorance of the human is that just as Christ had to fulfil the office of Mediator within the limitations of a human body, so he had to fulfil it within the limitations of a human mind. Part of the truth here is suggested by the first of the three temptations in the desert: 'tell these stones to become bread' (Mt. 4:3). The essence of the temptation was that the Lord disavow the conditions of the incarnation and draw on his omnipotence to alleviate the discomforts of his self-abasement. He could have turned the stones into bread; and he could (perhaps) have known the day and the hour of his parousia. But the latter would have undone his work as surely as the former. Christ had to submit to knowing dependently and to knowing partially. He had to learn to obey without knowing all the facts and to believe without being in possession of full information. He had to forego the comfort which omniscience would sometimes have brought. This, surely, was a potent factor in the dereliction (Mk. 15:34). The assurance of the Father's love, the sense of his own sonship and the certainty of his victory were all eclipsed, and he had to complete his obedience as the one who walked in darkness, knowing only that he was sin and that he was banished to the outer darkness. He suffers as the one who does not have all the answers and who in his extremity has to ask, Why? The ignorance is not a mere appearing. It is a reality. But it is a reality freely chosen, just as on the cross he chose not to summon twelve legions of angels. Omniscience was a luxury always within reach, but incompatible with his rules of engagement. He had to serve within the limitations of finitude.

Yet such limitations need not imply fallibility. Certainly, to err is human, but this argument, at least as sometimes used, proves too much. A statement is not bound to contain errors simply because it is human. For example, the idea that Scripture must be fallible since it is given through ordinary human personalities overlooks such facts as the almost invariable correctness of sports results on Saturday afternoon, despite their being compiled by fallible human beings. Besides, in the case of Jesus there are factors other than his humanness to take into account. For one thing, he was the Son of God and this should at least give us pause before accusing him of error. William Temple asserts that 'on all matters of mere information He shared the views of His time'.[34] This may be so, but there is nothing to substantiate it. Furthermore, the choice facing us need not be restricted to either assuming that Jesus was a flat-earther or assuming that he was conversant with the cosmology of Copernicus and the physics of Einstein. There is a third possibility: that Jesus knew the provisional nature of the science and metaphysics of his day and suspended judgment. If he knew that he did not know the day or the hour of the *parousia*, could he not also have known that he did not know the speed of light; and even that many questions relevant to the environment and to cosmic origins had not even been posed in the first century?

Temple quotes a certain Bishop Know to the effect that, 'The infallibility of Jesus ... was not due to the superseding of human fallibility by Divine Omniscience. It was due to the intimate relation between the Divine and human in one Personality, and was consistent with the full experience of His humanity.'[35] But the truth here needs to be formulated more precisely. Certainly, the infallibility of the Messiah is not that of divine omniscience. Neither, however, is it the result of the direct action of his divine nature on his human nature. These natures are not individual agents, capable of acting upon each other. The real premise of the Lord's mediatorial infallibility is that he was a prophet, indeed the Great Prophet, and as such specially endowed with the Holy Spirit. In principle, this endowment was no different from that enjoyed by other prophets whose utterances were clearly equated with the word of Yahweh. But this is not to say that there were no differences. Jesus could speak of the Father as his Father and of the Spirit as his Spirit in a way that no other prophet could.

Human emotions

'It belongs to the truth of our Lord's humanity', wrote B. B. Warfield, 'that he was subject to all sinless human emotions.'[36] This has been strongly emphasized in Protestant theology, particularly by John Calvin. 'Christ', he wrote, 'has put on our feelings along with our flesh.'[37] He develops this theme more fully in his exposition of Christ's agony in the garden, where, he says, Christ's mind was seized with a terror to which he had not been accustomed. This should cause us no embarrassment: 'those who imagine that the Son of God was exempt from human passions do not truly and sincerely acknowledge him to be a man'.[38] Certainly we must distinguish his weakness from ours. His passions were sinless and regulated by moderation. Nevertheless, says Calvin, 'the dreadful abyss of destruction tormented him grievously with fear and anguish', even to the extent that 'amidst the violent shock of temptation, he vacillated – as it were – from one wish to another'.[39]

Much has been made of the fact that Jesus is never said to have smiled or laughed. Linked to the description of the Servant as 'a man of sorrows and acquainted with grief' it has furnished a basis for the idea that Jesus' life was unremittingly joyless and stressful. But this is a serious over-simplification. Apart from all else, a joyless life would have been a sinful life. Would Jesus have been guilty of the anxiety he forbade in others (Mt. 6:25)? Would he have fallen short of Paul's attainment as one who had learned to be content whatever the circumstances (Phil. 4:11)? Or of the precept to 'rejoice always' (Phil. 4:4)? Could he have been filled with the Spirit and yet not have known the Spirit's joy (Gal. 5:22)? Could he have given rest and relief to others (Mt. 11:28) while remaining depressed and disconsolate himself?

Besides these general considerations there are clear and specific statements in the New Testament to the effect that Jesus experienced deep, habitual joy. In Luke 10:21, for example, he is described as 'full of joy through the Holy Spirit' (the verb used is *ēgalliasato*, from *agalliaomai*, to 'exult or be overjoyed'). In John 15:11 he refers to his own joy: 'I have told you this so that my joy may be in you and that your joy may be complete.' This clearly implies that the joy Jesus shares with his disciples is, in the first instance, his own. The immediate context makes plain that it was based on his sense of the Father's love and approbation, and, beyond that, on his obedience to the Father's commands. There is a similar reference in John 17:13, 'I am coming to you now, but I say these things while I am still in the world, so that they may have the full measure of my joy within them.'

There can be little doubt that, apart from the brief (although indescribably intense) moment of the dereliction on Calvary, Jesus was serene, contented and happy. He rejoiced, doubtless, in the being of his Father, meditating on him as an object of wonder and admiration; in his Father's love, approbation and constant help and presence; in the beauties and glories of his Father's creation; in doing his Father's will, promoting his glory and saving his people; in the friendship, company and conversation of those the Father had given to be with him; and in anticipating his return to the glory he had with the Father 'before the world began' (Jn. 17:5). Such joy was an indispensable element in the psychology of his obedience. He served not as a slave but as a Son.

Jesus also knew anger, indeed, blazing indignation, evoked sometimes by human evil and perverseness and sometimes by the sheer scale of the human tragedy. For example, in the synagogue at Capernaum he was angered by the congregation's attitude towards his healing the man with the withered hand: 'He looked round at them in anger ... deeply distressed at their stubborn hearts' (Mk. 3:5). What did he find so disturbing? Probably the legalism which saw the Sabbath in terms only of rules and regulations, completely oblivious to the needs of men and women and judging the Messiah himself solely by his attitude to their traditions.

Later (Mk. 10:13) he was indignant when the disciples discouraged the mothers who had brought their children to him. What stirred him? Was it the disciples' misguided attempts to protect him? Or the unnecessary hurt to the women? Most likely it was the disciples' complete misunderstanding of his kingdom, presuming that it could not be for the weak and frail and dependent. On the contrary, he said, it is precisely to such that the kingdom belongs.

But the most interesting reference to Jesus' anger is in the account of the raising of Lazarus. Overcome by the weeping of Mary and her fellow mourners 'he was deeply moved in spirit and troubled' (Jn. 11:33). Each of the verbs used expresses strong emotion; so much so, in fact, that some early versions and manuscripts, embarrassed by the attribution of such distress to Jesus, modified the passage to read, 'he was moved in spirit, as if he were troubled'.[40] *Enebrimēsato* means that he shuddered in indignation and outrage; *etaraxen heauton* that he was troubled in himself. Again, we have to ask, what caused this anger? The idea that it was the hypocrisy of the mourners is unlikely, since the weeping Jews are bracketed with Mary, whose sorrow was genuine enough. It is equally unlikely that he was angry because he was being forced to perform a miracle.[41] The lead-up to the incident (especially Jn. 11:23) strongly suggests that Jesus had come to Bethany with the express purpose of doing something extraordinary. The idea that he was angry because of the unbelief of Mary and Martha and the other mourners (grieving as if they had no hope, 1 Thess. 4:13) is more plausible. But the most likely explanation remains that of Warfield: 'The spectacle of the distress of Mary and her companions enraged Jesus because it brought poignantly home to his consciousness the evil of death.'[42]

Besides joy and anger, Jesus, equally clearly, experienced grief. He was not simply Man, but Sin-bearer, and as such liable to emotions 'which never would have invaded his soul in the purity of his humanity save as he stood under the curse incurred for his people's sins'.[43] Such grief is clearly implied in Jesus' weeping at the tomb of Lazarus (Jn. 11:35) and in his lament over Jerusalem (Lk. 19:41). But it becomes particularly clear in the account of Gethsemane where, as Calvin says, Christ 'allows the flesh to feel what belongs to it, and, therefore, being truly a man, he trembles at death'.[44] As Lohmeyer points out, 'The Greek words depict the utmost degree of unbounded horror and suffering.'[45] *Ekthambeisthai* (Mk. 14:33) describes someone in the grip of a shuddering horror or a terrified surprise. *Adēmonein* (also verse 33) occurs again in Philippians 2:26, referring to the distress of Epaphroditus. 'It describes', writes Lightfoot, 'the confused, restless, half-distracted state, which is produced by physical derangement, or by mental distress, as grief, shame. disappointment, etc.'[46] *Perilypos* (verse 34) indicates deep grief, intensified in this particular instance by the addition of the words 'unto death'. His distress is so acute as to threaten life itself (or, possibly, so acute that death itself would be preferable).[47]

But the narrative does not owe its force to the adjectives alone. The whole account resonates the acutest torment and anguish. This appears, for example, in the fact that he took Peter, James and John with him, not merely for companionship but so that they might watch and pray with him. It was of paramount importance for himself, for the universe and for mankind that he should not fail in his task, and the temptations that beset him on the eve of his agony represented a real threat to the completion of his obedience. Hell would do – was doing – all in its power to divert him from the Father's will. Hence the supreme urgency of watching and praying; and hence the need for the prayers of others. Could there be a more impressive witness to the felt weakness of Jesus than his turning to those frail human beings and saying to them, 'I need your prayers!'?

In the event they failed him. He had to watch and pray alone. Had the redemption of the world depended on the diligence of the disciples (or even on their staying awake) it would never have been accomplished. As Barth puts it in his probing exposition of Gethsemane:

> There is no one to bear the burden with Him. There is none to help. No Christian individual had the insight, and no Christian group put it into effect, that this was a matter for Christians and Christianity itself, that for their own sake Christians and Christianity had good reason to have a part in this prayer, to join with Jesus in crying to God.[48]

But the impressive thing is that he turned to them at all. How deep must have been his need and his fear!

It is impressive, too, that immediately after telling his disciples that his soul was filled with mortal fear he turned away from them and set his face towards God: 'He withdrew about a stone's throw beyond them, knelt down and prayed' (Lk. 22:41). There was nowhere else to go. Even the physical circumstances of his prayer make plain that it came out of a soul near the end of its resources. He throws himself prostrate on the ground. He is so exhausted by the first phase of his prayer that 'an angel from heaven appeared to him and strengthened him' (Lk. 22:43). And when he resumes his prayer, it is in anguish (*en agonia*), praying so earnestly that his sweat falls like drops of blood to the ground (Lk. 22:44). This is in line with the allusion to Gethsemane in Hebrews 5:7,[49] where the writer tells us that Jesus offered up supplications and entreaties to God 'with loud cries and tears'. Here is a man pouring his whole strength, physical and spiritual, into a plea that God would 'save' him.

It is clear from all the accounts that Jesus' experience of turmoil and anguish was both real and profound. His sorrow was as great as a man could bear, his fear convulsive, his astonishment well-nigh paralysing. He came within a hairsbreadth of break-down. He faced the will of God as raw holiness, the *mysterium tremendum* in its most acute form: and it terrified him. Long ago, at his baptism, he had publicly embraced the Messianic role, identifying himself totally with his people. In the temptations in the desert he had already faced some of the implications of his position, as the Enemy quickly unleashed three massive assaults. But the full implications of being the Servant and the Ransom (Mk. 10:45) dawned on him only gradually, as he reflected on the Scriptures, observed sin at work and communed with his Father. In Gethsemane the whole, terrible truth strikes home. The hour of reckoning has come. Now is the last moment to escape. Beyond it there can be no turning back.

When Moses saw the glory of God on Mount Sinai so terrifying was the sight that he trembled with fear (Heb. 12:21). But that was God in covenant: God in grace. What Christ saw in Gethsemane was God with the sword raised (Zc. 13:7; Mt. 26:31). The sight was unbearable. In a few short hours, he, the Last Adam, would stand before that God answering for the sin of the world: indeed, identified with the sin of the world (2 Cor. 5:21). He became, as Luther said, 'the greatest sinner that ever was' (*cf.* Gal. 3:13). Consequently, to quote Luther again, 'No one ever feared death so much as this man.'[50] He feared it because for him it was no sleep (1 Thes. 4:13), but the wages of sin: death with the sting; death unmodified and unmitigated; death as involving all that sin deserved. He, alone, would face it without a *hilasmos*, or 'covering', providing by his very dying the only covering for the world, but doing so as a holocaust, totally exposed to God's abhorrence of sin. And he would face death without God, *choris theou*,[51] deprived of the one solace and the one resource which had always been there.

The wonder of the love of Christ for his people is not that for their sake he faced death without fear, but that for their sake he faced it, terrified. Terrified by what he knew, and terrified by what he did not know, he took damnation lovingly.[52]

At one level, there is obvious discontinuity between the emotional state of Jesus in Gethsemane and the emotional crises faced by his people. The agony in the garden is indeed one of the great foundations of his compassion because there he plumbed the depths of our emotional weakness, but nowhere is it more important than here to distinguish between the Lord suffering *with* us and the Lord suffering *for* us. What he faced in Gethsemane (the cost of atonement and redemption) we shall never face; and we shall never face it precisely because he faced it, offering his body as the place where God should effect the condemnation of sin (Rom. 8:3). Gethsemane is as unique as Calvary exactly because, as much as the cross, it belongs not to church history but to salvation history.

Yet, remarkably, there is an emotional depth beyond Gethsemane: that of Golgotha itself. This is reflected particularly in the cry of dereliction, 'My God, my God, why have you forsaken me?' (Mt. 27:46). The state of mind indicated in these words is not coterminous with the crucifixion itself. The humiliation of Christ was not a point, but a line, beginning at Bethlehem and descending towards Calvary. But Calvary itself, in turn, is a line, as, on the cross, the Lord moves deeper and deeper into the abyss. The immolation itself took place at the third hour (Mk. 15:25). Between that and the sixth hour there took place the conversation with the penitent robber (Lk. 23:40ff.), in the course of which it becomes plain that Jesus is still sustained by hope ('Today you will be with me in paradise'). From the sixth to the ninth hour there was darkness over the land (Mk. 15:33). Shortly afterwards Jesus cried, '*Elōi, Elōi, lama sabachtani?*' and breathed his last. According to Luke's account, he did so in full repossession of his filial consciousness: 'Father, into your hands I commit my spirit'(Lk. 23:46).

The reason for labouring these details is that they underline the fact that Jesus was not forsaken all the time he was on the cross. The dereliction was only a moment in the long journey from the immolation to expiry. Yet it was the climactic moment, and a moment of incredible density; and it was so precisely because its agony was so compacted – so infinite – as to be well-nigh unsustainable. As an eighteenth-century Gaelic hymn expressed it, the whole entail of sin (pains and agonies it would have taken the world eternity to endure) were all poured on him in one horrific moment.[53]

What the emotional content of this forsakenness actually was, it is impossible for us to know. What is certain is that Golgotha was more awful than Jesus had envisaged in Gethsemane. He felt forsaken, and he *was* forsaken. This involved, among other things, Jesus experiencing the agony of unanswered prayer. In Psalm 22, this idea is expressed just beside the words quoted by Jesus on the cross:

> My God, my God, why hast thou forsaken me? …
> O my God, I cry by day, but thou dost not answer;
>   and by night, but find no rest.
>
> (Ps. 22:1–2, RSV)

What he prayed for is hidden from us. It may have been, once again, that the cup might pass; or, that there be some light; or, that he be given some token of the Father's love; or, that the pain might be over soon. We do not know. Whatever it was, there was no answer: only the echo of his own voice, the derision of those he had come to save, and the cruel taunts of hell.

Beside the unanswered prayer there was the loss of the filial consciousness. In the moment of dereliction, there is no sense of his own sonship. Even in Gethsemane, Jesus had been able to say, 'Abba!' But now the cry is, '*Elōi, Elōi*'. He is aware only of the god-ness and power and holiness and otherness of God. In his self-image, he is no longer Son, but Sin; no longer *Monogenēs*, the Beloved with whom God is well-pleased, but *Katara*, the cursed one: vile, foul and repulsive. Here it is helpful to recall a remark of the nineteenth-century Scottish theologian, Hugh Martin, stressing the connection between intellectual and emotional finitude. Christ's soul, he wrote, being a true human soul, 'could not possibly behold all elements of truth in one act of contemplation'. Hence, 'the object of dread for an instant engrossed the whole reflective faculty'.[54]

Corresponding to the loss of the sense of sonship there was a real abandonment by God. No-one was ever less prepared for such an experience than Jesus. As the eternal Word he had always been with

God (Jn. 1:1). As the incarnate Son the Father had always been with him (Jn. 16:32). They had gone up from Bethlehem to Calvary, like Abraham and Isaac, 'together' (Gn: 22:6, 8). But now, in the hour of his greatest need, God is not there. When he most needs encouragement, there is no voice to cry, 'This is my beloved Son.' When he most needs reassurance, there is no-one to say, 'I am well pleased.' No grace was extended to him, no favour shown, no comfort administered, no concession made. God was present only as displeased, expressing that displeasure with overwhelming force in all the circumstances of Calvary. Every detail in a drama which walked a fine line between chaos and liturgy declared, 'This is what God thinks of you and of the sin you bear!' He was cursed (Gal. 3:13), because he became 'the greatest thief, murderer, adulterer, robber, desecrator, blasphemer, etc., there has ever been anywhere in the world'.[55]

The paradox should not escape us. He was sinless. He was the Son of God. But there, on Golgotha, he was a sinner. He was sin (2 Cor. 5:21). Luther comments: 'He bore the person of a sinner and a thief – not of one, but of all sinners and thieves ... Therefore when the Law found Him among thieves, it condemned and executed Him as a thief.'[56] Barth has expressed the same truth equally forcefully: 'it is the Judge who in this passion takes the place of those who ought to be judged, who in this passion allows himself to be judged in their place ... He fulfils this judgment by suffering the punishment which we have all brought on ourselves.'[57] The great *for* of substitution enmeshes Christ in the guilt of his people and justifies God in treating him as sin deserves. He is damned and banished with the effect, as Calvin describes it, that 'he must also grapple hand to hand with the armies of hell and the dread of everlasting death ... suffering in his soul the terrible torments of a condemned and forsaken man'.[58] He was the scapegoat. He was 'outside', in the outer darkness. He was beyond the cosmos, the realm of order and beauty, sinking instead into a black hole which no light could penetrate and from which, in itself, nothing benign or meaningful could ever emanate. Here was a singularity where ultimate lawlessness (the sin that he was) met ultimate chaos (the Son forsaken by the Father). Here is the final anomalousness of sin. Impossible in itself, its existence immediately creates the possibility of further impossibilities, climaxing in the accursedness of the Son and the pain of the Father.

The 'Why?' of Golgotha is boundless, seeking the logic of sin and asking questions to which not even God himself could provide answers. Calvary, as a chaotic shambles, is God's supreme exposure of sin. Only when we have seen it as such – as the most awesome expression of both human viciousness and divine permissiveness (Acts 14:16) – can we begin to reflect on it as the focal point of redemptive grace.

Yet, even here, there are shafts of light. There can be no doubt that the Father loved him; here, at Golgotha, above all, because this was the magnificent climax of his obedience. Nor can there be any doubt that there was a ministry of the Holy Spirit which persisted even through the dereliction. Only through this ministry was he able to offer himself without spot to God (Heb. 9:14). More remarkably still, Jesus' own faith remained intact. Even at the lowest point, where he cannot say, 'Abba!' he says '*Elōi*!' ('*My* God!'). As Calvin put it: 'still in his heart faith remained firm, by which he beheld the presence of God, of whose absence he complains'.[59] It could not have been otherwise. To lose faith and lapse into despair would itself have been sin. But what a tribute it is to the spiritual strength of Jesus that even as he walks through this darkness he reaches out towards a God still perceived as his own.

Here, even more than at Gethsemane, we have to remind ourselves that Christ suffered vicariously. The gospel of the dereliction is not that Christ shares our forsakenness but that he saves us from it. He endured it, not *with* us, but *for* us. We are immune to the curse (Gal. 3:13) and to the condemnation (Rom. 8:3) precisely because Christ took them upon himself and went, in our place, into the outer darkness. It remains true, of course, that he sympathizes with us in even the most acute of our emotional traumas, but the learning of compassion was not the primary motive behind the dereliction, which involved a journey into territory ordinary men and women will never tread. What Golgotha secured for us was not sympathy but immunity.

The human will of Christ

It is in connection with Gethsemane that Calvin raises the issue of Monothelitism: Did Christ have one will or two? The Formula of Chalcedon (451) had laid down clearly that Christ had two natures. Where, then, was the principle of coherence? How could two natures function together as a single agency? How could we avoid the practice of attributing this action to one nature and that action to another?

One proposed solution was that Christ had but one will, providing a single 'energizing' for the entire person. This was Monothelitism. Debate on the matter was particularly fierce (and unedifying) in the seventh century, until the question was finally settled at the Third Council of Constantinople in 680.[60] This Council augmented the Chalcedonian Definition of the Faith (of which more later) by affirming that in Christ there were two natural wills (*duo physica thelēmata*) and two natural energizings (*duo physica energeiai*). These wills were distinct, yet inseparable; they always worked in harmony; and the human was invariably subordinate to the divine.[61]

Echoes of the extraordinary bitterness of this ancient controversy can still be heard in Calvin's comments on Jesus' words in Gethsemane, 'Yet not as I will, but as you will' (Mt. 26:39):

> This passage shows plainly enough the gross folly of those ancient heretics, who were called Monothelites, because they imagined that the will of Christ was but one and simple; for Christ, as he was God, willed nothing different from the Father; and therefore it follows, that his human soul had affections distinct from the secret purpose of God.[62]

Is this anything more than an arid scholastic debate, rendered even more distasteful by the fact that its progress and outcome were determined to a large extent by sordid political considerations? Not quite! For one thing, whatever doubts may attach to the definition of will, it is clear that there can be no true human nature without the ability to make human choices. Jesus had ordinary human desires, longings, preferences and aspirations. Just as truly, he had human aversions. Under these influences he made decisions and pursued options in the same way as we do ourselves.

This is clearly indicated in the Scriptures, not least in the way they distinguish between the will of Jesus and the will of God. This appears in, for example, John 6:38, 'I have come down from heaven not to do my will but to do the will of him who sent me.' Such language presupposes not only a metaphysical distinction between the will of Jesus and the will of the Father, but also the logical possibility that Jesus' natural preferences (based on personal self-interest) might not always coincide with the wishes of the Father. Indeed, it is this fact which creates the whole possibility of *kenōsis* or self-emptying. The Servant consults not his own interests but the interests of others (Phil. 2:4). This climaxes in Gethsemane, where the dilemma becomes almost unbearably acute. At a very basic level, Jesus does not want this 'cup'. His whole nature shrinks from it, and as he speaks to his Father he becomes acutely aware that there are two wills (and two ways): there is 'my will' and there is 'thy will'. Nor did Jesus find it easy to be reconciled to the Father's will. It literally terrified him, because here was the concentrated essence of the *mysterium tremendum*. It was eerie.

It was overwhelming. It was uncanny. Jesus' victory consisted not in merging his will with that of the Father or even in wanting specifically what the Father wanted. It came from choosing the Father's will rather than, and even over against, his own. He willed what he did not want, embarking on an astonishing course of altruism.

Sharing our environment

One final point may be made in connection with the humanity of Christ: he came into, and shared, our environment. This too, is made plain in John 1:14. He dwelt among us. This involved the most complete sharing of our experiences on the part of the Son of God, accentuated by the fact that he chose not simply to be born, but to be born in a low condition. Hence the 'low estate' of his mother (Lk. 1:48, KJV). Hence the manger. Hence the flight into Egypt. Hence Nazareth. Hence the homelessness (Mt. 8:20). Hence the penury which has no money to pay the temple tax (Mt. 17:24ff.) and no place to celebrate the Passover. Hence the reputed lack of learning and the scorn of the rulers (Jn. 7:48f.). Hence the notoriety gained through friendship with publicans and sinners.

For the Son of God, the incarnation meant a whole new set of relationships: with his father and mother; with his brothers and sisters; with his disciples; with the scribes, the Pharisees and the Sadducees; with Roman soldiers and with lepers and prostitutes. It was within these relationships that he lived his incarnate life, experiencing pain, poverty and temptation; witnessing squalor and brutality; hearing obscenities and profanities and the hopeless cry of the oppressed. He lived not in sublime detachment or in ascetic isolation, but 'with us', as 'the fellow-man of all men',[63] crowded, busy, harassed, stressed and molested. No large estate gave him space, no financial capital guaranteed his daily bread, no personal staff protected him from interruptions and no power or influence protected him from injustice. He saved us from alongside us.

7

CHALCEDON: "PERFECT IN GODHEAD, PERFECT IN MANHOOD"

As a result of the Docetic, Arian and Apollinarian controversies the church found itself, by the close of the fourth century, in secure possession of a two-nature Christology. Christ was truly and perfectly God; and Christ was truly and perfectly man. It fell to the theologians of the fifth century to debate the remaining question: What is the relation between these two natures? Do they represent separate persons or agencies? Are they mixed or commingled in one person? Or have they been fused together to produce a *tertium quid*, neither human nor divine?

Nestorianism

The first phase of the controversy began with the emergence in Constantinople of a school of thought which, allegedly, so stressed the humanity of Christ and so distinguished it from his divinity as to convey the impression that the Mediator was two separate persons, one the Son of God and the other the Son of Man. This is the heresy known as Nestorianism, but discussion of the issue is complicated by the fact that

Nestorius was almost certainly not a Nestorian.[1] He did, however, react badly to the situation he found in Constantinople on his appointment to the See in 428. The prevailing Christology appeared to represent the incarnation as a blending of the two natures in Christ, human and divine, to the confusion of both. At the same time, popular use of the term *theotokos* ('Mother of God') had reached the point where men dared to regard the Virgin 'as in some kind of way divine, like God'.[2]

At this distance in time it is not easy to decide how, exactly, Nestorius responded to the situation. His works were burned by Imperial decree and only fragments survive. His reinstatement at the hands of historian Bethune-Baker and others resulted largely from the discovery in the late nineteenth century of a Syriac manuscript of his lost apology, *The Bazaar of Heraclides*, but, as Frances Young points out, there is no guarantee that the position Nestorius took in this work coincides with the position he took at the height of the crisis.[3] It seems clear, however, that although he did not altogether condemn the term *theotokos* he strongly disliked it and showed little tact in saying so.

The reason for his aversion to the term was not primarily its tendency to encourage Mariolatry, but the threat it posed to the deity of Christ. If Mary were proclaimed as the Mother of the Word of God, would that not open the door to the old Arian notion that the *Logos* was a creature? On the other hand, it was important, according to Nestorius, to insist that the humanity which Christ assumed was complete. It was not defective, as argued by Apollinaris. Nor was it absorbed into the deity, as suggested by the monophysite tendencies prevailing in Constantinople.

It was this latter stress on the real and complete humanity of Christ which convinced some that Nestorius believed that after the incarnation there were two distinct subjects or agents in Christ, God and man, joined together in a graduated partnership or co-operative (servant and master) rather than united in one being. Nestorius himself claimed that his views were no different from those of his mentor, Theodore of Mopsuestia, who died, honoured and revered, in 428, but he had the misfortune to fall into the hands of an implacable enemy, Cyril of Alexandria, who, besides being one of the most able propagandists and most unscrupulous ecclesiastics in Christian history, had an in-bred suspicion of the See of Constantinople and a paranoid aversion to the Antiochene Christology of Theodore and Nestorius. The kind of feelings Cyril evoked can be gathered from a contemporary letter expressing heartfelt relief at his death, and suggesting that 'a large, heavy stone be placed at his tomb lest he provoke the dead so much that they send him back!'[4]

Cyril succeeded in convincing the church that Nestorius was a heretic, 'every way declaring two sons and dividing the one Lord Jesus Christ',[5] and had him deposed and condemned by the Council of Ephesus in 431.

Whether Cyril won the theological battle is a different question entirely. Relations between Alexandria and Constantinople remained strained for some time after the Council of Ephesus and although in the eventual reconciliation his own province had to disown Nestorius personally, there was nothing in the Formula of Reunion to which the alleged heresiarch would have taken exception. The Formula specifically acknowledges the Lord to be not only perfect God but 'perfect man made up of soul endowed with reason and of body'. It declares that the union between the natures 'involves no merging'. Above all, it carefully qualifies the term *theotokos*, explaining that it is applied to the Virgin only 'because God the Word was "made flesh" and "became man" and united to himself the temple he took from her as a result of her conception'.[6]

Eutychianism

The issue of the relation between the two natures in the person of Christ was still far from settled, however. If the tendency of the Antiochene theology was to overstress the humanity of Christ and thus the distinction between the natures, the tendency of the Alexandrian was to overstress the deity; and not merely to overstress it, but to insist on its dominant and determinant role within the person. In such a context (which had already produced Apollinarianism) the idea of a union of natures could easily be misunderstood as a *merging* of natures. On the whole, Cyril himself seems to have maintained a proper balance in this respect, but some of his statements are as open to misunderstanding as those of Nestorius, although in the opposite direction. In particular, he speaks more than once of the Son being one by nature (*mia physis*). For example, in his *Third Letter to Nestorius* (5) Cyril speaks of Christ 'being one Son by nature'; and in his *Letter to Acacius of Melitene* he declares that after the union 'the duality has been abolished and we believe the Son's nature to be one, since he is one Son, yet become man and incarnate'.[7]

Such statements reflect the monophysite strain inherent in Alexandrian Christology by the middle of the fifth century. Many of its representatives were unhappy with the reconciliation effected between Cyril and Antioch in 433 and continued to agitate against the two-nature doctrine. These extremists found a rallying-point in Eutyches. As

J. N. D. Kelly points out, it is far from clear what this 'aged and muddle-headed thinker' actually taught.[8] His most notorious statement was to the effect that while there were two natures before the union there was but one afterwards. The consensus among scholars appears to be that he believed that in the incarnation the deity of Christ completely absorbed the humanity. Later Eutychians were more consistent monophysites, arguing that the union of the two natures resulted in a compound which was neither human nor divine but formed some kind of *tertium quid*. Both formulations clearly implied a denial of the humanity of Christ.

Eutyches was deposed in 448 by the Standing Synod of Constantinople, meeting under the presidency of the Archbishop, Flavian. He appealed to Leo, the Bishop of Rome, complaining that Flavian had treated him unfairly. More or less simultaneously Flavian also wrote to Leo, putting his side of the case. In a letter to Flavian, written in June, 449, the Pope roundly condemned Eutyches as having utterly failed to grasp the mystery of the faith and went on to provide a magisterial survey of the Christological controversies, asserting the unity of the person of Christ, but insisting equally strongly that 'each nature retains without loss its own properties'.[9] 'In Christ Jesus,' concluded Leo, 'neither Humanity without true Divinity, nor Divinity without true Humanity, may be believed to exist.'

Eutyches, however, had influential friends, not least at court, and the Emperor Theodosius, in response to a request from Alexandria, convened a General Council. This council eventually met at Ephesus in August, 449. It was heavily biased in favour of Eutyches and the Alexandrians, but its proceedings came to an abrupt halt with the death of the Emperor in July, 450. A further council, the Council of Chalcedon, was convened by the new emperor and began its deliberations in October, 451. Besides ratifying the creeds of Nicea and Constantinople this council also endorsed both the Synodical Letters of Cyril (the *Second Letter to Nestorius* and the *Letter to John of Antioch*) and the *Tome* of Leo, thereby condemning both Nestorius and Eutyches. Positively, Chalcedon affirmed the unipersonality of Christ and the authenticity and perfection of both his natures, human and divine:

> Following, then, the holy Fathers, we all unanimously teach that our Lord Jesus Christ is, to us one and the same Son, the Self-same perfect in Godhead, the Self-same perfect in manhood ... before the ages begotten of the Father as to the Godhead, but in the last days, the Self-same, for us and for our salvation (born)

> of Mary the Virgin *Theotokos* as to the Manhood; One and the Same Christ, Son, Lord, Only-begotten; acknowledged in Two Natures unconfusedly, unchangeably, indivisibly, inseparably; the difference of the Natures being in no way removed because of the Union, but rather the property of each nature being preserved, and (both) concurring into One Prosopon and One Hypostasis.[10]

These were traumatic times for the church, and the story of the Christological controversies is not always an edifying one. The successful champions of orthodoxy were not unfailingly scrupulous in their methods of debate, nor guiltless of ambition and intrigue. On occasion, the vanquished heretic was much the more attractive and saintly personality. But through the collision of theories and the clash of personalities the basic axioms of Christology were laid down with such precision and clarity that they have served as parameters for all subsequent reflection.

Who became incarnate?

One of the factors clarified was the subject of the incarnation. Who, precisely, became flesh? It was not the godhead (the divine nature) itself. Neither was it God the Father, nor God the Holy Spirit. It was specifically God the Son. Cyril was both clear and emphatic on this: 'We do not mean that the nature of the Word was changed and made flesh or, on the other hand, that he was transformed into a complete man, but instead we affirm this; that the Word substantially (*kath' hypostasin*) united to himself flesh.'[11] This is clearly in line with the classic New Testament utterance on the incarnation, 'The Word became flesh' (Jn. 1:14). It was a person, not a nature, who became flesh, and this itself is probably sufficient to preclude understanding the incarnation as a conversion (of one nature into another). Beyond that, we have to insist that when we speak of the Son or the *Logos* as the subject of the incarnation we do not mean merely that he subjected himself passively to being made flesh. The incarnation was a personal act of the *Logos*. He took 'the form of a servant' (Phil. 2:7, KJV). He made himself poor (2 Cor. 8:9). The act of becoming flesh was deliberate, voluntary, sacrificial and dynamic.

But what is the sense of 'became flesh'? Christians have generally been more comfortable with the word 'assumed' (from Phil. 2:7) than with the word 'became', probably because of our embarrassment over the idea of divine mutability. 'Became' implies change and obviously threatens the prejudice that there is no becoming in God. Yet 'became' is the word John uses and we must do it justice. Whatever the process involved in the incarnation, it resulted in the fact that the Word was flesh and the Son was poor. This cannot imply change in the sense that the Son changed his identity. He remained Son. Nor can it imply change in the sense of his ceasing to be what he was. He continued to be divine, possessing all the attributes of God, performing all his functions and exercising all his prerogatives. In the words of Karl Barth,

> This work of God, the incarnation, does not include any renunciation by God of His deity. In it He does not change Himself into a man ... Everything depends upon the fact that in the doing of this work He is always the One He is, that He becomes and is man as God, and without ceasing to be God.[12]

Nevertheless, there is real change: change in the sense that in Christ God enters upon a whole new range of experiences and relationships. He experiences life in a human body and in a human soul. He experiences human pain and human temptations. He suffers poverty and loneliness and humiliation. He tastes death. He becomes son to Mary and Joseph, brother to James, friend to Peter and John, neighbour to the residents of Nazareth, adversary to the Pharisees. Before and apart from the incarnation, God knew such things by observation. But observation, even when it is that of omniscience, falls short of personal experience. That is what the incarnation made possible for God: real, personal experience of being human.

In the presence of these facts, immutability must be understood in the light of the incarnation rather than the incarnation constrained by an *a priori* understanding of immutability. The manger in Bethlehem says not only that God took but that God became. Karl Rahner argued for the formula, 'the immutable in itself can become mutable in another'.[13] But this does not meet the case. The Son did not become another; and it was not another who became. He himself became, and he became other. He became what he had never been before: flesh, poor, forsaken, dead. The basic form of immutability encountered here is the permanence of the divine freedom, the divine power and the divine love. God is immutably free and able to become what he needs to become in order to save the world. We may even say that only God could have undergone becoming on the scale implied in the incarnation. God was the only being who could have become man.

Theotokos

Chalcedon also confirmed the place of the word *theotokos* in the Christian credal tradition: 'for us and for our salvation (born) of Mary the Virgin *Theotokos* as to the Manhood'. It would be unwise, however, simply to walk away from Nestorius' reservations over this term. Its precise meaning is 'God-bearer', but we can be fairly confident that in fifth-century Constantinople it served as an emotionally charged slogan equivalent to 'Mother of God'. We can be even more confident that although to the theologians *theotokos* was a statement about Christ (affirming his divine identity), to the populace it was a statement about the Virgin Mary, just as it is today. Such language inevitably accelerated the tendency towards Mariolatry, and it is easy to imagine Nestorius' counter-preaching causing the same uproar at Constantinople as Paul's preaching had caused at Ephesus among the devotees of Diana (Acts 19:23ff.). Besides, although Nestorius may have presented his case tactlessly, he could point out in his own defence that Scripture never says that God was born of the Virgin (the New Testament speaks of the incarnation of the *Logos*, not of his birth); and that although such fathers as Origen and Athanasius had used the term *theotokos,* it had not been incorporated into either the Nicene Creed of 321 or the Constantinopolitan Creed of 381 (nor would it be used in the Anglican Articles or in the Westminster Confession).

The term *theotokos* encapsulated a great truth: the divine identity of the person born of the Virgin. Her child was the Son of God, a point which the annunciation itself had made clear: 'the child' will be called 'the Son of God' (Lk. 1:35, RSV). The question is whether *theotokos* was the best term to express this truth. It certainly tended to obscure the humanity of Christ. It also lent itself all too easily to the misunderstanding that Mary was the mother of the Godhead (or even the mother of the Trinity); and, beyond that, to the idea that she should herself be worshipped and adored. These considerations explain why even the Chalcedonian definition had to add the words 'as to the Manhood' immediately after *theotokos*. They also explain why, in the Formula of Reunion incorporated into his *Letter to John of Antioch*, Cyril had to be equally circumspect, carefully defining his use of the term: 'we confess the holy Virgin to be *Theotokos*, because that God the Word was incarnate, and lived as Man, and from the very conception united to Himself the temple which He took of her'.[14] They also explain later developments, particularly the fact that the adoption of the term *theotokos* was followed soon afterwards by the emergence of

Eutychianism, arguing for a one-nature Christ whose human being was completely eclipsed by his divine.

It is fascinating to reflect on the term *theotokos* in the light of a distinction drawn by Karl Rahner between what is objectively true and what is kerygmatically correct. 'Not every objectively true statement is also kerygmatically correct.'[15] Rahner cites as an example the fact that when Jesus prayed as a man he prayed to the three divine persons. Yet, he says, it would be kerygmatically incorrect to dwell on the fact that Jesus worshipped the Son of God. Instead, we must orientate ourselves to modes of expression current in the New Testament because otherwise we shall push the non-important things into the foreground and important things into the background.

All this is directly relevant to the term *theotokos*. It expresses the objective truth that the child Jesus was the Son of God. Its effect, however, is not to push this truth into the foreground. On the contrary, what it has pushed into the foreground is Mary herself, elevated to a prominence she never enjoyed in the New Testament. The Marian dogmas – the perpetual virginity, the immaculate conception and the assumption of the Virgin – are all derived from a non-kerygmatic understanding of *theotokos*: an understanding which has led to a form of Christianity which has *Ave Maria!* at its centre. The results of this are seen even in the judicious Rahner himself, leading him to exaggerate the contribution of Mary's faith and consent to the act of the incarnation[16] and even to the extraordinary position that because of her perfect personal holiness she needed no redemption by grace, but merely preservation by grace.[17]

In view of such developments it is difficult not to concede that Nestorius' apprehension was well justified. We certainly cannot feel free to use *theotokos* without careful elucidations and safeguards.

Hypostatic union

The term 'hypostatic union' (*kath' hypostasin enosis*) makes its first appearance in Cyril's *Second Letter to Nestorius* (3): the *Logos* united flesh to himself (*kath' hypostasin*). It also occurs several times in the *Five Tomes against the Blasphemies of Nestorius*. 'For the word of truth', he writes, 'sets forth that the Word of God has been *kath' hypostasin* united to the flesh.'[18] There is some doubt, however, as to whether Cyril set much store by the term. One of his most recent editors, Lionel R. Wickham, argues, for example, that although he invented it 'it was not for him a technical term and he dropped it quickly'.[19] It is certainly doubtful whether Cyril used it with the precision which came to be attached to it later. Wickham, for instance, translates *kath' hypostasin* as 'substantially' in the passage from the *Second Letter to Nestorius* cited earlier, and this is justified to the extent that Cyril did not draw a sharp distinction between *hypostasis* and *physis*. If the union was one *kath' hypostasin* it was also, as we have seen, one of *mia physis*. This interchangeability between *hypostasis* and *physis* explains the unease of Nestorius. It also explains the rise of Monophysitism among Cyril's most earnest disciples.

But whatever doubts surround its genesis the idea of the hypostatic or personal union firmly established itself in the language of Christology. As such it appears, for example, in the Second of the Anglican Articles: 'two whole and perfect Natures, that is to say, the Godhead and Manhood, were joined together in one Person'. It also occurs in the Westminster Confession (VIII.II): 'two whole, perfect, and distinct natures, the Godhead and the manhood, were inseparably joined together in one person, without conversion, composition, or confusion'.

The term 'hypostatic union' encapsulates three truths: that Christ is one person; that the union between his two natures arises from the fact that they both belong to one and the same person; and that this one person, the son of God, is the Agent behind all of the Lord's actions, the Speaker of all his utterances and the Subject of all his experiences.

This last emphasis is clearly required by the New Testament's statements on the incarnation. For example, in John's Prologue the person who was made flesh and who lived among us is the same *Logos* as we meet in the opening words, 'In the beginning was the Word, and the Word was with God, and the Word was God.' This is the very person who changed water into wine (Jn. 2:1–11), spoke to Nicodemus (3:1–21) and washed his disciples' feet (13:5). The same sequence is found in 2 Corinthians 8:9, the very Lord who was rich in his pre-existent state becoming poor in the incarnation. In Philippians 2:5ff., Paul highlights the same truth at greater length. The one who already existed in the form of God made himself nothing, took the form of a servant, submitted to crucifixion and was exalted by God the Father. In the whole sweep of mediatorial history, from pre-existence through humiliation to exaltation, the person acting and affected is the same.

This means that whenever we look at the life of Christ and ask, Who did this? Who suffered this? Who said this? the answer is always the same: 'The Son of God!' We can never say, 'The divine nature did this!' or, 'The human nature did this!' We must say, 'He did this: he, the Son of God!' He was born, baptized, tempted and transfigured. He beheld the city and wept over it. He agonized in Gethsemane. He was betrayed, arrested and condemned. He was flogged, immolated, crucified, dead and buried. He rose from the dead. He reigns. He will come again. He will judge the living and the dead. His was the blood shed, his the body broken, his the life poured out. He is our propitiatory. He is our ransom-price. He is the revealer of God: and the revelation. He is our Saviour: and our salvation. In him God acts, speaks and suffers for our redemption. In him, God provides and even becomes the atonement which he demands. In him (in his flesh, within the finitude of his life-time, the finitude of his body and the finitude of his human being) God dealt with our sin. He is a man: yet the man of universal significance, not because his humanity is in any sense infinite but because it is the humanity of God. In him, God adds human being to his divine being and human experience to his divine experience. In him, God lives a truly human existence. This is the heart of the miracle of incarnation: the Son of God 'exists not only in heavenly form, but also in earthly-historical form'.[20]

These great positive truths constitute the core of Christianity. Yet the phrase 'hypostatic union' always had a polemical edge. To Cyril, for example, it was a rebuttal of the notion (which he attributed to Nestorius) that the incarnation consisted merely of the *Logos* settling, externally, on an ordinary human person.[21] This polemical function of the term is still important. The union involved in the incarnation must be carefully distinguished from other unions. It must also be protected from misguided analogies. For example, the relation between the two natures in the person of Christ is entirely different from that between the Father, the Son and the Holy Spirit in the eternal Trinity. This latter relationship is inter-personal: I–Thou and face-to-face. As we shall see more fully later the human nature of Christ certainly did not stand in an I–Thou relationship to his divine. Equally, the union between divine and human in Christ does not correspond to that between soul and body in a human being.[22] In the incarnation, the person exists before the event and actively takes a human body and soul. In the human being, the soul does not take a body. On the contrary, the psychosomatic unity is given, involuntarily, from the beginning; and the union is not one between two natures but the coherent, integrated functioning of different components of one and the same nature.

Nor is it helpful to compare the personal union involved in the incarnation to the union established by grace between Christ and his people. The best known exponent of this comparison is Donald Baillie.[23] Baillie's starting-point is what he calls 'the central paradox' of grace. 'Its essence', he writes, 'lies in the conviction which a Christian man possesses that every good thing in him, every good thing he does, is somehow not wrought by himself but by God.' This is the doctrine of prevenient grace: God, in the language of Augustine, gives us what he commands us to have. Baillie continues:

> What I wish to suggest is that this paradox of grace points the way more clearly and makes a better approach than anything else in our experience to the mystery of the incarnation itself; that this paradox in its fragmentary form in our own Christian lives is a reflection of that perfect union of God and man in the Incarnation on which our whole Christian life depends, and may therefore be our best clue to the understanding of it.

Jesus, in other words, is the pre-eminent example of the principle laid down in Galatians 2:20, 'Christ lives in me.' Baillie concludes,

> If then Christ can be thus regarded as in some sense the prototype of the Christian life ... is it not the same type of paradox, taken at the absolute degree, that covers the whole ground of the life of Christ, of which we say that it was the life of a man and yet also, in a deeper and prior sense, the very life of God incarnate?[24]

It is important to note the caution with which Baillie introduces this analogy. He cites it only as 'a better approach than anything else in our experience' and calls it 'but a feeble analogue of the incarnate life'. Yet even with these qualifications it is seriously misleading. In particular it threatens the essential Christian emphasis on the uniqueness of Christ and the uniqueness of the incarnation.[25] There is, of course, continuity between Christ and the Christian disciple and this continuity includes the fact that he was the recipient of grace to the extent that his human obedience depended on the ministry of the Holy Spirit. But we cannot equate 'God was in Christ' with 'Christ lives in me'.[26] Even less could Christ say with respect to his deity, 'By the grace of God I am what I am' (a statement Baillie quotes more than once in reference to this comparison). The real effect of this whole approach is to convey the impression that Christ differs from ordinary believers only in degree, as the one who receives a special measure of grace and a special filling with the Holy Spirit.

There is a further element of instability in the comparison as well. Just as the spirit of the Enlightenment seeks to minimize the distance between Christ and other religious personalities, so it seeks to minimize the distance between Christians and non-Christians. Donald Baillie's brother, John, for example, argues that it is impossible to draw a clear line between grace and nature.[27] If this is so, there is no essential difference between Christians and others: that is, God's Spirit does not act on Christians in any special sense. If we then continue to take Donald Baillie's 'paradox of grace' as an illustration of the union effected between God and man in the incarnation, we shall find ourselves drawn inexorably to the view that the presence of God in Christ does not differ in principle from his presence in other men: God is immanent in all men, specially immanent in Jesus.

To affirm the hypostatic union is to protest against all such reasoning (which, after all, is only adoptionism with up-to-date bibliography). It is to say that in Christ godhead and manhood co-exist in one person and that Jesus is as divine as he is human. It is, of course, a great truth that God can come upon us and indwell us and empower and enable us. But as Barth points out, it is only a penultimate truth.[28] Beyond it there is the ultimate truth: Jesus Christ is Yahweh, God and man in one person. Without this there could not even be a 'paradox of grace'. And to this there can be no human analogy. It is 'a fact without precedence, parallel or repetition either in the divine sphere or (much less) in the human, natural and historical creaturely sphere'.[29]

It is equally confusing to compare the relation between the divine and the human in Christ to the presence of God in the church after Pentecost. Such Anglicans as Charles Gore, for example, have spoken of the church as an 'extension of the incarnation': 'The Church is the body of Christ. It is the extension and perpetuation of the Incarnation in the world. It is this, because it embodies the same principle and lives by the same life.'[30] Gore does not seem to mean by this anything more than that the church is the bearer of Christ, whose Spirit perpetuates the presence of the Son of Man in the world. It is totally misleading to refer to this as an incarnation. The Spirit is not enfleshed and the church is not divine. God is incarnate in Jesus Christ. He is merely present in and to his church, and no matter how real or dynamic we make that presence it falls far short of an incarnation. The effect of such language as Gore's is only to minimize the uniqueness of Bethlehem, placing it close to the category of general religious experience. This is not what Gore intended, but it is the inevitable kerygmatic effect of his terminology.

The term 'hypostatic union' emphasizes that Christ is or has one self. But what does this imply for the self-consciousness of Jesus? Jesus has two levels of consciousness. He is aware of the Father, of himself, of the universe and of other men as God; and he is equally aware of them as man. This latter includes the fact that he has a human consciousness of being the Son of God. It also includes the fact that his human consciousness is (not merely was) a developing one. Like any normal human child he became more and more aware of his surroundings. He also became more and more aware of his own uniqueness, growing in consciousness of his divine sonship as he talked to his mother, read the Scriptures and communed through prayer with his Father in heaven. There is little record in the New Testament, however, of the course of this development. By the time we meet him in the synoptic account he is already in secure possession of the filial consciousness. God is 'Abba'. The only moment we see that consciousness eclipsed is in the cry of dereliction. On the other hand, it is equally clear that his consciousness of sonship could be an occasion of temptation. He could be tempted to doubt it: 'If you are the Son of God ...' (Mt. 4:3). He could also be tempted to become obsessed with it as the question to be settled before anything else could be attempted (hence the placing of the temptations immediately after the baptism and just before the public ministry). Above all, it could become an argument to deviate from the path of humiliation and to mitigate the cost of incarnation. If he was hungry, could he not, as God's Son, command the stones to become bread? Could he not, if he were in peril, send for twelve legions of angels (Mt. 26:53)? Here, too, in being vulnerable to being tempted through his sonship, he is one with us.

None of this means that in Jesus there are two self-consciousnesses, but it does mean that there are two levels of consciousness of the one self. There is a divine consciousness that he is the eternal Son of God and there is a human consciousness of the same fact. These two forms of consciousness remain distinct, united in the one person, communicating through the Holy Spirit.[31]

Communion in attributes

Closely linked to the doctrine of the hypostatic union is the idea of the communion in attributes (*communicatio idiomatum*). The starting-point for this notion is the belief that in Christ there is a communion of natures (*communio naturarum*). But what is the relation between these natures? They are not merged. Neither, on the other hand, are they merely juxtaposed, lying side by side in the one person without contact or interaction. In the words of Leo (*Tome*, 3), 'the properties of both natures and substances were preserved and coexisted in One Person'. Some of the Fathers hinted that the relation between the two natures was one of *perichoresis*. They interact with, and flow into, each other. John of Damascus, for example, writes: 'He imparts to the flesh His own attributes by way of communication in virtue of the inter-penetration (*perichoresis*) of the parts one with another.'[32] However, the idea of *perichoresis*, as we have seen, quickly became a trinitarian rather than a Christological term, and the concept of a *perichoresis* between the two natures in the incarnate Mediator was never developed. Instead, the church adopted the idea of the communion in attributes. Each nature, it was insisted, retained its own distinctive attributes, but between them there was some kind of communion. What kind?

First, there was universal agreement that the attributes of both natures were attributes of the person. Leo gave eloquent expression to this in a famous passage of his *Tome* (3):

> Since then the properties of both natures and substances were preserved and co-existed in One Person, humility was embraced by majesty, weakness by strength, mortality by eternity; and to pay the debt of our condition the inviolable nature was united to a passible nature; so that, as was necessary for our healing, there was one and the same "Mediator between God and men, the man Jesus Christ," who was capable of death in one nature and incapable of it in the other. In the complete and perfect nature, therefore, of very man, very God was born – complete in what belonged to Him, complete in what belonged to us.[33]

Cyril expressed the same idea: 'He made the properties of the flesh his own.'[34] He was the Son of God and, as such, without ceasing to be divine, he took on the qualities of human nature: createdness, finitude, dependence, ignorance, mutability, embodiedness and even mortality. Simultaneously, of course, he also possessed divine attributes and the classical theologians did not shrink from the resulting paradox. Christ was simultaneously visible and invisible, comprehensible and incomprehensible, temporal and eternal, servant and master, passible and impassible, mortal and immortal.[35] This was no merely verbal *communicatio*. It was real.

Secondly, there was communion between the two natures in the work of Christ as Mediator. This is the so-called *communicatio apotelesmaton*. According to this doctrine, the Agent involved in all the Mediator's acts and the subject of all his experiences as the incarnate

Son was the God-man. In these acts and experiences, both natures are involved, each in its own distinctive way. There is a divine loving and a human loving; a divine willing and a human willing; a divine self-abnegation and a human self-abnegation; a divine surrendering to suffering and a human surrender to suffering; a divine sovereignty and a human sovereignty. 'In fact,' wrote the sixteenth-century Reformed theologian, Zanchius, 'Christ the Mediator never did or does anything according to his humanity, in which the divinity too did or does not co-operate, and achieved nothing according to His Deity, which His humanity did not subserve or agree to.'[36] Barth writes to similar effect: 'God Himself speaks when this man speaks in human speech. God Himself acts and suffers when this man acts and suffers as a man. God Himself triumphs when this One triumphs as a man.'[37]

Thirdly, orthodox Christology has spoken confidently of a communion in graces (*communio gratiarum*) between the two natures of Christ.[38] He was uniquely endowed, and he was so because of the grace of union, which, as traditionally understood, involved both the condescension of the *Logos* in uniting himself to human nature and his generosity towards that nature. Confining ourselves for the present to the latter part of this idea, there is, of course, no doubt that the Mediator was richly and habitually endowed with the graces of faith, hope and love, and also with the charismata necessary to one who was prophet, priest and king. The question is whether these were due simply to the union of the human with the divine. If we take Scripture as our guide, it is much more likely that these endowments were due to something much more dynamic: the ministry of the Holy Spirit. This was well expressed by John Owen, who, referring to the Lord's human nature, wrote: 'Filled it was with light and wisdom to the utmost capacity of a creature; but it was so, not by being changed into a divine nature or essence, but by the communication of the Spirit unto it without measure.'[39] This accords well with such an incident as the agony in the garden, where Jesus appeals not to the 'grace of union' but to 'him who was able to save him' (Heb. 5:7, RSV), so that at last, through the eternal Spirit, he offered himself unblemished to God (Heb. 9:14). It also accords, of course, with the fact that the Saviour is, *par eminence*, the Christ, the Anointed One. This pre-eminence in unction itself rested on his unique identity as the Son and his unique responsibility as Mediator. Yet it was neither static nor one-sided. It was a function of the communion between the incarnate *Logos* and the Holy Spirit: a communion which rested on a shared commitment to the glory of the Father and the salvation of his church; and a communion which was mediated through the Son's own faith and prayerfulness. Just as it would later be true that Christ himself would dwell in his people's hearts through their faith, so the Holy Spirit dwelt in his heart by faith. This indwelling, rather than any grace of union, is the biblical explanation for the moral and spiritual pre-eminence of Christ.

There remains a further question. Granted that the attributes of both natures are communicated to the person, can we also say that the attributes of one nature are communicated to the other? This became a matter of sharp debate between Calvinists and Lutherans at the time of the Reformation. Calvinists freely admitted that in the New Testament the attributes and experiences of one nature were predicated of Christ denominated according to the other nature. Calvin, for example, sees an instance of this 'communicating of characteristics or properties' in Acts 20:28, where God is said to have purchased the church with his own blood.[40] Calvin also instances 1 Corinthians 2:8 (referring to the Jews crucifying the Lord of glory) and 1 John 1:1 (referring to the handling of the Word of life). But Calvinists insisted that such a *communicatio* was purely verbal. To quote Calvin again:

> Surely God does not have blood, does not suffer, cannot be touched with hands. But since Christ, who was true God and also true man, was crucified and shed his blood for us, the things that he carried out in his human nature are transferred improperly, although not without reason, to his divinity ... because the selfsame one was both God and man, for the sake of the union of both natures he gave to the one what belonged to the other.

The position of later Calvinists was clearly stated by Heidegger: 'This communication of attributes is real in respect of the person, verbal in respect of the natures.'[41] In the nineteenth century, W. G. T. Shedd spoke to similar effect: 'While the acts and qualities of either nature may be attributed to the one theanthropic person, the acts and qualities of one nature may not be attributed to the other nature.'[42]

Lutherans, on the other hand, insisted that there was a real communication of the attributes of the divine nature to the human. The reason for the sharp difference in opinion lay in the divergent doctrines held by the two traditions with regard to the Lord's Supper. The Reformed spoke of the presence of Christ in the sacrament as 'spiritual'. Lutherans, insisting on a literal acceptance of the words, 'This is my body', spoke of it as physical: the body of Christ is received in, with and under the elements (the doctrine which later came to be known as 'consubstantiation'). This had clear implications for Christology. If there were to be a physical presence of Christ in the sacrament, then his humanity must be in some sense omnipresent. This was secured by the peculiarly Lutheran doctrine of the *communicatio*, referred to as the *genus majesticum* because according to it the Son of God communicated his divine majesty to the flesh he assumed, with the result that even the human nature of Christ 'is in full possession, and capable of full use, and participant in the full glory of the divine'.[43] In particular, according to Lutherans, the properties of omniscience, omnipotence and omnipresence were communicated to the Saviour's human nature. It was also, because of its participation in the divine glory, entitled to worship and adoration.

It is difficult to see how such a doctrine can be defended. For one thing, Lutherans refuse to admit a reciprocity in this communion of attributes. The divine nature communicates its properties to the human, but there is no corresponding communication of the human to the divine. This refusal is all the more striking in view of the Lutheran argument that the whole doctrine of the incarnation hinges on this *communicatio*. The modern Lutheran, John T. Mueller, writes, for example: 'If the incarnation is at all real, then also the communication of divine attributes to the human nature must be real, since by the personal union not only the person, but also the divine nature, which cannot be separated from the person, has entered into communion with the human nature.'[44] If the communion between the two natures self-evidently implies the impartation of divine properties to the human nature, must it not also imply the impartation of human properties to the divine nature? Conversely, if we can maintain the personal union between the natures despite the fact of the divine nature remaining unchanged, can we not also maintain it despite the human nature remaining unchanged?[45] In fact, if we look at the New Testament there is much more evidence of human properties being predicated of the divine than of divine properties being predicated of the human. Certainly, if such phrases as 'the blood of God' and such statements as, 'They have crucified my Lord' were taken at face-value they would lend support to the idea of the humanization of the divine rather than to that of the divinization of the human.

It is also difficult to avoid the conclusion that the Lutheran doctrine involves the destruction of the human nature. A humanness which has divine attributes is not humanness at all. For example, to attribute omniscience to the human nature of Jesus is disastrous for his manhood not only because it excludes him from our human experience of learning and knowing but because it completely changes his emotional and volitional life. Both our feelings and our choices are conditioned by the finitude of our knowing: and to eliminate this is to eliminate human psychology altogether. A humanness which possessed divine properties would represent not an incarnation (the enfleshment of the Son of God) but a conversion (of humanity into deity).

Again, this Lutheran theory is inconsistent with the New Testament doctrine of the glorification of Christ. According to Lutheranism the human nature of Christ is glorified in the personal union: from the very moment of conception he possesses the majesty of the divine. It is a sufficient answer to this that his human nature, far from being divinely glorified, was mortal. But over and above that, the New Testament clearly shows that Christ was glorified only in that complex act of exaltation which comprised the resurrection, the ascension and the heavenly session. He himself while on earth prayed for such a glorification (Jn. 17:1); and the New Testament specifically attributes it to him, telling us, indeed, that he was 'hyper-exalted' (Phil. 2:9, my translation). Such a glorification would have been impossible if the human nature of Christ were already in possession of the divine majesty simply by virtue of the incarnation itself.

But then, not even the glorification of Christ involves the impartation of divine properties to his humanity. Even in the case of the Mediator there are clear limits to the idea of *theiosis*. His human body and human soul can be glorified to a degree far beyond what they possessed on earth and even far beyond what Adam possessed in Paradise. They can undergo a transformation which far exceeds anything we can imagine. His humanity can share in the glory of God and in the blessedness of God and in the sovereignty of God. It can serve as the revelation of God. It can subdue all creation to itself and exercise dominion over heaven and earth. It can sit in the very centre of the throne (Rev. 7:17). But it remains human, and not even the most extravagant language used of the glory of Christ should betray us into forgetting that.

If, however, we are ever tempted to forget it, the language used by the New Testament about ourselves should call us back. We are to be with Christ where he is (Jn. 17:24). We are to receive the very glory which the Father has given him (Jn. 17:22). We are even to be participants in the divine nature (2 Pet. 1:4, a passage which so astonished John Calvin that he commented, 'it is, so to speak, a kind of deification'). This verse is probably the closest we come in the New Testament to the Lutheran idea of the *communicatio idiomatum*, but it applies not to Christ but to believers. It sets forth a magnificent promise. Yet we know at once that it does not imply that one day we shall receive the attributes of the divine nature. In the case of Jesus, similarly, glorification brings his humanity to its Omega-point, but it remains humanity, finite, time-bound and space-bound, even though it is the humanity of God. To render it omnipotent, omniscient and omnipresent is to destroy it.

It is important to remember, however, that although his human nature is neither omnipotent, omniscient or omnipresent, he himself is. This is particularly relevant to the question which lies at the heart of the Lutheran–Calvinist debate: the nature of Christ's presence in the Lord's Supper. This is not an issue on which either side has achieved great clarity, but we are probably closest to the truth when we say that although the body of Christ is not present, he himself is. His personal presence is not limited to his bodily presence. His humanity is limited and localized, but it exists only in union and conjunction with his deity. Shedd ventured, in the light of this, to affirm, 'The humanity is in effect ubiquitous, because of its personal connection with an omnipresent nature, and not because it is in itself so immense as to be ubiquitous.' He continued: 'Christ's deity is never present anywhere in isolation and separation from his humanity, but always as united with and modified by his humanity.'[46] The key word here is 'modified'. What we have now, in the Lord's Supper, is a form of the divine presence modified (perhaps even *mode*-ified?) by the enfleshment of God in Christ. It is the divine presence with a whole new dimension: the dimension of human being and human experience, remembering that we are dust, knowing our frame, sympathizing with our weaknesses and familiar with our temptations. The one who is with us is the one seated at the right hand of the Majesty on High. But that very one is also the dust of the earth: transfigured dust, but still dust. It is as such, as the God-man, that he gives us the privilege of eating and drinking not merely in remembrance of him, but with him, at his table. Neither the divine nor the human is now excluded from anything he does.

Anhypostasia

It is easy enough to summarize the doctrine laid down by Chalcedon: two natures in one person. But even such a bald statement immediately presents a problem. How can two natures constitute one person? This difficulty led to the introduction of yet another technical term, *anhypostasia*, into the language of Christology. The incarnate mediator, the God-man, remains one person because the human nature he assumed is 'anhypostatic' or 'impersonal'.

It is difficult to be sure who first used the term. The concept was implied in the Apollinarian thesis that Christ did not have a human mind;[47] and it was explicit in the Christology of Cyril of Alexandria, who insisted that although the *Logos* united himself to human nature (*humanitas*) he did not unite himself to a man (*homo*). Even after the incarnation the Mediator's one personhood was that of the *Logos*: 'All the sayings contained in the Gospels must be referred to a single person, to the one incarnate hypostasis of the Word.'[48]

Yet the Christological use of the precise term *anhypostatos* is surprisingly rare in Patristic Greek.[49] It appears to occur no earlier than Leontius of Byzantium (485–543), and even he took it up only to reject it as inadequate. By the time of the Reformation, however, the idea had become a staple element in orthodox dogmatics. The consensus is expressed by Heppe: 'The humanity taken up into the person of the Logos is, then, not a personal man but human nature without personal subsistence.'[50]

More recent Christology has tended to be distinctly critical of the idea of an impersonal humanity. According to R. C. Moberly, for example, 'There is, and there can be, no such thing as an impersonal humanity ... Human nature which is not personal is not human nature.'[51] H. R. Mackintosh concurred: 'no real meaning could be attached to a human "nature" which is not simply one aspect of the concrete life of a human person'.[52] These sentiments were endorsed by Donald Baillie, who concluded that few theologians would now defend the phrase 'impersonal humanity' or hesitate to speak of Jesus as a man, 'a human person'.[53]

These objections seem to rest, largely, on misunderstanding. *Anhypostasia* was not a denial of the individuality of Jesus. Clearly he was neither Peter nor Paul nor James nor Mary. He was Jesus of Nazareth. Orthodoxy was emphatic on this, as Heppe points out: 'Christ's human nature is of course an *individuum*, an exposition of human nature in individual form.'[54] Similarly, *anhypostasia* is perfectly compatible with the idea that Christ has a human 'personality' in the modern sense of that term. To us, as A. N. S. Lane points out,[55] 'person' has strong psychological overtones and 'personality' indicates the complex of characteristics which distinguish one person from another. In that sense, Jesus certainly had a personality. He was sinless, authoritative, meek, humble, compassionate, patient and prayerful. His sayings and his teaching-methods were highly individualistic, marking him off from all his predecessors and all his successors.

Anhypostasia did not deny any of this. What it did deny was, first of all, the independent, autonomous existence of his human nature. In this respect, *anhypostasia* was linked to Cyril's denial of the adoptionism he attributed to Nestorius. Christ took human nature, but he did not take a man. He took *the form of a servant* (Phil. 2:7), but not *a servant*. He did not even take an existing human genotype or embryo. He created the genotype in union with himself, and its 'personality' developed only in union with the Son of God. His human nature certainly did not exist in an I–Thou relationship to his divine nature: such an understanding would plunge us into the most unambiguous Nestorianism.

Donald Baillie objects that when the gospels record Jesus as praying we can hardly maintain that it was the Second Person of the Trinity praying to the First Person.[56] Why not, particularly since he characteristically addresses him as Father? Once we affirm that the Lord's human nature was a person we must either argue that he was two individuals (the Son of God, and a man) or we must save his unipersonality by denying that he was a divine person (and find ourselves in serious trouble over the question, Who became incarnate?). It is far safer to insist that he is a divine person who, without 'adopting' an existing human person took our human nature and entered upon the whole range of human experiences.

Yet even before the rise of modern psychology and the resultant confusion between person and personality, there were suspicions that *anhypostasia* was not the best term to apply to the humanity of Christ. This is why many theologians have preferred to speak of it as *enhypostatic* or *in*-personal. The term appears to have been introduced to Christology by Apollinaris, who used it, along with *teleios*, to describe the completeness and perfection of the divine and human natures of our Lord.[57] But what has been of particular interest to theologians is the use made of the term by Leontius of Byzantium, who introduced it into his *Adversus Nestorianos et Eutychianos* to convey the idea of two natures existing in a person. For Christology this meant that the two natures, divine and human, were hypostatized in the one hypostasis of the *Logos*. This allowed Leontius to avoid the Nestorian error of two hypostases, while at the same time countering the Monophysite argument that there can be no such thing as a nature without a person (*physis anhypostatos*): 'Nature can only exist individually in an individual, and hence a nature without hypostasis would be an abstraction.'[58]

John of Damascus incorporated both the word and the concept, *en-hypostatos*, into his *Exposition of the Orthodox Faith*. The holy Virgin, he writes, 'was overshadowed by the enhypostatic Wisdom and Power of the most high God'.[59] He clarifies the concept in the remainder of the *Exposition*, the fullest statement being in Book III, Chapter IX:

> For the flesh of God the Word did not subsist as an independent subsistence, nor did there arise another subsistence besides that of God the Word, but as it existed in that it became rather a subsistence which subsisted in another, than one which was an independent subsistence. Wherefore, neither does it lack subsistence al-together, nor yet is there thus introduced into the Trinity another subsistence.

The import of *enhypostatos* is that the human nature of Christ, although not itself an individual, is individualized as the human nature of the Son of God. It does not, for a single instant, exist as *anhypostatos* or non-personal. As embryo, foetus, infant, child and man it is *hypostatos* in the Second Person of the Trinity. The flesh is his. The form of a servant is his. The likeness of men is his. The obedience unto death is his. At every juncture, as Barth points out, we have to do not with a man into whom God changed himself, but with God himself. He is a real man only as the Son of God.[60] Nor is his humanity mere attribute, an accident of his existence. It is part of his essence or being. He became man; and he is, irrevocably and inalienably, man. Everything he is and does is modified by his humanity as surely as by his divinity. He thinks and loves and wills as man, as surely as he thinks, loves and wills as God.

Two further points may be made in connection with *enhypostasia*.

First, against the background of biblical anthropology the assumption of human nature into union with the divine is not at all as incongruous as might appear at first sight. Man was made in the image of God (Gn. 1:27). As such he possesses spirit and reason (*logos*). As such, too, he possesses the capacity for fellowship with God. These considerations mean that, in becoming man, God is not identifying with something that is a contradiction of himself. Human nature has the capacity for sharing in the divine (2 Pet. 1:4) and this implies that there is in the incarnation an element of appropriateness which would not exist in the case of a union between God and any other creature.

Secondly, *enhypostasia* represents a limiting and defining of Christ. His humanity is that of Everyman. But he is not Everyman. He is the man, Christ Jesus; and the only humanity united to him hypostatically is his own. This must control our understanding of such a concept as the vicarious humanity of Christ. J. B. Torrance, for example, writes:

'When Jesus was born for us at Bethlehem, was baptised by the Spirit in Jordan, suffered under Pontius Pilate, rose again and ascended, we were born again, baptised by the Spirit, suffered, died, rose again and ascended in him.'[61] But who are the 'we' and 'us' referred to here? Was Judas Iscariot born again at Bethlehem or Adolf Hitler baptized by the Spirit in Jordan or Joseph Stalin raised from the dead on Easter morning? We can entertain such notions only in defiance of *enhypostasia*. It was not the human race but the specific, personalized humanity of Christ that suffered under Pontius Pilate. We have already seen that the *Logos* cannot be identified with the godhead (*ho theos*, Jn. 1:1). No more can Jesus be identified with the whole of humanity. Christ is true God, but he is not the whole godhead; and he is true man, but he is not the whole of humanity. It is, therefore, no more legitimate to say that Judas Iscariot was born again at Bethlehem than it is to say that God the Father was crucified on the cross of Calvary. The humanity was hypostatized in the person of the Son, not in the person of the Father; and godhead was united to manhood not in the person of Everyman but in the person of Jesus Christ.

This means that we have to think very carefully of the nature of the union between Christ and men. The hypostatic union does not by itself secure the *theiosis* of every human being. In fact, it did not by itself secure the *theiosis* of even our Lord's human nature. He was glorified not because he was God incarnate but because he finished the work given him to do (Jn. 17:4).

For us, the urgent question remains: How does the blood of this man avail for me? In him, godhead and manhood co-exist as one. But how can I share in such reconciliation? It is perfectly possible to be human and yet not be in Christ, because although the incarnation unites Christ to human nature it does not unite him to *me*. I become one with him only in the compound but yet single reality of covenant-election-calling-faith-repentance-sealing. Certainly, we become one flesh with Christ (Eph. 5:31f.). Significantly, however, that language occurs in a context where Paul compares the relationship between Christ and the church to a marriage; and, just as in human marriage, the union depends not on the sharing of a common nature but on the consent of both parties. I have to say, 'I do!' to this real man, the Son of God, who asks whether I take him as my Saviour, Redeemer and Friend. Then, but only then, in that faith which is both his gift and his demand, do he and I become one.

8

KENŌSIS: MAKING HIMSELF NOTHING

Historically, discussion of the incarnation has been dominated by the Gospel of John, particularly by John 1:14, 'the Word became flesh'. The only passage to rival this one in importance is Philippians 2:6–11. In fact, it is from Paul's statement here that we derive the idea of the incarnation as an *assumption* of human nature. Christ made himself nothing, taking or *assuming* the form of a servant (Phil. 2:7).

The Kenotic Theory

Unfortunately, reflection on the theological significance of this passage has been overshadowed since the mid-nineteenth century by the Kenotic Theory of the incarnation, according to which Christ's assumption of humanity involved his 'emptying' himself, in some way or other, of deity. The first notable exponent of this theory was the German theologian, Thomasius, whose *Christi Person und Werk* was published at Erlangen between 1853 and 1861. Thomasius argued that in becoming incarnate Christ abandoned the relative attributes of deity, such as omnipotence and omniscience, while retaining the essential attributes of holiness and love. As a result of this contraction, his life on earth was lived entirely within the conditions of manhood.

Thomasius' compatriot, Gess, went further, arguing that the *kenōsis* was absolute, involving the abandonment of the essential as well as of the relative attributes. This self-reduction affected even the internal relations of the trinity: during the earthly life of Christ both the eternal generation of the Son by the Father and the cosmic functions of the Son himself underwent a temporary interruption.[1]

The Kenotic Theory has enjoyed a considerable vogue in British theology, due largely to the advocacy of the Anglican, Charles Gore. Gore was not by temperament either a radical or a heretic. On the contrary, he was a cautious churchman, jealous for orthodoxy; so much so, indeed, that in 1918 he led the opposition to the consecration of Hensley Henson as Bishop of Hereford on the ground of Henson's professed agnosticism on the two great miracles of the Creed, the virgin birth and the resurrection. But Gore had other concerns beyond a passion for credal fundamentals. He was anxious to effect a synthesis, or at least a reconciliation, between Anglo-Catholicism and Liberalism, especially in the area of biblical criticism. From this point of view, Gore's theory has been aptly described as 'an hypothesis to account for a difficulty'.[2] The difficulty was that with regard to the authorship of certain Old Testament books Christ had made statements which, *prima facie*, were inconsistent with the pronouncements of modern scholarship. The Kenotic Theory appeared to offer a way out of the difficulty by suggesting that as a result of the incarnation Christ's knowledge on such matters was no different from that of his contemporaries.

Gore believed unreservedly in the Christology of Nicea and Chalcedon. He saw no inconsistency, however, in linking this belief to a theory of the incarnation very similar to that of Thomasius. The language in which he expresses his theory varies, betraying symptoms of incoherence and uncertainty. Sometimes he speaks of Christ 'refraining from the exercise of what He possessed, or from the divine mode of action'.[3] At other times he speaks of the Lord abjuring equality with God and laying aside the divine mode of existence (Gore's preferred translation of the phrase *to einai isa theō*, Phil. 2:6). But he can also speak of Christ ceasing to exercise such divine functions as omniscience; and even of his abandoning his divine prerogatives. 'Thus,' he writes, 'remaining in unchanged personality, He abandoned certain prerogatives of the divine mode of existence in order to assume the human.'[4]

Whatever the words used, this process of self-abnegation had as its result that Christ lived his earthly life entirely within the conditions of humanity. Indeed, Gore's guiding principle, so far as the content of the *kenōsis* was concerned, was that Christ laid aside whatever was 'incompatible with a truly human experience'.[5]

If we ask, 'Emptied himself of what?' the picture which emerges is a puzzling one. Gore does not appear to have held that Christ laid aside his divine consciousness or his divine will. Nor did he succeed in convincing himself that the self-emptying involved Christ's laying aside his cosmic functions. The one clear emphasis that shines through his exposition is that Christ laid aside his omniscience. In a key passage in his famous essay in *Lux Mundi* ('The Holy Spirit and Inspiration') he wrote: 'He willed so to restrain the beams of Deity as to observe the limits of the science of His age, and He puts Himself in the same relation to its historical knowledge.'[6] In a footnote Gore indicated the bearing of this on biblical studies: 'He never exhibits the omniscience of bare Godhead in the realm of natural knowledge; such as would be required to anticipate the results of modern science or criticism.'

The Kenotic Theory also had its advocates in the Free Churches, most notably in P. T. Forsyth's Congregational Union Lecture, *The Person and Place of Jesus Christ*. Forsyth gave a clear definition of *kenōsis*. 'The suicide of God', he wrote, 'is no part of the kenotic idea, which turns but on self-divestment as a moral power of the eternal Son; who retains his consciousness but renounces the conditions of infinity and its procreate form.'[7] When it comes to deciding what this self-divestment involves, Forsyth follows a path similar to Gore's, using some verbal sleight-of-hand in the process. An attribute, he affirms, cannot be laid aside, because 'it is only the Being Himself in a certain angle or relation'. But there are, he says, 'accidental relations which determine the form in which the attribute exists'. This allows Forsyth to argue that omniscience, omnipotence and omnipresence may be retracted, since they are 'not so much attributes as functions of attributes, or their modifications'.

As in the case of Gore, Forsyth was particularly interested in the implications of such kenoticism for Christ's views on matters connected with biblical criticism. 'It need hardly be pointed out', he wrote, 'how free such views leave us in regard to those ignorances and limitations in Christ which make so much more trouble to us than they did to the evangelists; those errors, in respect of the form of the future no less than the history of the past, which he shared with his time and race.'[8] Referring more particularly to biblical studies, Forsyth declared: 'it is no way to deal with so great a blessing as criticism arbitrarily to challenge or curb its rights. The way is to fix our faith beyond its reach.'[9] This seems all very well (although the idea of placing our faith beyond the reach of criticism is itself an implicit rejection of incarnation), but behind it lies the conviction that Christ's knowledge of the history of the past was only that of his own time and of his own race; and the further conviction that this ignorance extended equally to 'the form of the future'. As for the idea that this was an ignorance merely of the human nature, Forsyth rejects it uncompromisingly: 'There could not be two wills, or two consciousnesses, in the same personality, by any psychological possibility now credible. We could not have in the same person both knowledge and ignorance of the same thing. If he did not know it he was altogether ignorant of it.'[10]

Another major British theologian to espouse the Kenotic Theory was H. R. Mackintosh, although there is some evidence that he later abandoned it.[11] To Mackintosh, the kenotic idea was

> a conception of immense religious significance ... So dear were human souls to God that he travelled far and stooped low that He might thus touch and raise the needy. Now this is an unheard-of truth, casting an amazing light on God, and revolutionising the world's faint notions of what it means for Him to be Father.[12]

The stooping itself consisted in his laying aside the glory, prerogatives and privileges of deity, and it resulted in 'a life wholly restrained within the bounds of manhood. Outside the conditions imposed by the choice of life as man the Son has no activity or knowledge.'[13]

Mackintosh had little patience with the argument that such a *kenōsis* should be discounted simply because it was incompatible with 'the changelessness of the Absolute'. 'What is immutable in God', he wrote, 'is the holy love which makes His essence. We must let Infinitude be genuinely infinite in its moral expedients.'[14] He also rejected the idea of the abandonment of this or that attribute on the part of the eternal Son as 'a conception too sharp and crude, too rough in shading, for our present problem'.[15] It is difficult to avoid the suspicion, however, that the idea which was shown out by one door was quickly readmitted by another: 'Still, though not parted with, attributes may be transposed.' The Son, according to Mackintosh, possessed all the attributes of Godhead 'in the form of concentrated potency rather than of full actuality'.[16] In practice, Mackintosh drew a sharp distinction between 'holy love' and other attributes of the deity; and in his view, however subtly qualified, the earthly Christ was neither omnipresent, omnipotent or omniscient. There dwelt in him 'no power which a perfect manhood could not mediate'.[17]

Critiques of the Kenotic Theory

There is no shortage of critiques of the Kenotic Theory, those of Bruce, Temple and Baillie being especially noteworthy.[18] Detailed evaluation would therefore be a work of supererogation. The following are the main difficulties.

First, as has often been pointed out, the theory has no answer to the objection posed by William Temple:

> What was happening to the rest of the universe during the period of our Lord's earthly life? ... to say that the Creative Word was so self-emptied as to have no being except in the Infant Jesus, is to assert that for a certain period the history of the world was let loose from the control of the Creative word, and 'apart from Him' very nearly everything happened that happened at all during thirty odd years, both on this planet and throughout the immensities of space.[19]

It is difficult to evade the force of this. The New Testament makes clear that Christ is the One who sustains all things (Heb. 1:3) and the One in whom all things hold together (Col. 1:17). Apart from him, the universe has neither Preserver nor Governor; and apart from omniscience and omnipotence its preservation and government are beyond him. Any form of kenoticism which involves the idea of a depotentiated *Logos* ('one who had no power which a perfect manhood could not mediate') would be fatal to the Lord's competence to carry out his cosmic functions.

Secondly, despite the orthodoxy of its main British exponents, the Kenotic Theory sits uneasily with the Christology of Chalcedon. It is to the credit of Gore and his associates that they took the humanity of Christ seriously, but in their anxiety to emphasize this aspect of the incarnation they portrayed his divinity as one which, at least for the duration of his earthly life, was seriously truncated. Indeed, much of the language of kenoticism is monophysitic, starting from the premise that the idea of two consciousnesses and two minds and two wills in one person is simply absurd. An authentic human life is possible on such terms only at the expense of the divine: if he was man, he could not have been God. From this point of view, the price paid for an authentic humanity was too high. Christ had the human property of ignorance, but not the divine property of omniscience. How, then, can we speak, with Chalcedon, of 'one and the same Son, the same perfect in Godhead and the same perfect in manhood, truly God and truly man' or profess that each nature, the divine as well as the human, retained its own distinctive properties even in the hypostatic union? An incomplete godhead is as incompatible with Chalcedon as an incomplete manhood.

Besides, if the idea of two distinct natures in one person is simply impossible psychologically, does this mean that after Jesus is glorified he is no longer man? If so, the Kenotic Theory, in the words of William Temple, 'makes the Incarnation episodic'.[20] This is a radical departure from the earlier orthodoxy which spoke of Christ as 'God and man in two distinct natures, and one person, for ever' (*Shorter Catechism*, Answer 21).

Thirdly, the Kenotic Theory makes it difficult to maintain continuity between the pre-existent and the incarnate Son. Up to the moment of his enfleshment, according to this theory, the Son was omniscient. At that fateful moment, however, his knowledge suddenly contracts: from infinity to that of a first-century Jew. That represents a degree of amnesia to which there can be no parallel. He forgot virtually everything he knew. Nor is the contraction a matter merely of information. It carries with it a profound change in mental equipment and outlook: so profound, indeed, as to represent a hopeless breakdown in the consciousness of the Son. At the very least, after an eternity of divine self-awareness he would suddenly not know who he was. Indeed, considering the importance of memory to personal identity, he would not even be who he was. Supposing Einstein had suddenly been reduced to a mollusc, the shock could not have been greater.

Fourthly, the Kenotic Theory would drive a fatal wedge between the Jesus of history and the Christ of faith. The earthly Jesus would have no divine attributes, perform no divine functions, enjoy no divine prerogatives and possess no divine consciousness. For the Kenoticist, as Ritschl put it, 'Christ, at least in His earthly existence, has no Godhead at all.'[21] This totally contradicts the evidence of the gospels, where Christ knows that he is the eternal Son; shows complete mastery over the forces of nature ('Even the wind and the waves obey him', Mk. 4:41); claims to be able to carry the burdens of the whole world (Mt. 11:28); looks forward to judging the entire moral universe; and accepts, without embarrassment, the kind of adoration due to God alone. It was from such evidence, pointing clearly to the conclusion that Jesus saw himself as divine, acted as one who was divine, portrayed himself as divine and was seen as divine, that the church derived its belief in the deity of Christ. That belief is essential to the life and worship of the church: and fatal to the Kenotic Theory. Whatever the lowliness into which Christ stooped by his incarnation it was not such as to prevent his disciples seeing his glory (Jn. 1:14). If it had been – if the earthly life had disclosed nothing but 'human likeness' (Phil. 2:7) – Christ would never have been worshipped and Christianity would never have been born.

Finally, the position that the Lord was fallible in literary and historical matters yet infallible spiritually and morally is an extremely precarious one.[22] Whether Jesus ever pronounced on the authorship of any Old Testament book is a moot point, but this is no longer (if indeed it ever was) the charge brought against him by critical scholarship. The charge is that he was entirely mistaken about the nature of the Old Testament. He regarded it as proceeding 'from the mouth of God' (Mt. 4:4), he believed in its jot-and-tittle authority (Mt. 5:18) and he averred that it could not be broken (Jn. 10:35). The estimate of professional scholars is radically different. Even Liddon could point out in his day that the scholars were proclaiming 'the legendary and immoral character of considerable portions of those Old Testament Scriptures upon which our Lord has set the seal of His infallible authority'.[23] In our own day, even so conservative a theologian as Karl Barth has spoken of Scripture in terms which are far from flattering, declaring it the product of 'fallible, erring men like ourselves' and insisting that its capacity for error extends even to 'its religious and theological content'. It contains 'lacunae, inconsistencies and over-emphases', sometimes it alienates and sometimes it is downright offensive.[24]

All this means that if the Kenotic Theory was 'a hypothesis to account for a difficulty', the difficulty has increased significantly since the hypothesis was formulated. The question is not, any longer, how Jesus could be wrong on the authorship of Deuteronomy or the unity of Isaiah, but how he could be so blind and how his moral sense could be so dull as not to notice the moral and theological lacunae, inconsistencies and errors which are so plain to the merest freshman in today's seminaries. Modern scholarship has arraigned Jesus on the charge of culpable deficiency in theological and moral sensitivity. It will take more than the Kenotic Theory to vindicate him.

One cannot help thinking that 'criticism' has treated the Kenotic theologians with cruel ingratitude. Such men as P. T. Forsyth argued, very persuasively, that the new discipline should be allowed to pursue its course unchallenged and uncurbed. Christians should seek no more than to place their faith beyond its reach. Instead, the critics placed Christ beyond our reach, blowing him (so they thought) out of sight and proving to their own entire satisfaction that the Jesus of history is as elusive as the Christ of faith. From this point of view the Kenotic Theory was a tragic failure.

True *kenōsis*

This does not mean, however, that we can dispense with the idea of *kenōsis*. No Christology can ignore the fact that Christ 'emptied himself' (Phil 2:7, RSV); or that, being rich, he made himself poor (2 Cor. 8:9). As Donald Mackinnon puts it, 'it is the notion of *kenōsis* which more than any other single notion points to the deepest sense of the mystery of the incarnation'.[25]

This still leaves us, however, with the question, What does the idea of *kenōsis*, particularly as defined in Philippians 2:6ff., involve?

It involves, first, the fact that the pre-incarnate Christ occupied a position of the highest imaginable eminence. In Pauline terms, he was 'in the form of God' (*en morphē theou hyparchon*, Phil. 2:6). The meaning of *morphē* in this connection has been much discussed, particularly since J. B. Lightfoot's note in his *Commentary on Philippians* (pp. 127–133). The core of Lightfoot's argument was that *morphē* is sharply contrasted with *schēma*, the latter referring to what is accidental and outward, the former to what is intrinsic and essential. This conclusion was based on a survey of these terms as used by the Greek philosophers, for whom, argues Lightfoot, *morphē* was the specific character of an object or entity. The New Testament, he concluded, used it in the same sense: 'Thus *morphē* refers to the divine attributes.'

Lightfoot's theory was, naturally, widely accepted. It is doubtful, however, whether we can draw such a clear distinction as he alleges between *morphē* on the one hand and more visual terms such as *schēma*, *homoiōma* and *eikōn* on the other. *Morphē* occurs as a component of several New Testament verbs such as *symmorpheō* and *metamorpheō*, usually translated as 'conformed' (or 'being made like', *e.g.* Phil. 3:10) or 'transformed' (Rom. 12:2). These verbs clearly imply a change in *morphē*, but hardly a change in specific character or essential attributes. This is particularly true of the transfiguration of Christ, which clearly involved a change in *morphē* (*metemorphōthē*, Mk. 9:2) but equally clearly did not involve a change in essence. It can even be argued that the change in *morphē* occurred precisely to disclose the underlying essence.

Even more interesting (and fatal to Lightfoot's argument) is the use of *morphē* in the longer ending of Mark: he 'appeared in a different form [*morphē*] to two of them' (Mk. 16:12). The idea that Jesus changed his essence or his specific character in between his resurrection appearances is, surely, absurd. In this context at least, *morphē* is indistinguishable from *homoiōma* and *schēma*.

Lightfoot's argument was based, as we have seen, on the use of *morphē* in the Greek philosophers. The range of occurrences surveyed was, however, very narrow; and in any case there is no guarantee that when Paul used the word *morphē* he used it in the same sense as Aristotle. After all, a modern Christian theologian may not mean by the word *nature* the same as it means in the work of A. N. Whitehead. An alternative approach, suggested by H. A. Kennedy[26] and developed more fully by R. P. Martin,[27] is to focus on the use of *morphē* in the Septuagint. Although the data are scarce they seem to warrant three conclusions: first, that in the few passages where *morphē* is used it 'denotes the form, appearance, look or likeness of some one, that by which those beholding him would judge him';[28] secondly, that *eikōn* and *morphē* are used as interchangeable terms in the Greek Bible;[29] and, thirdly, that *eikōn* and *doxa* are also equivalent terms.

Taking these facts together, it seems clear that *morphē* belongs to a group of words which describe God not as he is in himself but as he is to an observer. To an angel, for example, God has a form, an image, a likeness and a glory. He makes himself accessible in his form. What the New Testament does is to insist that this form (Phil. 2:6), image (Col. 1:15) and glory (Jas. 2:1) belong to 'Christ Jesus' in exactly the same way and to the same degree as they do to God the Father. He is God (Jn. 1:1); and he has the image and the glory and the likeness and the form that go along with it. The *morphē* is not the essence, but it presupposes the essence, and 'truly and fully expresses the being which underlies it'.[30] The subject of the *kenōsis*, therefore (the one who 'emptied himself'), is one who had glory with the Father before the world began (Jn. 17:5). He was, in the words of Frank Houghton's hymn 'rich beyond all splendour' (2 Cor. 8:9). He possessed all the majesty of deity, performed all its functions and enjoyed all its prerogatives. He was adored by his Father and worshipped by the angels. He was invulnerable to pain, frustration and embarrassment. He existed in unclouded serenity. His supremacy was total, his satisfaction complete, his blessedness perfect. Such a condition was not something he had secured by effort. It was the way things were, and had always been; and there was no reason why they should change.

But change they did, and they changed because of the second element involved in the *kenōsis*: Christ did not insist on his rights. In the context, this is the main point Paul is making. The church at Philippi was threatened by a lack of lowliness of mind. In their vainglory, its members looked at their own selves, each thinking they were somebody important and insisted on their rights. Hence the appeal to the very different mind-set of Jesus: he did not regard being equal with God as a *harpagmos*.

This word occurs only here in the New Testament, never in the Septuagint and only rarely in secular Greek. Its meaning has been, and still is, the subject of intense debate.[31] The theological starting-point must be that Christ already had an equality with God (*isa to theō*). As such, he had rights: to be recognized; to be revered; to be served by angels; to be immune from poverty, pain and humiliation. Had he been motivated by vainglory, he would have insisted on such rights. Instead, he did not regard them as something to be clung to (*harpagmos*). He could have rejected the proposal that he become servant; or, he could, while consenting to be sent forth, have insisted that it should be in a manner consistent with his dignity. He could have insisted on coming, not *incognito*, but in the full blaze of divine paraphernalia and insignia: as Yahweh came on Mount Sinai (Ex. 19:16ff.); or as he himself would one day come in the glory of the parousia; or as the Tempter suggested in the desert, immune to weakness, renowned as a potentate, guarded by angels; or at least in the glory he enjoyed momentarily on the Mount of Transfiguration, receiving from God the Father honour and acclamation (2 Pet. 1:17). These were his rights, but, being in the form of God, he did not insist on these rights.

The usual way of reading this is that *although* Christ was God he did not insist on his rights. C. F. D. Moule, however, suggests an alternative understanding: 'precisely *because* he was in the form of God he recognized equality with God as a matter not of getting but of giving'.[32] This suggestion has no particular support from the grammar, neither is there anything in the context to require it, but it is interesting to compare it with the account of Jesus washing the disciples' feet (Jn. 13:2ff.). What is particularly fascinating is John's preface to the story: 'Jesus knew that the Father had put all things under his power, and that he had come from God and was returning to God; so …'. At the moment when Jesus decided to perform this service he was clearly aware of his own unique status. The narrative suggests, at the very least, that Jesus saw nothing un-Godlike in washing disciples' feet. But it probably also suggests something more: that at this moment Jesus was driven by a desire to do something 'matchless, God-like and divine' and saw the performance of this menial service as the action which, above all others, conformed to the fact that it was from God he had come and to God he was returning. This accords well with Moule's idea that it was precisely because he was God that he did not insist on his rights.

There is a clear link between Philippians 2:6ff. and John 13:2ff. in the fact that foot-washing was a servile act, indeed, 'a task normally reserved for the lowliest of menial servants.'[33] The conclusion to which this leads us is that the impulse to serve lies at the very heart of deity. God is not self-centred and self-absorbed. As love, he is pure altruism, looking not on (or at) his own things, but at the things of others. From this point of view the idea of *kenōsis* is revolutionary for our understanding of God. It is his very form to forego his rights.

The third element in the *kenōsis* is that Christ made himself nothing. Both the Revised Version and the Revised Standard Version translate *ekenōsen* (Phil. 2:7) literally: 'he emptied himself'. The Vulgate had done the same (*se ipsum exinanivit*) and this is echoed by many of the older theologians. John Owen, for example, writes: 'that in general which is ascribed unto him is kenosis, exinanition, or self-emptying; he emptied himself'.[34] However, in virtually every other instance of its occurrence in the Greek Bible the verb requires to be rendered metaphorically. For example, in Jeremiah 14:2 the RSV rendering is, 'Judah mourns and her gates languish' (*cf.* Je. 15:9). In 2 Corinthians 9:3 the RSV reads, 'I am sending the brethren so that our boasting about you may not prove vain'.

There can be little doubt that a similar translation is required in Philippians 2:7. The KJV's 'made himself of no reputation' is good, the NIV's 'made himself nothing' even better. But the nuance of vanity and futility should not be lost. The lowest point of the *kenōsis* is the cross, and the cross is the ultimate in vanity and futility. Here, the Life becomes dead and the Eternal Word is reduced to silence. Here the career of the Son of Man runs into the sand, disgraced, discredited and meaningless. He has achieved nothing and the grim words, 'All is vanity!' run round the universe with a new depth of meaning.[35]

But how did Christ effect such *kenōsis*? The idea that the emptying is to be understood as 'the renunciation of the *morphē theou*' is still canvassed,[36] but there is nothing in the language or context of Philippians 2:7 to justify it. Instead, the passage emphasizes two things: first, that it was *himself* he emptied and, secondly, that the way he emptied himself was by taking the form of a servant. This latter may not express the whole truth about the mode of the *kenōsis*, but it certainly expresses the central element. It is what Christ *assumes* that humbles and impoverishes him: hence the justice of Augustine's comment that he emptied himself 'not by changing His own divinity but by assuming our changeableness'.[37]

According to Philippians 2:7ff., this addition by which Christ made himself nothing involved three movements.

First, he took 'the form of a servant'. Here, the parallel with the 'form of God' is important. He became a servant as surely and as truly as previously he had been God. The term *doulos*, too, is important. Christ came into an entirely new relationship with the Father. From eternity he was a Son. Now, he becomes a servant, under the law, bound to obey, charged with a work given him to do (Jn. 17:4) and threatened with the direst consequences for himself and all connected with him should his obedience falter. He became a slave, without rights: a non-person, who could not turn to those crucifying him and say, 'Do you not know who I am?'

Secondly, Christ assumed a public image which was entirely and exclusively human. He took the likeness (*homoiōma*) and the appearance (*schēma*) of men. Paul does not choose such language in order to suggest that the humanness of Jesus was less than real.[38] It can hardly be doubted that he believed him to be in the truest and completest sense a man. His reason for choosing the words 'likeness' and 'appearance' is, rather, that he wishes to highlight the impression made by Jesus. How did people find him (Phil. 2:8)? Those who were causing concern in the church at Philippi were suffering from vainglory. They were concerned about their image, anxious to make a good impression and keen to be recognized as people of consequence. By contrast, the one who really was Somebody put himself in a position where people completely misunderstood him and underestimated him. They looked, and saw nothing but a man. There was nothing in his appearance to distinguish him from anyone else. There was no halo, no glow, probably not even anything that made him particularly handsome or striking. Not a head would have turned as he walked. He looked utterly ordinary.

Thirdly, Christ took death, 'even death on a cross' (Phil. 2:8). The subject of this dying – the One who dies – is God the Son. He obeys unto death. In his original form he was immune to death, but he deliberately assumed a form that was mortal. He went towards death, choosing it and tasting it, deciding not to be its master but its victim, and accepting a destiny according to which it would be a sin for him not to die. The Son of Man must suffer. Death was obedience; *not dying* would be disobedience. Besides, it is death in its most aggravated form, not merely because the cross involved indescribable physical pain, but because in his case it was the occasion, the instrument and the symbol of the curse due to sin. He experienced death unmitigated and unqualified: death with the sting; a death without light, comfort or encouragement. The long, long journey from Caesarea Philippi to Calvary was a journey into a black hole involving not only physical and emotional pain but a spiritual desertion beyond our imagining. In his agony, he would cry and not be heard. He would lose all sense of his divine sonship. He would lose all sense of his Father's love. Into that tiny space (his body, outside Jerusalem) and into that fraction of time (the ninth hour, on Good Friday) God gathered the sin of the world; and there and then, in the flesh of his own Son, he condemned it (Rom. 8:3). On that cross, at its darkest point, the Son knew himself only as sin and his Father only as its avenger. Here was a singularity. The *Logos*, the ground of all law, became lawlessness (*anomia*), speechless in a darkness beyond reason. He so renounced his rights that he died; and he so made himself nothing that he died *that* death. He did not shrink from the connection with flesh. When a second great step was called for, he shuddered, yet resolutely accepted the connection with death. He became flesh, then went deeper, tasting death.

Deeper principles

Beneath these three great movements there lie other, even deeper, principles.

For example, the principle of *krypsis*. The *kenōsis* involved an obscuring of the divine glory of Christ. 'Christ, indeed, could not divest himself of godhead,' wrote Calvin,[39] 'but he kept it concealed for a time, that it might not be seen, under the weakness of the flesh. Hence he laid aside his glory in the view of men, not by lessening it, but by concealing it.' Luther had written earlier to similar effect:

> ... this is the most profound *incognito* and the most impenetrable impossibility of recognition that can be; for the contrast between God and an isolated individual human being is the greatest possible contrast; it is infinitely qualitative. This, however, is His will, His free will, and therefore it is an *incognito* maintained by omnipotence.[40]

Neither Luther nor Calvin meant, of course, that the incarnation consisted merely of *krypsis*. On the contrary, it was a real assumption of real flesh. But this itself involved the veiling of the glory. In becoming incarnate God not only accommodates himself to human weakness: he buries his glory under veil after veil so that it is impossible for flesh and blood to recognize him. As he hangs on the cross, bleeding, battered, powerless and forsaken, the last thing he looks like is God. Indeed, he scarcely looks human. He looks like nothing but a hell-bound, hell-deserving derelict. Everything about him says, 'An atheist and a blasphemer!' At last, his identity was obscured even from himself.

We should notice, too, that the *kenōsis* involved the willingness to go ever lower. Behind it, there lay two great decisions. The first, pre-temporal, was the decision of the eternal Son to assume the form of a servant and the likeness of men. The second, taken once he was incarnate, was the decision to humble himself even further. From this point of view, the humiliation of Christ was not a point, but a line. Its greatest single step was that by which he became the child in the manger. The condescension involved in that is beyond imagining. Yet it was only the beginning of the long downward journey through homelessness, poverty, exhaustion, shame and pain to Gethsemane; and beyond that to Calvary.

And even then, Calvary, as we have seen, was not a point but a line. From the third to the sixth hour the agony was one of relative serenity, punctuated by the three-fold chorus of derision from the passers-by, the scribes and Pharisees and those crucified with him (Mk. 15:29ff.). From the sixth to the ninth hour there was darkness: possibly symbolic of the darkness in the Saviour's soul; or, alternatively, pointing to the fact that the Light was almost exhausted in its struggle with the Darkness. At the ninth hour came the dereliction, when there was nothing but darkness and emptiness: no hearing, no loving, no 'withness'. He was alone with the world's sin and with God; experiencing the presence of the Holy as a dreadful forsakenness.

But at the ninth hour, the dereliction ceased. The curve moved no longer downwards, but upwards, the humiliation passing imperceptibly into exaltation. As he died, his dawn was already breaking: 'Father, into your hands I commit my spirit' (Lk. 23:46).

Every moment in that journey from Bethlehem to Calvary was chosen; and every moment on the cross, from the third to the ninth hour, was chosen. Every day of the Lord's life he re-enacted the *kenōsis*, renewing the decision which had made him nothing and choosing to move further and further into the shame and pain it involved. He loved his own, and when eventually it became clear what that love would cost he went forward, trembling, to be what his people's sin deserved.

Even as he did so, he revealed another side to the *kenōsis*: the willingness to cast himself unreservedly on the love and care of his Father. In the descent into the abyss, the Servant was renouncing control over his own destiny, performing what Balthasar calls the 'genuinely human act of trusting self-abandonment to a future that is not at one's own disposal'.[41] This is highlighted in the abrupt change of subject in Philippians 2:9: 'wherefore, God hyper-exalted him' (my translation). He made *himself* nothing. But he did not exalt himself. Indeed, he could not. The body placed in the tomb could never have raised itself. It was raised only when God was satisfied; and only by his power.

From this point of view the obedience of Jesus involved breath-taking risks. He put his destiny wholly in the hands of the Father and willed to die unrecognized, disgraced and accursed. He committed himself to him who judges justly (1 Pet. 2:23), staking everything on the belief that his Father, a God of absolute integrity, governed in the interests of moral order. However terrifying the penultimate word – the word of the cross – the ultimate word would be one of vindication. But it would be a vindication not in his own hands. In the words of a forgotten Scottish preacher, James McLagan, he had to 'touch the very brink of danger, though not be swept away by it, and feel all the horror of the precipice, but without falling over'.[42]

Indeed, at a deeper level still, he even had to place his faith in the servant-form he had assumed, venturing all on its power to sustain the shocks and pressures to which the journey into the far country would subject it. To quote McLagan again:

> the failure but for one moment of his human endurance and resolution, must effect not only the universal and eternal triumph of wickedness and misery, but what it is fearful to name, even while we know it can never happen – the defeat of His Father's counsel – the failure of His Father's truth – and the desecration of His Father's Godhead![43]

Finally, *kenōsis* involves real renunciation. To this extent Gore was correct in insisting that the language of Paul 'expresses something very much more than the mere addition of a manhood to His Godhead'.[44] Over against kenoticism, however, we have to insist that it is perfectly possible to speak of real renunciation without defining it as renunciation of deity. Indeed, theologians who had probably never heard of kenoticism spoke freely of such renunciation. Hugh Martin, for example, described Christ as 'not drawing on his divine might and energies, but denying himself their exercise and forth-putting ... withdrawing from the field of action those prerogatives and powers of Deity, which in the twinkling of an eye might have scattered ten thousand worlds and hells of enemies'.[45]

It is probably impossible to formulate a theory which will account fully for the total situation we encounter here (making himself nothing while at the same time retaining the form of God). Some progress, however, is possible, particularly in view of the pointers available in the accounts of the temptation in the desert. When the devil put to Jesus the proposal, 'Tell these stones to become bread!' there can be no doubt that Jesus had the power to perform such a miracle. He clearly exercised it when, for example, he fed the five thousand. But there was a crucial difference between the two incidents. In the first, Jesus was tempted to use his power for himself. In the second, he used it for others. He denied himself the exercise of his divine might and energies, but in other directions these energies were frequently put forth: for example, in performing the cosmic functions of the *Logos*, in healing the sick and in destroying the works of the devil. But they were not put forth in his own interest. In particular, they were not put forth to protect him from the implications of his decision to become incarnate and bear the sin of the world. Never once does he in his own interest or in his own defence break beyond the parameters of humanity. He had no place to lay his head; but he never built himself a house. He was thirsty; but he provided for himself no drink. He was assaulted by all the powers of hell; but he did not call on his legions of angels. Even when he saw the full cost of *kenōsis*, he asked for no rewriting of the script. He bore the sin in his human body, endured the sorrow in his human soul and redeemed the church with his human blood. The power which carried the world, stilled the tempest and raised the dead was never used to make his own conditions of service easier. Neither was the prestige he enjoyed in heaven exploited to relax the rules of engagement. Deploying no resources beyond those of his Spirit-filled humanness, he faced the foe as flesh and triumphed as man.

9

THE SINLESSNESS OF CHRIST

The humanity of Jesus, as C. F. D. Moule points out, 'is both continuous with and discontinuous from that of the rest of mankind'.[1] One of these points of discontinuity, the virgin birth, we have already seen. The humanity of Jesus came into being in a way to which there is no analogy in ordinary experience.

The second point of discontinuity is the sinlessness of Christ. The New Testament insists on this. He was tempted, but without sinning (Heb. 4:15). He was 'holy, blameless, pure' (Heb. 7:26). He could fearlessly challenge his enemies, 'Can any of you prove me guilty of sin?' (Jn. 8:46).

This sinlessness involves two elements.

First, Christ was free of actual sin. He betrays no consciousness of guilt. He never prays for forgiveness. He never confesses short-coming. On the contrary, all he did, thought or said conformed exactly to the will of God. He fulfilled all righteousness (Mt. 3:15).

Secondly, he was free from inherent sin. Nowhere in the structures of his being was there any sin. Satan had no foot-hold in him.

There was no lust. There was no affinity with sin. There was no proclivity to sin. There was no possibility of temptation from within. In no respect was he fallen and in no respect was his nature corrupt.

Until the nineteenth century this was the virtually unanimous confession of the church. Since then, however, there has been a growing tendency to speak of Christ as taking a fallen human nature. Otherwise, it is said, he would not have been fully human, he could have felt no sympathy with us and human nature would not have been redeemed.

It was Edward Irving, a nineteenth-century Scottish theologian, who first began to give passionate expression to this point of view.[2] As a result, he was deposed from the ministry of the Church of Scotland in 1833, the specific charge against him being that he denied the sinlessness of Christ and argued that he was tainted with original sin. It should be noted that even those who were most disturbed by Irving's teaching respected his piety and acknowledged his devotion to Christ.[3] It should also be noted that Irving vehemently affirmed his personal belief in the sinlessness of Christ. 'The soul of Christ', he wrote, 'did ever resist and reject the suggestions of evil.' 'I believe it to be necessary unto salvation', he continued, 'that a man should believe that Christ's soul was so held in possession by the Holy Ghost and so supported by the divine nature, as that it never assented unto an evil suggestion, and never originated an evil suggestion.' Jesus, he declared unambiguously, 'differed from all men in this respect, that He never sinned'.[4]

On the other hand, there can be no doubt that Irving used extremely provocative language. 'The flesh of Christ,' he declared, 'like my flesh, was in its proper nature mortal and corruptible.'[5] It was liable to all forms of evil suggestion and temptation, through its participation in a fallen nature and a fallen world.[6] That what he took was our fallen human nature was, according to Irving, 'most manifest', 'because there was no other in existence to take'.[7] The fact that he did not commit actual sin was due, not to any intrinsic quality of his own person, but to the ministry of the Holy Spirit. This is what really set Christ apart: 'no one was ever thus anointed with the Holy Ghost'.[8] Without this restraint, the corruption of his fallen human substance would have erupted. 'I have the Holy Ghost manifested', wrote Irving, 'in subduing, restraining, conquering the evil propensities of the fallen manhood, and making it an apt organ for expressing the will of the Father.'[9]

Irving's pulpit and private utterances were even more extreme. One hearer was horrified to hear him refer to Christ's human nature as 'that sinful substance'.[10] In a subsequent conversation Irving was challenged as to whether he believed that Christ, like Paul, had 'the law of sin' in his members, bringing him into captivity. 'Not into captivity,' Irving replied, 'but Christ experienced everything the same as Paul did, except the "captivity".'[11]

The early response to Irving was almost entirely critical.[12] In 1938, however, Karl Barth, in the second part of the first volume of his *Kirkliche Dogmatik*, enthusiastically espoused the idea that Christ took a fallen humanity. In doing so he acknowledged the work of Irving.[13] Barth went on to expound the idea zestfully. It meant a corrupt nature (*natura vitiata*); one which is obnoxious (liable?) to sin; and one which exists in a vile and abject condition. He wrote:

> There must be no weakening or obscuring of the saving truth that the nature which God assumed in Christ is identical with our nature as we see it in the light of the Fall. If it were otherwise, how could Christ be really like us? What concern could we have with Him? We stand before God characterised by the Fall. God's Son not only assumed our nature but He entered the concrete form of our nature, under which we stand before God as men damned and lost.[14]

Inevitably, many others took their cue from Barth. This appears, for example, in C. E. B. Cranfield's *Commentary on Romans*. Commenting on Paul's use of the phrase, 'in the likeness of sinful man' (Rom. 8:3), Cranfield writes: 'By *sarx hamartias* Paul clearly meant "sinful flesh", i.e., fallen human nature.' Cranfield rejects the traditional interpretation ('that he used *homoiōma* in order to avoid implying that the Son of God assumed *fallen* human nature') on the ground that 'it is open to the general theological objection that it was not unfallen, but fallen, human nature which needed redeeming'.[15] T. F. Torrance writes to similar effect: 'the incarnation is to be understood as the coming of God to take upon himself our fallen human nature, our actual existence laden with sin and guilt, our humanity diseased in mind and soul in its estrangement or alienation from the Creator'.[16] J. B. Torrance follows Irving even more enthusiastically. Commenting on Athanasius' classic treatise, *De Incarnatione*, he declares:

> Christ does not heal by standing over against us, diagnosing our

> sickness, prescribing medicine for us to take, and then going away, to leave us to get better by following his instructions – as an ordinary doctor might. No, He becomes the patient! He assumes that very humanity which is in need of redemption ... That was why these fathers did not hesitate to say, as Edward Irving the great Scottish theologian in the early nineteenth century and Karl Barth in our own day have said, that Christ assumed 'fallen humanity' that our humanity might be turned back to God in him by his sinless life in the Spirit, and, through him, in us.[17]

The case for a *fallen* human nature

In favour of the idea that Christ took fallen human nature it is argued, first of all, that it follows from the principle that 'the unassumed is the unhealed'. But this is an illegitimate use of a form of words which has a very definite function in the history of Christology. The first occurrence of the phrase is in Gregory of Nazianzen's *First Letter to Cledonius* and its specific import was to negate the heresy of Apollinaris. The context makes this clear: 'If anyone has put his trust in Him as a man without a human mind, he is really bereft of mind, and quite unworthy of salvation. For that which He has not assumed He has not healed'.[18] It is quite perverse to suggest that 'the unassumed' in this statement is 'fallen human nature'. What Gregory has in his sights is the Apollinarian insistence that Christ did not assume a human mind: 'If he has a soul,' he asks, 'and yet is without a mind, how is he man, for man is not a mindless animal?'

All this is quite irrelevant to the much later idea that Christ assumed a fallen nature. None of Irving's opponents denied the completeness of our Lord's humanity; and conversely none of the fathers held that Christ took fallenness. Indeed, the pointers we have from the fathers are in the opposite direction. Cyril, for example, in his *Answers to Tiberius* (13) declared: 'though he clothed himself, as they say, in Adam, he was not, as Adam was, of the earth earthy, but was celestial and so incomparably superior to what was earthy'.[19] The Western fathers were of the same mind. 'For there was born,' wrote Augustine, 'not a nature corrupted by the contagion of transgression, but the one only remedy of all such corruptions.'[20] Leo, in his *Tome*, expressed it more epigrammatically: 'Nature it was that was taken by the Lord from His mother, not defect.'[21]

It is argued, secondly, that Christ's humanity must have been fallen because it was taken from the substance of his mother. 'This', wrote Irving, 'is the first point in the mystery of Christ's constitution, His taking the substance of the fallen Virgin Mary.'[22] The premise, of course, is correct, and none of Irving's opponents denied it. Indeed, they strove to do justice to the mystery of the umbilical cord and no one has ever expressed it better than Marcus Dods: 'she imparted to her Son all that other mothers impart to their children'.[23] But this phrase, too, had its own historical context: it was a protest against Docetism with its suggestion that Christ's humanness had no real physical connection with his mother's. Against this background the insistence that Christ was born 'of the Virgin Mary, of her substance', was never intended to suggest that Christ's humanity was fallen. It signified only that it was real. 'The Holy Spirit', wrote Leo, 'made the Virgin bring forth, but it was a real body taken from her body.' Through the umbilical cord Christ was keyed into the genetic stream of mankind: related even to the dust of the ground and to the whole world of matter. But he never existed except as a 'holy thing' (Lk. 1:35, KJV). The divine act that made his humanity made it holy. He was born of a fallen and sinful mother, but he was born of her 'without sin'.

Thirdly, Irving argued that unless Christ was fallen he was not like us. But surely all the identity we need is secured by the fact that he 'became flesh and made his dwelling among us' (Jn. 1:14)? He took a true body. He took a reasonable soul. He lived in our physical, social and spiritual environment. He shared our pains, our sorrows and our fears: even the loss of God. What more can we ask? On the other hand, even on Irving's own terms there is significant discontinuity between us and Christ. He never sinned, 'for, if he sinned, atonement and reconciliation are made void for ever'.[24] He had a unique measure of the Holy Spirit ('no one was ever thus anointed with the Holy Ghost').[25] He had a unique self-consciousness. Any one of these, let alone all of them together, would be sufficient to break the continuity between Christ and us.

It is argued, yet again, that Christ must have taken fallen human nature because that is the only human nature there is. Does this mean that unless he were fallen he would not be human: that fallenness is part of the definition of human nature? Surely not! If it were, then the First Adam was not a man. Indeed, on these terms God did not create a man at all. What he created became a man only by falling. The same conclusion would apply at the other end of human destiny. Glorified man would not be human. Any premise which leads to such conclusions is patently absurd. It is perfectly possible to be a man and yet to be unfallen.

Above all, Irving argued that if Christ did not have a fallen humanity he could not have been tempted. Indeed, he seems to have regarded 'unfallen' and 'not liable to temptation' as convertible terms. It is important, of course, to acknowledge unreservedly that Christ was tempted and that these temptations were absolutely real. He felt the appeal of the sinful proposals put to him and he had to struggle with all his might to repel them. John of Damascus was quite wrong to suggest that Jesus dispelled the devil's assault 'like vapour'.[26] He stood only by the power of the Holy Spirit: not by some effortless, Samson-like omnipotence, but by the power of a relationship with God which was moral and personal and which meant that he was invincible in faith, hope and love.

But in one crucial respect Christ was not like us. He was not tempted by anything within himself. He was not dragged away by his own evil desire and enticed (Jas. 1:14). There was no law of sin in his members (Rom. 7:23). There was no predisposition to sin, no love of sin and no affinity with sin. The 'prince of this world' had no foot-hold on him (Jn. 14:30).

What, then, did the devil work on? Part of the answer is that although Jesus had no vices he did have sinless human weaknesses. He could be tempted (and clearly was) through hunger, through the fear of pain and through love for a friend. It is not a mark of fallenness to feel any of these, and yet each of them could generate strong pressure to deviate from the path prescribed for him.

Jesus also had holy affections, feelings and longings which, in the course of his work, he had to thwart. Foremost among these was the longing for communion with God. Is it any wonder that in the Garden of Gethsemane the prospect of losing this communion almost overwhelmed him? He was not being called upon to mortify a lust. He was being called upon to frustrate the holiest aspiration of which man is capable. What he wanted and what his Father directed were in conflict. Hence the 'loud cries and tears' (Heb. 5:7).

Again, Christ could be tempted through his sonship. This was clearly the focus of the temptations in the desert (Mt. 4:1–11 and parallels), where the devil insinuates doubt as to whether he were the Son at all: 'If you are the Son of God …'. The Tempter could certainly point out that the circumstances of the Lord's life could not support any assurance on this score. He had no bread. He had no kingdom. But there was also something deeper: the temptation to be obsessed with the question of his own sonship. The third temptation revolves around the question of a sign. If Jesus throws himself from the pinnacle of the temple, angels will bear him up and he will suffer no injury. What is envisaged here is not some portent to impress others with the glory of Christ. There were no others present. The sign was for himself: a temptation to seek reassurance, as if to say, 'The real question is my own sonship. I must forget all else and all others and all further service until that is clear!'

The sinless, unfallen One could even be tempted through his very self-renunciation. The essential meaning of the incarnation was that Christ took the nature and condition of men and the road to death. In the first temptation, the devil attacked him precisely at this point, tempting him to step out from among the men with whom he has identified in baptism, to use his personal power and authority to mitigate the implications of his humiliation, to refuse the experience of hunger and to end his dependence on ordinary, vulnerable, sources of supply. Significantly, Jesus' answer began with the word 'man': '*Man* does not live on bread alone.' That is what he has become, a man, and he must accept not only the appearance but the reality.

This attack is resumed in Peter's vehement rejection of the idea that the Messiah should be crucified: '"Never, Lord!" he said' (Mt. 16:22). That these words struck a raw nerve in the psyche of the Saviour is clear from the vehemence of his reaction: 'Get behind me, Satan!' (Mt. 16:23). On a later occasion, Peter once again became (perhaps unconsciously) the voice pleading for an abandonment of the path that was leading to the cross: 'You shall never wash my feet' (Jn. 13:8). But the final, full-scale assault came in Gethsemane, where the full implications of the cup finally dawned on Jesus. Soon, he would be sin. Soon, he would be in the far country. Soon, he would face that unimaginable moment when the Father would not be there. He would cry and God would not answer. In Gethsemane, there was still time to turn back, and the arguments for such a course were strong and plausible. How could Love face the loss of Love? *Should* Love face the loss of Love, even *choose* it? He was, as we saw, despondent, close to despair, afraid and almost overwhelmed. But he stood. He took the cup, confirming and re-enacting his decision to be nothing. He rose, with invincible resolution (Mk. 14:42), to face damnation and anathema. From that point onwards, there was not a falter.

We must be careful not to misconstrue the effect of Jesus' sinless integrity at this point. Far from meaning a shorter, painless struggle with temptation it involved him in protracted resistance. Precisely because he did not yield easily and was not, like us, an easy prey, the devil had to deploy all his wiles and use all his resources. The very fact that he was invincible meant that he endured the full force of temptation's ferocity, until hell slunk away, defeated and exhausted. Against us, a little temptation suffices. Against him, Satan found himself forced to push himself to his limits.

Difficulties in Irving's position

Besides the weakness of the evidence alleged in its support, there are two serious intrinsic difficulties in Irving's idea that Christ took a fallen humanness.

First, he has no answer to the charge of Nestorianism. What was fallen? Was it the person? This would lead to the conclusion that the Son of God was fallen: a conclusion Irving, quite rightly, was not willing to draw. 'What was holy', he wrote, 'was His person.'[27] What then was fallen? The human nature! But this means that Irving had to separate that nature sharply from the person:

> Whenever I attribute sinful properties and dispositions and inclinations to our Lord's human nature, I am speaking of it considered as apart from Him, in itself ... we can assert the sinfulness of the whole, the complete, the perfect human nature, which He took, without in the least implicating Him with sin.[28]

This is surely hopeless. How can the nature be fallen without implicating the person? Only if the humanness is an agent in its own right, acting independently and autonomously: so independently, indeed, that the Son carries no responsibility for his human nature. That is absurd.

Secondly, there is the difficulty of the historical connotation of 'fallen'. That can be clearly seen in, for example, the Westminster Assembly's *Shorter Catechism*: 'Our first parents ... fell from the estate wherein they were created by sinning against God' (Answer 13). To be 'fallen', therefore, is to have sinned against God; and to be 'fallen' is to be in a state of sinfulness, devoid of righteousness and 'wholly defiled in all the faculties and parts of soul and body' (*Westminster Confession*, VI.II). How can any of this apply to Jesus? It is impossible to maintain a distinction between 'fallen' and 'sinful'. Fallen Adam is sinful Adam. Fallen nature is sinful nature, dominated by 'the flesh' (in the Pauline sense) and characterized by total depravity. A. B. Bruce was perfectly correct, then, to declare that Irving's theory 'requires that original sin should be ascribed to Christ; for original sin is a vice of fallen human nature; and the doctrine that our Lord's human nature was fallen, means, if it means anything, that it was tainted with original sin'.[29] Irving would have been as well, then, to argue that Christ took *sinful* human nature 'because there was no other human nature to take'. He held back from this only because he knew that it was totally incompatible with the New Testament's description of Christ as the one 'who had no sin' (2 Cor. 5:21).

But if we cannot use the word 'fallen', how, then, are we to describe Jesus? We cannot improve on the traditional terminology: he was man in a state of humiliation. This contrasts with other possible human states. He was not in a state of primitive bliss, like the First Adam. Nor was he in a state of glorious exaltation comparable to that which he now enjoys as the risen Saviour. He was in an altogether unique position: unfallen and sinless, and yet sharing his mother's 'humble state' (Lk. 1:48). Nothing that was human was alien to him. He was liable to all the miseries of this life; he was vulnerable to all its darker emotions; he was destined to lose communion with God; and he was mortal.

But why? Not because he was fallen, but because, prompted by love, he freely chose to suffer with the fallen and, at last, to suffer *for* the fallen. He was crucified between two thieves, but he was no thief. He was made sin (2 Cor. 5:21), but he was no sinner.

Able to sin?

Finally, how are we to express the sinlessness of Christ? Is it enough to say that he was *able not to sin* or must we also say that he was *not able to sin*? The former is the truth about the First Adam. As created by God he was very good (Gn. 1:31). He had the freedom and power to do what was good, but he had it mutably. He could fall from it (*Westminster Confession*, IX.II). With regard to the Last Adam, however, we must take higher ground. He was not able to sin. 'His holy behaviour was *necessary*,' wrote Jonathan Edwards: 'It was *impossible* it should be otherwise, than that he should behave himself holily, and that he should be perfectly holy in each individual act of his life ... it was *impossible* that the Messiah should fail of persevering in integrity and holiness, as the first Adam did.'[30]

The crucial issue is whether Christ could have willed to sin? The answer rests entirely on his identity. He was the Son of God, 'very God of very God'. If he sinned, God sinned. At this level, the impeccability of Christ is absolute. It rests not upon his unique endowment with the

Spirit nor upon the indefectibility of God's redemptive purpose, but upon the fact that he is who he is. 'When the Logos', wrote W. G. T. Shedd, 'goes into union with a human nature, so as to constitute a single person with it, he becomes responsible for all that this person does through the instrumentality of this nature ... Should Jesus Christ sin, incarnate God would sin.'[31]

We may link the subject 'God' with many predicates. The Son of God may suffer, may be tempted, may be ignorant and may even die. But we cannot link God with the predicate 'sin'. God cannot in any situation or for any purpose commit a transgression of his own will. He absolutely cannot be guilty of lawlessness.

It does not follow, however, that when Christ was tempted he was always aware, at the human level, that the Tempter could never conquer him. We know that the devil could, on occasion, put a big *if* against his consciousness of sonship (Mt. 4:3). He would have found it equally easy to question his sinlessness. It would certainly be unwise to conclude that at every single point Jesus was in full possession of the whole truth about himself.

It is helpful to recall here Dr John A. Mackay's distinction between the view from the balcony and the view from the road.[32] To the angels on the balcony (as to theologians in their armchairs) it may have been perfectly clear that Jesus could never sin. To himself, engaging the devil on the road, the outcome may have been far from clear. Never once, as we observe him struggle with temptation, do we see him deriving comfort from the fact of his own impeccability. All that we see is his having recourse to the very same weapons as are available to ourselves: the company of his fellow-believers (Mk. 14:33), the word of God (Mt. 4:4) and prayer (Mk. 14:35).

10

NO OTHER NAME: THE UNIQUENESS OF CHRIST IN MODERN THEOLOGY

During the twentieth century Christological discussion has continued unabated. It would be a serious exaggeration to suggest that all the outstanding contributors have turned their backs on Chalcedon's conclusions. Roman Catholic theologians have, in the main, adhered to the Formula of Chalcedon, as have such Anglo-Catholics as E. L. Mascall and the not inconsiderable band of conservative evangelicals (most notably B. B. Warfield, G. K. Berkouwer and D. F. Wells). Barth and Brunner, too, have operated, more or less, within the framework of Chalcedon, while such scholars as Cullman, Pannenberg and Moltmann have sought to build on it rather than abandon it.

Nevertheless, those who have set the agenda have generally been those who repudiate Chalcedon. Sometimes, the repudiation is only implicit (for example, in the denial of the pre-existence of Christ). But in countless instances, modern theologians repudiate Chalcedon explicitly. John A. T. Robinson, for example, can scarcely conceal his disgust:

> Not only does it use categories that almost inevitably suggest

> that the human centre of consciousness was replaced or displaced by the divine, but it gives the impression to a modern man that Jesus was a hybrid: the very idea of a God-man, with two natures in the same person, evokes the picture of a sort of bat-man or centaur, an unnatural conjunction of two strange species.[1]

Albert Schweitzer described the two-nature doctrine as a deception by which self-contradiction was elevated into a law: 'This dogma had first to be shattered before men could once more go out in quest of the historical Jesus, before they could even grasp the thought of His existence.'[2] John Knox asks: 'Do we find it literally, word for word and phrase by phrase, credible or even intelligible? Must we not confess that we do not?'[3] Don Cupitt dismisses it as simply obsolete: 'The classical doctrine of the incarnation belongs, not to the essence of Christianity, but only to a certain period of church history, now ended.'[4] And John Hick argues that orthodoxy has never been able to give the doctrine of the two natures any meaning: 'For to say without explanation that the historical Jesus of Nazareth was also God is as devoid of meaning as to say that this circle drawn with pencil on a paper is also a square.'[5]

Paradoxically, however, many of those theologians who have rejected the Formula of Chalcedon have continued to profess themselves worshippers of Jesus Christ. This clearly implies that they still regard Christ as in some sense special: so special, in fact, that he may be accorded divine honours. But how can this be, if he is not God incarnate?

Rudolf Bultmann

One of the most influential answers to that question has been Rudolf Bultmann's. We have already seen something of Bultmann's programme of demythologization and may well ask, Once the mythology is stripped away, what is left? The answer appears to be, 'The Christ-event!' The interpretation put upon this, however, is highly idiosyncratic. It does not mean the sequence of events we usually associate with Jesus, particularly cross and resurrection. These events, so far as Bultmann is concerned, have no redemptive significance. The Christ-event is the *kerygma* itself. However, this *kerygma*, too, has two levels.

First, the preaching of Jesus. This immediately strikes one as inconsistent with Bultmann's starting-point. If we can know nothing of the life or personality of Jesus, how can we know what he taught? Part of Bultmann's answer to this is that we can be much more certain with regard to Jesus' teaching than we can with regard to his life and personality.[6] The other, more radical, part is that if the teaching came from someone else, what does it matter? 'Whoever', he writes, 'prefers to put the name of "Jesus" always in quotation marks and let it stand as an abbreviation for the historical phenomenon with which we are concerned, is free to do so.'[7] It is the message, not the person or his history, that constitutes the Christ-event. Jesus or 'Jesus' announced that the Day of Decision had come; and Jesus or 'Jesus' summons us to repentance and love.

The second phase of the *kerygma* is the preaching of the early church. According to Bultmann, this had clear mythological elements such as the claim that Jesus had risen from the dead and the assertion that he was the Lord and the Son of God. But when the myths are stripped away, an essential core remains. God has acted decisively in history: not, however, in some past event, but in the preaching itself. This preaching calls us to decision, and the decision has two foci: the cross and the resurrection. But these, too, must be radically reinterpreted. To believe in Easter is merely to believe in preaching;[8] and to believe in the cross means only to be willing to be crucified with Christ.[9] There is no objective (or verifiable) Christ-event. There is only *preaching*, proclaiming that God has acted decisively, that every hour is the last hour and that we are called to decision.

It is always difficult to be sure that one has understood Bultmann correctly. Indeed, his own work is probably in greater need of a hermeneutic than the gospels he was so keen to demythologize. But if the above summary of his thought is substantially correct, Bultmann's theology clearly labours under enormous difficulties.

First, is it *gospel* at all? The gospel, after all, is good news; and it consists of indicatives. Bultmann, by contrast, is low on indicatives and high on imperatives. Our salvation (whatever that means) depends on our compliance with the demands made in the *kerygma*: we must come to a decision; we must repent; we must love (with all the rigour that 'Jesus' imparted to that concept); and we must be crucified with Christ. By any standard, these are tall orders, particularly when (in accordance with the programme of demythologization) no supernatural help (*grace*) is available to us. Far from giving peace, such a gospel could easily become the stuff of a new bondage. And to make matters worse, we face these challenges to decision, penitence and love with little to encourage us. There is no risen Saviour in control of the universe. There is no high priest to sympathize with us in our weaknesses. There is no comfort in bereavement because our dead are simply dead and we have no hope of ever seeing them again. There is no heaven, and all that talk about sharing the glory of Christ is mere whistling in the dark. And there is little purpose in prayer since God never interferes in the time–space continuum. In fact, by eliminating both dogma and eschatology, Bultmann has reduced Christianity to Stoicism. History is hard, but history is all we have, and all we shall ever have. All we can do is take a deep breath and make a decision to be loving and penitent until the candle goes out.

Secondly, Bultmann's *kerygma* appears to be completely detached from historical norms. By his own admission, it is discontinuous, in virtually every detail, with the message of the apostles. What they thought to be central, he deems peripheral. What he deems central, they scarcely mention. But the problem does not end there. There is also a gulf between the early Christian *kerygma* and the preaching of 'Jesus'; and probably another between 'Jesus' and Jesus. As far as Bultmann is concerned, it is not simply difficult to ascertain how the *kerygma* originated. The quest itself is illegitimate, because we would then have found a logical, humanist basis for our faith: 'That would be to tie our faith in the word of God to the results of historical research. The word of preaching confronts us as the word of God. It is not for us to question its credentials. It is we who are questioned, we who are asked whether we will believe the word or reject it.'[10] We cannot say, 'The *kerygma* is true because this is the essential core of what Jesus taught.' It is simply true, in the moment of encounter; and to seek any means of verifying it is to destroy its very nature. Confronted with the *kerygma* we simply know that this is, for us, the last hour, the moment of decision.

Of course, it would be sheer rationalism to seek to rest our faith on evidence alone. But it is sheer *irrationalism* to divorce it from evidence entirely. Unfortunately for himself, Bultmann has already deprived himself of the only solution to this dilemma. He cannot appeal to the inner witness of the Holy Spirit because the Spirit is a myth.

Thirdly, it is extremely difficult to see how, on Bultmann's assumptions, Christ can be deemed unique, or even special. He is obviously not unique in any metaphysical sense. He is not pre-existent. He is not redeemer: the idea that his cross had special redemptive significance is a myth. He cannot be regarded as sinless (after all, we know nothing of his life or personality). He is not unique in being in any meaningful sense post-existent (risen and ascended, head over all things, dwelling with his people, coming again in a glorious *parousia*). Nor can we deem him unique in the sense of his being the object (rather than the example) of Christian faith and devotion. The later Christian *kerygma* certainly equated 'faith' with faith in Jesus Christ, but he himself did not (according to Bultmann, he preached not himself, but God the Father). We cannot say that it was his person that gave significance to his work.[11] We cannot even allege (in possible desperation) that he is unique because the *kerygma* derived, ultimately, from him. We simply cannot be sure. The furthest we can go is that it came from 'Jesus'.

What we are left with is the impression that what is unique is simply the *kerygma*: the act of preaching. This cannot be preaching *about* Jesus because we know nothing of Jesus. Nor can it be preaching which asks for faith in Jesus and trust in his work: such preaching was an invention of the early church. It cannot even be preaching authenticated by its continuity with that of Jesus because we have to remain in ignorance of the historical genesis of this preaching.

What is the meaning of it all? That Christ exists only in the *kerygma*, and indeed never existed anywhere else (although Jesus did)? Or, that we have to live like the early Christians, showing our superiority to them by the fact that our faith, unlike theirs, does not have the comfort of such props as the myths of redemption and eschatology?

John Hick and *The Myth of God Incarnate*

Another scholar who, rejecting Chalcedon, has had to struggle with the question of Christ's uniqueness is John Hick. Hick, and those associated with him in the publication of *The Myth of God Incarnate*, agree fully with the historical scepticism of Bultmann. They also agree that the incarnation is a myth, that is, a story which is not literally true, but which is told to elicit a particular response from the hearers. This particular myth arose, they say, because the tendency to exalt the founder is characteristic of all religions. In the case of Christianity, believers gradually began to apply to their founder concepts he had not applied to himself. This process was completed when 'the Son of God' became 'God the Son'. This transformation is most apparent in the Gospel of John and became indigenized in the church as a result of the uncritical (or pre-critical) acceptance of this gospel. The Council of Nicea put the finishing touches to this by promulgating the doctrine of the *homoousion*: the historical Jesus of Nazareth was one and the same in substance with God the Father. In Hick's view, such a statement is as meaningless as saying that a circle is also a square: 'orthodoxy has never been able to give this idea any content. It remains a form of words without assignable meaning'.[12]

The first response to this must be that it is by no means proven that Jesus never applied to himself the titles and concepts applied to him by later orthodoxy. Such a conclusion requires a discontinuity between Greek Christianity and Aramaic Christianity which Hick simply takes for granted. As we have seen, however, a strong case can be made that the most august Christological titles go back to the original Jerusalem church; and an equally strong case can be made that Jesus saw himself as the pre-existent Son of Man and as the only Son of God. It can even be argued with considerable plausibility that he saw himself as Lord, with all that that title meant in the various strands of Judaism.

This is recognized, at least to some extent, by Hick's associate, Dennis Nineham, who writes: 'no one doubts that a figure very remarkable, morally and in many other ways, is required to explain the appearance of the early Christian church and the writings it produces'.[13] Such an observation justifies C. F. D. Moule's claim that 'development is a better analogy for the genesis of Christology than evolution'.[14] There is no doubt that the Christology of John is an advance on that of Peter's sermon at Pentecost (Acts 2:14–36). But it is not a new species: 'rather, communities and individuals gained new insights into the meaning of what was there all along'.[15] Hick certainly has no right to dismiss without argument the possibility that, whatever the difference in terminology or even in profundity, there is a direct continuity between the later Christology and what was preached at the beginning: between Mark and Chalcedon.

Secondly, Hick's account of the origin of the doctrine of the incarnation is itself highly mythical. It arose, he argues, because people found in Jesus one who answered their own spiritual needs.[16] He evoked total discipleship because he had a 'specially intimate awareness of God', he exuded authority and he had the power to give new life. These qualities led to his being hailed as Messiah and, later, to his being deified.

But why, we may ask, if that is all there was to it, did the myth of incarnation attach itself to this man in particular: a man so apparently uninteresting that his followers remembered nothing of his life or personality? Why was St Paul not deified, or St John, or Muhammad, or John Wesley? Are we really to believe that the eventual development of Christology had no connection at all with Jesus' self-understanding, that he was crucified only because he offered a decisive encounter with God and that men and women laid down their lives for him merely because he enlarged and transformed their conceptions of the deity?

One of many bizarre moments in *The Myth of God Incarnate* is the point where Hick attributes the triumph of the myth of the incarnation to the inherent conservatism of religion.[17] A first-century Jew who believed in the enfleshment of God and in plurality within the godhead was not by any stretch of the imagination a conservative. He was a radical, taking a quantum-leap into a belief-system that contradicted his every instinct. It must have taken an immense force of fact and circumstance to produce such a revolution.

Then there is the problem of the resurrection. Hick can argue with at least some plausibility that the myth of the incarnation appears only at the very close of the apostolic era: even that it was an invention of Nicea. But it is impossible to make such a suggestion with regard to the resurrection. It was there from the beginning, in every strand of the tradition. No fact is more certain. Under the very noses of his executioners, those who had fled from his cross in despair and from his empty tomb in panic, proclaimed that he was risen. Nor is this a matter merely of the empty tomb and the post-resurrection appearances. It is a matter of the most basic elements in Christian self-understanding. Those early disciples believed that they were united to Christ, that he dwelt in them and lived in them and that he imparted such power that through him they could do all things (Phil. 4:13).

Why did this 'myth' develop so early? And why, if the whole tendency of the early Christology was toward Hellenization, did this most un-hellenistic idea of bodily resurrection take root so quickly?

Hick is forced to concede some of the force of this evidence: 'That there was some kind of experience of seeing Jesus after his death, an appearance or appearances which came to be known as his resurrection, seems virtually certain in view of the survival and growth of the tiny original Jesus movement.'[18] But he denies that the resurrection, however understood, can be taken as proof of Jesus' deity. It would not have been seen as such even by his contemporaries. That may be so, although the appearance of the risen Christ certainly had overwhelming evidential force for Saul of Tarsus. But the resurrection gives coherence to the entire New Testament: to the story of the virgin birth, to the miracles, to the transfiguration, to the titles ascribed to Jesus, to the worship accorded him, to Pentecost, to the idea of '*en Christo*', to the perception of his death as an atoning sacrifice, to the expectation of the *parousia*, to the hope of resurrection and to the belief in a final judgment. It explains the disciples' faith and martyrdom, the survival of the church, the expansion of Christianity and the existence of the Gospel of John. Precisely because it is so efficient as a principle of coherence it has a high degree of probability. Without it, Nicea (considered purely as an event) is unintelligible.

But what is the import of this for Christology? At one level, only that historical scholarship requires a Jesus of sufficient magnitude to explain why he became the object not only of intense fascination but of Christian belief. But there is something deeper still. There is cogent evidence that the resurrection is not myth but fact; and if the resurrection be fact, why not the incarnation? It is possible to isolate virtually all the other insignia of majesty in the synoptic tradition and pick them off one by one: the virgin birth, for example, the stilling of the tempest and the transfiguration. But if, in the last chapter of the story, we come across a fact such as the resurrection, then we have to roll back all our earlier scepticism and reinstate every pointer to the glory of this man, Jesus. The empty tomb is the Last Word (even though it has already been spoken); and what it says it says, in vindication of Jesus. It is the assertion of moral order;[19] and the moral order it asserts is one which affirms the crucified blasphemer as the Messiah to whose claims God takes no exception.

Hick objects that the idea of a God–man is as absurd as a square circle. But the comparison is inept. The real question is whether God has the right and the power to become man. Can he live in the form of the creature whom he deliberately created in his own image? Can he practise *kenōsis*? Can he make himself poor? Can he go towards pain and even towards death? Or is there, on the contrary, something which his love will not and cannot do; and if so, is he really God?

Not to me. God is that than which a greater cannot be conceived, and once I stumbled upon the concept of incarnation I could never venerate one who could not, or would not, become man.

The myth of Christian uniqueness

Beside the myth of the incarnation, however, there lies another, according to Hick: the myth of Christian uniqueness.[20] Hick rejects outright the exclusivism according to which God is adequately known only through Jesus Christ and Christ is preached as the one and only source of human salvation. He also rejects, however, the *in*clusivism which recognizes that salvation is taking place within other religions but only because, unknown to their adherents, Christ is secretly working among them.[21] Instead, Hick opts for pluralism, arguing that 'tremendous revelatory moments' lie at the basis of all the great world faiths, that salvation is experienced within all religions, that the superiority of Christianity to other religions is far from self-evident, that we cannot say that all who are saved are saved by Jesus of Nazareth and that Christian mission should aim not at replacing the religious life of 'unbelievers' but merely at deepening it.[22]

In support of this position, Hick offers a series of arguments ranging from the destructive effects of Christian imperialism, through the failure of Christianity to produce more saints than other religions, to the fact that it is absurd to place the whole range of ethnic religions outside the sphere of salvation. 'Is it credible', he asks, 'that the loving God and Father of all men has decreed that only those born within one thread of human history shall be saved?'[23] On the contrary, Hick believes, God is at work within the total religious life of mankind. Christianity is only one of many streams and we must accept the independent validity of other faiths.

This is not the place for an extended response to Hick's arguments.[24] Our concern is limited to those which have a bearing on Christology.

First of all, the belief that Jesus Christ is universal Lord and the only Saviour does not imply that Christianity has a monopoly of truth. It shares many of its values (for example, love of one's neighbour, concern for the poor and belief in the sanctity of life) with other world-faiths. It also shares with some of those faiths a significant body of theological belief. This is particularly true of its relationship with Judaism and Islam, both of which derive from the Old Testament. But it is also true in relation to faiths which have no connection with the Book. Belief in one personal creator and in life after death is not confined only to religions which derive from the Bible.

Such facts, however, are not in the least inconsistent with the claim that Jesus is the only way to God. Christianity has never believed that God reveals himself only through the New Testament or only through Jesus Christ. It has always believed in revelation through the Old Testament; and equally in revelation through creation (see particularly Rom. 1:18–32). The invisible things of God are revealed through the things that are made (Rom. 1:20). This explains the overlap between Christianity and world religions; and the even more significant overlap between Christianity on the one hand and Islam and Judaism on the other. Orthodox Christianity has no difficulty assimilating these facts. It believes that no man knows the Father except through the Son (Mt. 11:27), but it also believes that the Old Testament is revelatory precisely because the Spirit of Christ spoke in the prophets (1 Pet. 1:11); and that creation is revelatory precisely because the aeons were made through the divine Son (Heb. 1:2).

We may even, possibly, go further. John speaks of 'the true light that gives light to every man', and many theologians of unobjectionable orthodoxy have taken this to refer to a work of Christ, the eternal *Logos*, in the heart of Everyman. For example, John Calvin's interpretation of the passage is that 'from this *light* the rays are diffused over all mankind'. He continues:

> For we know that men have this particular excellence which raises them above other animals, that they are endued with reason and intelligence, and that they carry the distinction between right and wrong engraven on their conscience. There is no man, therefore, whom some perception of the eternal *light* does not reach.[25]

The presence of this *light* gives a perfectly coherent explanation, from the standpoint of Christian exclusivism, for all that is true and valuable in the religions of the world.

Yet, when it comes to questions of *fact*, Christianity and those other faiths are in open collision. The central fact, of course, is Christ. If Jews and Muslims are correct in their estimate of him, Christianity collapses. If Christians are correct, then Christian exclusivism is fully justified.[26] This is the crux of the matter. As Newbigin points out, we may be pluralists with regard to values, but we cannot be pluralists with regard to facts.[27] Consequently, it is only by stripping Christianity of its facts and focusing solely on its values that we can incorporate it into any kind of pluralism. To do so, however, is to destroy Christianity, which consists not in the statement of eternal truths but in the telling of a story. In Jesus Christ God took our nature. In Jesus Christ God lived an earthly historical existence. In Jesus Christ God made atonement for our sins. In Jesus Christ God tasted death and conquered death.

It is as impossible to be pluralist on such matters as it is to be pluralist on the date of the Battle of Hastings. Either God was incarnate in Christ or he was not. Either the tomb was empty or it was not. We certainly cannot unite in one global religion those who regard Jesus as the Son of God and those to whom the very idea is repugnant; or those who regard him as the only object of worship and those who see him as only one of many roads to the true Object of Worship.

In the last analysis, there is a blatant hypocrisy in Hick's position: under the language of pluralism there lurks a most dogmatic exclusivism. Far from gazing admiringly on all the world's religions, Hick is standing on the vantage-point of modern western humanism, giving a nod of approval to the few elements in each religion which agree with his own philosophy and dismissing the rest with unconcealed contempt.

'All the great faiths lead to God!' becomes at last, 'A plague on all your houses!' Hick does not believe, with the Jew, that Yahweh is God and that Israel is his people; or with the Muslim that Allah is God, Muhammad his prophet and the Q'ran his infallible revelation; or with the Christian that Jesus is Lord and his cross the one place of atonement. He believes all of these claims to be, equally, nonsense. The real prophets are Hume, Kant and Lessing; the real truth is Liberty, Equality and Fraternity; and the real kingdom came with the Enlightenment. To have Christianity sit in judgment on such a religion is, to Hick, unthinkable; and to entertain even the possibility that the incarnation might be a fact and the resurrection a real event is to put one's mentors to an open shame. How could one ever again look Goethe in the face if one came to believe that a dead man had risen?

Hick's argument is entirely circular: if the resurrection were fact, it would confirm the entire Christian worldview. But it cannot be a fact precisely because it would confirm that worldview. It is easier for a camel to pass through the eye of a needle than for a worshipper of the Enlightenment to enter the kingdom of God.

The Anglican Unitarians

Another modern approach to the problem of Christology is represented by a group of theologians who may, not unfairly, be labelled 'Anglican Unitarians'.[28] This group includes John A. T. Robinson, G. K. W. Lampe, Don Cupitt, John Knox, Norman Pittenger, Denis Nineham and Maurice Wiles.

The main driving force behind their attempted reformulation of Christology is a paranoid aversion to Docetism, leading to an obsessive preoccupation with the humanity of Christ and a tendency to suggest that pre-twentieth century Christology (including that of the ecumenical creeds) minimized, if it did not quite destroy, the manhood of Jesus. Such an outlook is obviously ill at ease with Chalcedon. But the unease does not end there. These scholars deny key features of historical orthodoxy.

First, they deny the doctrine of the incarnation itself. Maurice Wiles, for example, regards the incarnation as only one possible interpretation of the significance of Jesus; one which is not presented directly in Scripture (even in the Gospel of John); and one which has no intelligible meaning.[29]

Secondly, Anglican Unitarians deny the pre-existence of Christ. We have already seen the emphatic denial by John Knox.[30] Similarly,

G. K. W. Lampe dismisses pre-existence as 'a misleading way of acknowledging the divine quality of the human character of Jesus.'[31]

Thirdly, these scholars deny the *post*-existence of Christ. This, again, is particularly explicit in Lampe, who dismisses the ideas of physical resurrection and heavenly ascension and concludes, 'Resurrection is the liberation of the life of the individual Jesus to become the life of all men whom God's Spirit that was in him refashions according to his likeness.'[32]

Fourthly, they deny traditional trinitarian formulations. In Lampe, for example, the distinct personality of the Holy Spirit is lost in the concept of *God as Spirit* which in turn is reduced to the idea of 'the continual descent of transcendent deity into immanence which is involved in the process of creation'.[33] E. L. Mascall charitably suggests that the anti-trinitarianism of such scholars is 'unconfessed'.[34] But Lampe certainly comes within a hairsbreadth of confessing it, declaring that 'the Trinitarian model is in the end less satisfactory for the articulation of our basic Christian experience than the unifying concept of God as Spirit'. He concludes: 'I shall certainly not claim that the views I have expressed are compatible with the way in which the ancient creeds articulate our faith.'[35]

Finally, Lampe and his associates deny the uniqueness of Christ. Maurice Wiles, for instance, recognizes that to abandon the concept of incarnation would inevitably lead to other changes in the outlook of the church. 'The most likely change', he continues, 'would be towards a less exclusive insistence on Jesus as *the* way for all peoples and all cultures.' This, he contends, does not involve the conclusion that all religions are of equal value. Nevertheless, 'It does rule out the judgment of the superiority of one religion over another in advance of an informed knowledge of both faiths. Such a change can only be regarded as a gain.'[36] Lampe speaks to similar effect:

> God in his creativity, that is, God as Spirit, addresses and inspires all men everywhere at all times, enabling the fruit of the Spirit to grow in them. The modes of his approach to the human spirit are manifold, including non-Christian faiths ... The mission of the Church is misconceived if its purpose is supposed to be to bring God into areas of the world from which he has hitherto been absent, or to introduce him to people who have until now been strangers to him.[37]

The logical path for such scholars to follow would be to renounce

Christianity altogether since on their premises it is impossible to regard Jesus as Lord or to worship him as God. How far, after all, can we bow the knee to one who no longer exists; and who, even when he did, was not at all unique? Yet none of these Anglicans has taken this road. They have remained within the church; they have continued to profess themselves Christians; and they are persistent in seeing a divine quality in Jesus. How is all this to be understood?

One clue lies in the peculiar tendency of Anglican modernism to represent God and man as continuous, if not indeed indistinguishable.[38] According to this point of view, *divine* and *human* are not mutually exclusive terms. On the contrary, God and man are indissolubly related, so that in the highest human life we find the disclosure of the inmost nature of the divine. We may even say (as H. D. A. Major did) that 'there is only one substance of the Godhead and the Manhood'.[39]

Important consequences follow from this approximation of the human and the divine. First, on this premise God is revealed in every man (and woman); secondly, it becomes impossible to believe that God is fully incarnate in Jesus Christ and not incarnate in anyone else; thirdly, it is by being Man that Jesus reveals God; and, finally, the justification for according him divine worship is merely that he is the highest representative of humanity.

The influence of this idea is clear in the thinking of more recent Anglican Unitarians. It explains how Lampe, for example, can speak of 'the divine quality of the human life of Jesus'.[40] It also underlies J. A. T. Robinson's *The Human Face of God*. Robinson argues that Jesus was totally and utterly a man: a man who had never been other than a man or more than a man.[41] But this man 'so completely embodies what was from the beginning the meaning and purpose of God's self-expression ... that it could be said, and had to be said, of that man, "He was God's man", or "God was in Christ", or even that he *was* "God for us".'[42] Divorced from their context such statements suggest considerable eminence for Christ. But *in* their context they are meaningless: God was in Christ without his ever having been more than a man.

Two responses may be made to this.

First, the belief that God is *other* than man surely requires no defence. All religion rests on the fact that in the presence of God man feels himself confronted by the *mysterium tremendum*. If *Creator* and *creature* do not represent a radical qualitative difference, words have no meaning.

Secondly, to the extent that Anglican Unitarians share the assumptions of radical gospel criticism they have cut themselves off completely from the humanity of Jesus and thus rendered their own Christological method inoperable. Maurice Wiles recognizes this. Having quoted R. H. Lightfoot's famous dictum that 'the form of the earthly no less than of the heavenly Christ is for the most part hidden from us', he concludes: 'Even if Jesus be the Son of God incarnate and his life was a humanly perfect one, that perfect manhood is not directly available to us as an absolutely authoritative model for our own lives.'[43]

This idea of continuity between the human and the divine, however, is only one element among many used by these scholars to justify their clinging to some respect for Jesus while rejecting the orthodox Christian view of his status and identity.

For example, in several of these writings there is a strong strain of adoptionism. This is most apparent in Robinson and Lampe, although it takes a different form in each. According to Robinson, Jesus was a man who became in some sense God. For example, commenting on the teaching of St Paul, he writes, 'It is not a heavenly being who becomes human, so much as a man who enters into the office of Son of God marked out for him from all eternity.'[44] His conclusion is unashamedly adoptionist: although Jesus was never anything more than a man he nevertheless 'embodied the divine initiative and presence so completely that he was declared at his baptism and confirmed at his resurrection to be everything God himself was'.[45]

This really is impossible. How could Christ be declared to be God if he was never anything more than a man? And how could he be 'everything God himself was' if he was not pre-existent?

In Lampe's formulation there is no becoming, no entering into office, no declaring and no confirming. Instead, Christ is God only in the sense that he is the focal point of the continuous descent and ascent of transcendent deity. In other words, he was a Spirit-filled man (or a God-inspired man: Lampe rejected the idea of the distinct personal existence of the Holy Spirit). This was not unique to Jesus, however. In creation 'there is a continuous *kenōsis* of God as Spirit'[46] in the sense that 'God is continuously involved in the evolution of the cosmos and especially in the emergence within it of free persons with whom he enters into communion at the personal level.'[47] Christ is only one such free person. He may be seen as a special moment within an everlasting continuum but not as 'an altogether fresh and discontinuous intervention of God in history'.[48] The same idea can be expressed in terms of *Logos* or *Wisdom*, but the result is the same: 'To recognize in Jesus the presence of the divine Logos or Wisdom is to acknowledge that God's action in Jesus is one with his continuing creativity from the beginning.'[49]

It is remarkable that theologians should seek contemporary relevance by trying to fuse a twentieth-century programme of demythologization with the myths of primitive adoptionism. The formulations of Robinson and Lampe are no more coherent than those of Theodotus or Paul of Samosata. A man cannot be or become God; and at the end of all the coruscating phraseology that is all that we have: a man, Jesus.

This is fatal to Christianity for two reasons.

First, it illegitimates the worship of Jesus. He cannot on such premises be the object of our faith or the one for whom we renounce all or the one to whom we pray or the one to whom we sing hymns and offer doxologies. He cannot be our *Kyrios* and we cannot be his *douloi*. At the very most we can only worship God through him. To worship him himself would be idolatry.

Secondly, adoptionism means that it is not God himself who comes towards us in Jesus Christ, taking our nature, sharing our pain and bearing our sins. It is at best only a *simulacrum* of the divine. The great invitation, 'Come to me, all who are heavy laden!' would no longer be the voice of the divine; and union with Christ would no longer mean union with God (assuming we could attach any meaning at all to the notion of *en Christō* in a thought-world where Christ has no post-existence). We could not even see Christ as in any meaningful sense the revelation of God, since denial of his eternal deity means that 'we could not think of God as being in himself what he appears to be in his manifestation toward us in Jesus Christ'.[50]

We may take matters further still. Robinson borrows from Hick the idea that we can express Jesus' relation to God in terms of *homoagapē*: 'he is *homoagapē*, of one love, with the Father'.[51] But this is precisely what we cannot say if we hold that he was no more than a man (even an inspired man or a Spirit-filled man). The *homoagapē* requires the *homoousion*. Without that, we cannot say that God loved me and gave himself for me (Gal. 2:20); or that the love of God constrains us (2 Cor. 5:14); or that God loved the church and gave himself for it (Eph. 5:25). We can say only that a man called Jesus loved us (adding, pathetically, a man who no longer exists, having been destroyed by the forces of evil). Such a position may be true, but if true it is fatal to Christianity.

Functional Christology

In the last analysis Anglican Unitarianism has to find refuge in a functional Christology: a development prompted by Oscar Cullmann's insistence that the New Testament has little interest in ontology, being concerned only with the divine action and self-communication: 'all abstract speculation about the "natures" of Christ is not only a useless undertaking, but actually an improper one. By the very nature of the New Testament Logos one cannot speak of him apart from the action of God.'[52] Accordingly, we can speak of the deity of Christ only in the sense that he is the centre of divine revelation: 'Jesus Christ was God in so far as God reveals himself to the world.'[53]

In response to Roman Catholic critics, Cullmann later made plain that his brand of functionalism meant only that the New Testament had no interest in the being of Christ outside of his mediatorial work and no interest in his natures apart from their manifestation in the history of salvation. He also made plain that New Testament functionalism presupposed 'the divine being and the divine person of the pre-existent Christ'. Besides, far from seeing any opposition between Chalcedon and the New Testament, Cullmann insisted that, 'The moment the question of the natures, though it is not itself present in the New Testament, is raised, the dogma formulated by this Council corresponds to what the Christology of the New Testament presupposes.'[54]

For Robinson and Lampe, however, functionalism is an alternative to Chalcedon and its confession of the pre-existent deity of Christ. For the former, Jesus embodies 'the divine initiative and saving presence' and reveals, through his self-surrender, 'the glory of God as utterly gracious, self-giving love'.[55] The latter declares: 'I believe in the divinity of our Lord and Saviour Jesus Christ in the sense that the one God, the Creator and Saviour Spirit, revealed himself and acted decisively for us in Jesus.'[56]

We cannot, however, separate ontology from revelation in this way. Christ reveals God only because he is God: the revealer, the revelation and the revealed one are the same. This is the point made with repeated emphasis by Karl Barth in discussing the root of the doctrine of the Trinity: 'Revelation is *Dei loquentis persona*' (the person of God speaking/God speaking in person); 'revelation is the self-interpretation of this God'; 'Revelation in the Bible means the self-unveiling, imparted to men, of the God who according to his nature cannot be unveiled to man.'[57] The point is made even more forcefully by Wolfhart Pannenberg, who insists that we cannot set 'presence as appearance' over against 'identity of essence'.[58] On the contrary, we can define revelation as the self-disclosure of God only if appearance and essence belong together: 'the concept of God's self-revelation contains the idea that the Revealer and what is revealed are identical'.[59] This lies at the very core of Pannenberg's Christology. Jesus reveals God because he is

God: 'If God is revealed through Jesus Christ, then who or what God is becomes defined only by the Christ event. Then Jesus belongs to the definition of God, and thus to his divinity, to his essence.'[60]

This clearly accords with the New Testament presentation: Jesus reveals God because he is the *Logos* and as the *Logos* he is divine (Jn. 1:1). We cannot reverse this and say instead that he is divine because he reveals God. He was *Logos* and God 'in the beginning' (Jn. 1:1). This is why the Johannine Christ can say, 'Anyone who has seen me has seen the Father' (Jn. 14:9). But such an emphasis is not confined to John. The Christ of Hebrews, through whom God has spoken his last word, is one who as Son is the brightness of the Father's glory and the express image of his being (Heb. 1:3, KJV). The Pauline Christ is the form of God, the image of God, the likeness of God and the glory of God. These expressions are all highly visual, yet all suggest that Christ gives God visibility only because of who and what he is. He is the self-disclosure of God: God in his revelation.

In the same way, the other functions of Christ are clearly rooted in ontology. This is true, for example, of his role in creation. It was through him that God made the ages: but it was through him as Son (Heb. 1:2). Similarly, his *authority* is rooted in his identity. He has authority over all flesh because the Father has crowned him with the glory he had as Son before the world came into being. Even his work of atonement comes under the same rubric. He is himself the propitiation (1 Jn. 2:2); and his blood cleanses from all sin precisely because it is the blood of the Son of God (1 Jn. 1:7).

Whether as prophet, priest or king, then, Christ's authority and competence rest four-square on his identity. He can reveal, reconcile and rule only because first of all he is the Son of God. Otherwise, we merely return to Arianism with its contention that the Son was created by God to perform divine functions such as creation.

Cullmann's contention that the New Testament has no interest in the 'natures' of Christ, concerning itself only with his actions, hardly fits the facts of the case. Mark prefaces his story by defining it as the beginning of the gospel of Jesus Christ, the Son of God; all the accounts of the baptism contain the heavenly acknowledgment of Jesus as the divine Son; the accounts of the transfiguration do the same; and John's Gospel was written with the express purpose of convincing readers that Jesus is the Son of God.

The epistles, too, contain significant statements on the identity of Jesus, some of these (Rom. 1:3f.; 9:5; Phil. 2:5–8) deliberately distinguishing his divine status from his human and several of them

(Rom. 9:5; Tit. 2:13; 2 Pet. 1:1) containing explicit assertions of his deity.

Furthermore, not only does the New Testament contain the materials out of which a doctrine of the incarnation can be built (by, for example, the Council of Chalcedon): it contains the explicit doctrine of the incarnation itself, declaring that the Word was made flesh, that the One who was in the form of God took the form of a servant and that all the fullness of the godhead dwelt in Christ bodily.[61]

Functional Christology focuses on the activities ascribed to Christ. It would have kept itself from serious imbalance if it had also focused on the activities ascribed to the church. The church worships him, invoking him in prayer and pouring out its heart in doxology addressed to him as Lord. If Christ is merely God's agent; if he is merely *in loco Dei*; if he is no more than God's vicar and ambassador: then all such worship is idolatrous. When our knees bow we need a confession that is ontological: Jesus Christ is Lord.

Christology and Process Philosophy

Underlying Anglican Unitarianism is a deep-seated mistrust of the idea of divine intervention in human affairs. This is one reason why Maurice Wiles, for example, is suspicious of the idea of incarnation: it grew up in a context where belief in divine intervention was widespread.[62] G. K. W. Lampe expressed similar reservations: the model of a descent and an ascent of the Son of God serves only to confuse our Christology; the affirmation of Christ's descent into this world from another is mythological; and,

> We should try to set the 'Christ-event' within the perspective of a continuous process of which we can discern neither the beginning nor the end, and to avoid the idea that in Christ God has broken into that creative process in which he is always immanent, and radically altered his own relationship to his human creation.[63]

The strongest assertions of this position come, however, from W. N. Pittenger, an Anglican who sought to marry the modernism of Hastings Rashdall and J. F. Bethune-Baker[64] to the Process Philosophy of Whitehead and Hartshorne. In accordance with this metaphysic, Pittenger objects that, 'The language which has been used about Jesus Christ has almost consistently been such that he has been made to look like an "intrusion" or "eruption" from outside into the sphere of human life and experience.'[65] If, as Process Philosophy alleges, God and his creation are 'in continued and intimate relationship' then what we need is a Christology 'which makes it possible to state clearly and definitely that our Lord is not an intruder into the creation, a "divine rescue expedition", but is tied in with and expressive of the whole God-world and God-man relationship, even while he is also genuinely new and the saviour from sin'.[66] Pittenger even contends that the idea of the incarnation as an 'intrusion' 'has no conceivable meaning save on a deistic conception of God as himself "outside" the world'. On the contrary, he argues, 'the Incarnation neither demands nor implies "miracle" in the vulgar sense of the disruptive violation of the relatively settled order of nature which is God's way of working in his world'.[67]

This line of argument appears to rest on *a priori* reasoning as to what is possible and not possible in God's relations with the world. It says, in effect, 'God cannot'; and to this extent, as B. L. Hebblethwaite points out, it is an objection to God *tout court*.[68] This is all the more precarious in view of the huge questions about space and time raised by modern physics. Who is in a position to pontificate about God's relation to either when as yet we have no clear idea as to what the concepts actually mean? What is possible for God can be known only through revelation; and, if Jesus Christ is the revelation of God, it is absolutely certain that God is capable of effecting a unique entry to a particular place at a particular time. He is capable of advent; and he is capable of *parousia*.

In any case, to represent the incarnation as the arrival of an alien intruder is to parody the position of orthodoxy. The idea that God is present in his creation always and everywhere, preserving and governing, lies at the very heart of Christian theology. Besides, the doctrine of the immanence of the *Logos* is most prominent precisely in those parts of the New Testament which give most emphasis to the incarnation. The very Paul who tells the Colossians that all the fullness of the godhead dwells in Jesus bodily also tells them that in him all things are held together (Col. 1:17); and John, the most eloquent preacher of incarnation, reminds us not only that the *Logos* indwells every man (Jn. 1:9), but also that when he came into the world he came to what was his own (Jn. 1:11). The intervention, then, if intervention it is, is not that of an alien or outsider, but that of the Maker and Preserver who never let go of his creation. He comes to it as a Father coming to his children. In such a light, the incarnation is entirely appropriate.

Pittenger's position reflects the early twentieth-century mind-set of the natural sciences, thirled to the idea of physical uniformity and regularity. Such an attitude is impatient of any kind of uniqueness or singularity: events must fall out in predictable sequence and according to a regular pattern. It is interesting to turn from this to John Polkinghorne's reminder that 'an important criterion of the personal is its uniqueness'. 'Personal experience', he continues,' does not repeat itself – we hear a Beethoven quartet differently each time we listen to it, even if we play the same disc. On the other hand, impersonal experience is essentially repeatable, because it is relatively invulnerable to minor variations of context.'[69]

Precisely because God is personal he is able to do what is unique and unrepeatable. He can create something radically new (man). He can divide the Red Sea. He can become flesh. He can choose to forgive sin. Divine faithfulness, as Polkinghorne points out, is not a kind of dreary uniformity: 'There may well have been throughout (cosmic history) … a succession of particular critical points at which divine influence was exercised in particular ways.'[70]

There is nothing capricious about such intervention, especially if we recognize that the moral universe is in a disordered state and in urgent need not only of continuous care but of divine redemption. Such a redemption would inevitably involve a series of singularities, and against such a background the incarnation is perfectly intelligible, especially when we remember that man is made in the image of God and that, therefore, in becoming man and in living among men God was relating to that element in creation which most closely resembles himself.

But why should such a special presence as is involved in the incarnation be necessary at all? There have been those in the Christian tradition who have viewed the incarnation as the result of a divine impulse to be one with creation and who have argued, consequently, that it would have occurred even if man had never sinned. But the prevailing conviction has been that the incarnation was a remedial act made necessary by the fall. Significantly, rejection of the idea of an intrusive incarnation usually goes hand in hand with either a demythologizing, or an outright denial, of the fall. But this is to rend the incarnation out of its biblical context and deprive it of its primary rationale. The total credal position is not that Christ descended out of heaven but that he descended *for us men and for our salvation.* This presupposes that the world is not in a normal state (facile tolerance of the Manichean notion that the world was always 'fallen' and therefore essentially evil is one of the most intriguing features of modern theology). It also presupposes that man is in a desperate plight. Indeed, we might well put to those who deny the incarnation the point made long ago by Anselm: *Nondum considerasti quantum ponderis sit peccatum* ('You haven't yet realized the gravity of sin'). Behind the drama of the incarnation there lies the catastrophe of the fall. The one is the divine response to the other. We might well admit that if we were living in a normal universe a step of the magnitude of the incarnation would have been impossible. But we are not. We are living in a world ruined by sin. If we ignore or deny or minimize this fact we shall never see the appropriateness of the incarnation. But if we admit it, the claim makes perfect sense. We had to be 'rescued' (Col. 1:13) from the power of darkness, and that could be achieved only by the coming of the Son of God to grapple personally with the forces of evil.

This rejection of the idea of redemptive divine intervention rests at last on a worldview which precludes all catastrophism and clings instead to an evolutionism which argues that progress is achieved by a long series of minute, imperceptible changes. Even in its own proper sphere (biology) such a paradigm faces serious difficulties. Unfortunately, its advocates have sought to apply it far beyond Darwin's original intention: to politics, art and technology, among other things. Yet a moment's reflection will show that progress in all these fields has been achieved not by evolution but by revolution. This accords perfectly with the Bible's portrayal of the relation between God and his universe. Indeed, it is very curious to hear Process theologians repudiating simultaneously both Deism and Interventionism. Darwinian evolution (the backdrop to the theology of all the Anglican Unitarians) was unashamedly deistic: natural selection was completely ateleological and achieved its results purely accidentally by means of long series of random mutations. God was entirely absent from the evolutionary process (that is what made the hypothesis so attractive). In Christianity, by contrast, God is not only a constant invisible presence: as Redeemer he is an incorrigible interventionist. The reason, is not, however, that he botched the original work of creation, but that man by his sin threw the moral universe into chaos. The Maker had to take dramatic remedial action. The great moment of incarnation-atonement is the climax of that action.

Christ in Liberation Theology

At first sight, Liberation Theology seems an unlikely soil for an innovative Christology. For one thing, its leading exponents are all

Roman Catholic clergy, committed to the tradition of the church (including the Formula of Chalcedon). For another, the movement professes little interest in purely theological questions; and even when it does take them up, its natural preoccupation is with the work, rather than with the person, of Christ.

Nevertheless, Liberation Theology, as Jon Sobrino, one of its most articulate exponents, points out, does have profound Christological implications.[71] Indeed, it is rooted in a very specific Christology, derived from Marx's principle that we come to know reality only insofar as we come to realize the necessity of transforming it.[72] This means that Christ is not known through 'static contemplation' or cultic activity. We know him only as we follow him, particularly as we involve ourselves in implementing his programme.[73] From this standpoint, *orthopraxis* is more important than *orthodoxy*.

In the precise context of South America this means that we know him only within the struggle for liberation. This liberation is sharply distinguished from its alternatives: *exploitation* (what the poor have long suffered at the hands of their oppressors); and *development* (offered by modern capitalism, but serving only as a palliative which in the long term exacerbates dependency). The great paradigm of liberation is the exodus, understood by such theologians as Gustavo Gutiérrez in unashamedly political terms:

> The liberation of Israel is a political action. It is the breaking away from a situation of despoliation and misery and the beginning of the construction of a just and fraternal society ... The Exodus is the long march towards the promised land in which Israel can establish a society free from misery and alienation.[74]

Sobrino is equally explicit. Jesus' most fundamental gesture, he writes, 'is taking sides with human beings in a concrete situation where the existing politico-religious structure has dehumanised people. It has turned those with power into brutes, while alienating and oppressing everyone else.'[75]

This preoccupation with Christ as Liberator gives a sharp focus to the Christology of Sobrino and his associates. Whatever is unrelated to liberation is ignored and the emphasis falls, instead, on those elements in the life and teaching of Jesus (particularly the resurrection and the kingdom of God) which might serve as paradigms of liberation, and on those of his activities which highlight practical ways of achieving liberation.

The net effect of these concerns is that Liberation Theology is interested only in the Jesus of history. This preoccupation is especially noteworthy in Sobrino, who argues that, 'Whenever Christian faith focuses one-sidedly on the Christ of faith and wittingly or unwittingly forgets the historical Jesus, and to the extent it does that, it loses its specific character as Christian faith and turns into religion.'[76] This leads to an intriguingly ambivalent attitude towards the resurrection on the part of Liberation theologians. On the one hand, it is 'the major event that serves as the ultimate ground for faith in Jesus of Nazareth'. On the other, it is

> what makes it possible for Christian faith to stop being Christian and turn into a version of religion. I want to show historically that the most radical temptation facing Christianity is the temptation to focus one-sidedly on the risen Christ, and that the way to overcome the temptation is to go back once again to the historical Jesus.[77]

The reason for this approach is not, however, any special interest in the historical Jesus as such, but rather the basic preoccupation of Liberation Theology, namely, the need to transform the socio-political situation in Latin America. The Christ of faith is, rightly or wrongly, deemed irrelevant to this task and the stress falls, therefore, on the historical Jesus, seen as the pathway to liberation. Pressed to its particulars, this means that it is the historical Jesus who both defines the meaning of liberation and illustrates how it may be achieved.

There is much in Liberation Theology that one may happily applaud, particularly its bias towards the poor.[78] Jesus himself was one of the poor, he pronounced the poor blessed and he stood in a prophetic tradition which had long argued the case for the oppressed. Besides, in a seminal definition of his own ministry he had declared (in the words of Isaiah) that the Lord had sent him to preach good news to the poor, to proclaim freedom for the prisoners and to release the oppressed (Lk. 4:18). His public ministry ended on exactly the same note, when he closed his Olivet discourse by affirming that at the last judgment men's destinies would depend on their attitudes to the hungry, the thirsty, the naked, the sick and the imprisoned (Mt. 25:35f.).

Similarly, Liberation Theology is correct to draw attention to the political attitudes of Jesus.[79] Far from adopting the detached stance beloved of Evangelical clergy, Jesus clearly conducted himself in such a way as to risk being confused with the Zealots, the advocates of violent

Jewish revolution. This appears, for example, in Acts 5:33ff., where Gamaliel specifically compares him to the notorious insurrectionists, Theudas and Judas the Galilean. Yet he never endorsed the Zealots, nor indeed any of the political parties of his day. Instead, he publicly confronted all the major power-blocs in Jewish society. He refused to sanction the narrow nationalism of the Zealots, warned them against resisting evil (Mt. 5:39) and told them to pay tribute to Caesar (Mt. 22:21). He called Herod a fox (Lk. 13:32), classed the tax-gatherers with the heathen (Mt. 18:17), roundly denounced the Pharisees and argued that Caesar was to be obeyed only as far as was consistent with the prerogatives of God. He never condoned unreserved submission to the state.

As Leonardo Boff points out, none of this constituted a specific programme.[80] Instead, it prescribed an attitude. 'His most fundamental gesture', writes Sobrino, 'is taking sides with human beings in a concrete situation where the existing politico-religious structure has dehumanised people.'[81]

The reassertion of this stress on 'the least of these brethren of mine' is most welcome, particularly after centuries of blind support for the forces of 'law and order', regardless of deeper issues of social justice. As Jurgen Moltmann points out, Christ became the brother of the despised, abandoned and oppressed: 'Thus Christian theology must be worked out amongst these people and with them. It is the "contemporary" theology when its thought is conducted in the sufferings of the present time, and this means in concrete terms, amongst and with those who suffer in this society.'[82]

Dietrich Bonhoeffer gave memorable expression to this Christian perspective, just before being swept away by the torrents of hatred and terror which marked National Socialism. 'There remains', he wrote, 'an experience of incomparable value. We have for once learned to see the great events of world history from below, from the perspective of the outcast, the suspects, the maltreated, the powerless, the oppressed, the reviled – in short, from the perspective of those who suffer.'[83]

Other aspects of Liberation Theology also have their attraction: for example, the insistence that sin is not merely a matter of individual action but also of social structures.[84] This problem is particularly acute when, as in Latin America, the oppressive structures have been erected by professed Christians and even claim the personal sanction of Christ. In such a context, the preacher of redemption must inevitably become a preacher of political liberation, not least because of the tendency of power to corrupt all who hold it, including the redeemed.

It would be a serious mistake, too, to dismiss Liberationists as theologically unsophisticated. On the contrary, Sobrino and Boff are master theologians, both at the level of erudition and at the level of creativity. This is particularly evident in Boff's *Trinity and Society*.[85] Among its many helpful contributions is the suggestion that the Trinity (particularly the idea of perichoresis) may serve as a model in the struggle for liberation. He writes:

> For those who have faith, the trinitarian communion between the divine Three, the union between them in love and vital interpenetration, can serve as a source of inspiration, as a utopian goal that generates models of successively diminishing differences. This is one of the reasons why I am taking the concept of perichoresis as the structural axis of these thoughts. It speaks to the oppressed in their quest and struggle for integral liberation. The community of Father, Son and Holy Spirit becomes the prototype of the human community dreamed of by those who wish to improve society and build it in such a way as to make it into the image and likeness of the Trinity.[86]

Nevertheless, to the extent that it is proposed as a self-contained alternative to the church's traditional understanding of the gospel, Liberation Theology is open to serious criticism. For the moment, we must limit ourselves to those which relate to Christology.

First, it is unbalanced in its treatment of Jesus' attitude to the poor. As Yves Congar points out, 'we cannot, in the name of the Gospel, somehow canonise poverty in the economic sense of the word'.[87] It may have been true, in the early phase of his ministry, that 'the common people heard him gladly', but it is no less true that at its close they cried, 'Crucify! Crucify!' (Mk. 15:13); and as he suffered on the cross the ordinary passers-by joined the religious leaders in the great chorus of derision (Mk. 15:29). On the other hand, Jesus did not refuse to associate with the rich and the powerful. He ate with tax-collectors as well as with sinners, made friends with Zacchaeus, availed himself of the hospitality of Lazarus' home in Bethany and numbered among his associates women of sufficient wealth to own expensive perfumes and afford spices to anoint his body (Mk. 16:1). He was admired by one member of the Sanhedrin, Nicodemus; and laid in the tomb of another, Joseph of Arimathea.

None of this comports with the picture of a man who refused on principle to associate with any but paupers and vagrants. Indeed, Ruth

Page is perfectly right to remind us that many of Jesus' stories and parables contain 'authority figures' with whom the property-owning classes could easily identify.[88] The parables of the talents, the prodigal son, the labourers in the vineyard and even the good Samaritan presuppose a *bourgeois* background, where the key figures are individuals of wealth and substance. The same is true of many of Jesus' healings. Such beneficiaries as Jairus and the Centurion (Mt. 8:5) were hardly members of an underclass. The truth is not that Jesus was concerned only with the poor, but that he was completely indifferent to distinctions of class.

We must not take this to mean, however, that the church should speak equally for the rich and for the poor. It must have a bias in favour of the oppressed, and even overstate their case, precisely because the rich have the resources (financial, political and communicative) to speak for themselves. What we have to guard against is such revolution as turns the former oppressor into the cruelly oppressed.

Secondly, Liberation Theology shows a surprising willingness to endorse some of the key concepts of the older Liberalism. This is particularly true of the insistence, found repeatedly in Sobrino, that Jesus 'did not preach about himself'.[89] Only the most radical historical scepticism can hold such a position. Even the ministry of John the Baptist had its focus in the person of Jesus: 'After me will come one more powerful than I, the thongs of whose sandals I am not worthy to stoop down and untie' (Mk.1:7). Jesus clearly focused on his own role at crucial points in his ministry. At the close of the Sermon on the Mount, for example, he made clear that what will be absolutely decisive for our final destiny is whether he 'knew' us (Mt. 7:23). Similarly, in Matthew 11:28 he extended his invitation in the most personal terms: 'Come to me, all you who are weary and burdened, and I will give you rest.' Even in the conclusion of the great Olivet discourse, where the focus fell so clearly on issues of social justice, the underlying thrust is Christological. The Son of Man will sit on his throne, all nations will be gathered before him and even the poor derive their significance from the fact that they are his brothers and sisters (Mt. 25:1–46).

This is why, before it is anything else (even before it is liberation) Christianity is worship: the worship of Jesus. We forsake all and follow him. We call him Lord. Indeed, the effect of Sobrino's view of the preaching of Jesus is to dissolve the problem of Christology rather than to solve it. The problem is precisely that he preached himself, even to the extent of making himself equal with God. What kind of man was that?

Thirdly, Liberation Theology works with an indefensible understanding of the kingdom of God. Sobrino declares this to be the movement's 'most all-embracing theological concept' and goes on to define it as follows: 'The Kingdom of God expresses man's utopian longing for liberation from everything that alienates him, factors such as anguish, pain, hunger, injustice and death, and not only man but all creation.' It is impossible to reconcile this with key elements of the New Testament description of the kingdom. For one thing, the kingdom is a present reality: it has come in the person of Christ.[90] It would be quite impossible to translate Mark.1:15 as, 'The hour has come! Utopia is here! Repent and believe the gospel!' Similarly, a utopian, this-worldly understanding of the kingdom is incompatible with Jesus' insistence to Nicodemus that the only way of entering it is by means of radical, inward new birth (Jn. 3:3). Liberation from hunger and poverty can be achieved by political means (as has happened, for example, in both Ireland and the Scottish Highlands). But to enter the kingdom of God we must be born from above.

It is clear, too, that whatever Jesus promised to those who entered his kingdom, it was not Utopia. On the contrary, to follow him was to sign one's own death-warrant: 'Take up your cross and follow me.' Far from guaranteeing economic liberation discipleship as envisaged by Jesus involved renouncing houses and lands for his sake (Mt. 19:29). Few of the early disciples escaped the promised deprivations. The glory of the kingdom lay on the far side of a tribulation which no believer could circumvent (Acts 14:22). This means that we must leave the Beatitude, 'Blessed are you who are poor!' (Lk. 6:20) just as it stands. They are blessed while they are poor, not once they have entered Utopia. This does not, of course, give us a right to abuse the dictum, 'The poor you will always have with you' (Mt. 26;11). It remains incumbent on all those possessed of power (including the institutional church) to assume responsibility for the elimination of poverty and injustice. Nevertheless, the achievement of such a goal would not itself be equivalent to the establishment of the kingdom.

Above all, however, Liberation Theology cannot give a coherent theology of the cross. This is not to say either that it lacks interest in the subject or that it handles it superficially. Sobrino devotes over fifty pages to the question of *The Death of Jesus and Liberation in history*.[91] Much of this discussion follows the lines laid down by Moltmann in *The Crucified God*: 'on the cross of Jesus God himself is crucified. The Father suffers the death of the Son and takes upon himself all the pain and suffering of history'.[92] In this way, God becomes part of the process of protest, rather than remaining above it. Even more important, the cross becomes our profoundest revelation of God: 'What is manifest on the cross is the internal structure of God himself.'[93] What exactly this 'internal structure' is, however, is far from clear. It appears to mean that God lets himself be affected by history through the Son; that the world is gathered up into the love between the Father, the Son and the Spirit; that from this love there flows a force which will ensure that 'external history can be a history of love rather than a history of domination'; and that the cross incorporates us as human individuals into God's own attitude to the world.

So much I can understand. But when Sobrino writes that, 'The eternal love between Father and Son is seen to be historically mediated in the presence of evil, and hence it takes the paradoxical form of abandonment', I am lost; and in that lostness I have lost, I think, the core of his argument.

There is much more in the same vein, exploring the implications of the abandonment of the Son by the Father. No justice is done, however, to the centrality of the death of Christ. According to the New Testament, Christ came into the world with the deliberate intention of sacrificing his life as a ransom for the many (Mk. 10:45). Sobrino, by contrast, sees the cross as in some sense the failure of his mission: 'The death he died was not only the death of his person but also the death of his cause.'[94] It is difficult to find even traces of such a point of view anywhere in the New Testament. In Gethsemane, the cross is 'the cup', the will of his Father (Mk. 14:36). In John's Gospel, it is his glorification: 'Now is the Son of Man glorified' (Jn. 13:31).

But the construction of the cross as the failure of Jesus' mission rests on something deeper: the inability of Liberation Theology to do justice to the specific link between the cross and liberation. The cross itself liberates. The New Testament terminology of redemption is steeped in this idea. The cross is a ransom. It redeems the captive. It buys back the slave. Hence such language as St Paul's, 'Christ redeemed us from the curse of the law by becoming a curse for us' (Gal. 3:13); or again, 'It is for freedom that Christ has set us free. Stand firm, then, and do not let yourselves be burdened again by a yoke of slavery' (Gal. 5:1); or yet again, 'In him we have redemption through his blood, the forgiveness of sins' (Eph. 1:7).

The fact alluded to in all these passages is that on the cross the definitive act of liberation has already occurred. Christ has paid the ransom. Christ has conquered the darkness. Christ has bound the powers. Christ has secured the ministry of the Holy Spirit. As a result, his people are free from the guilt of sin, the power of sin and the fear of its consequences. They have no Master but God; and to him they are not slaves but sons and daughters.

It is easy to say, 'Ah! But all that refers only to individual sin and leaves the sinful structures unchallenged!' It remains true, nonetheless, that those so liberated are free, as Paul was free and Martin Luther was free. It is also true that those who are thus free become themselves an irresistible force for social change. They can never themselves become oppressors of others; or remain idle spectators of the oppression of others; or be cowed into silence by the blusterings of earthly potentates. The saving grace which produces free individuals also produces free communities. Was this not what happened when Martin Luther's theology of the cross swept across Europe in the sixteenth century? Where it found a foothold it created spiritual freemen who rejoiced in the priesthood of all believers, accepted responsibility for their own religion and inevitably went on to claim responsibility for their own political destiny. The Christian is free: free because Christ died. It is the life lived out of this freedom (including our prophetic witness, our cross-bearing and our willingness to be nothing) which changes the sinful structures.

But the Christian is not *moving towards* liberation. He is starting from liberation, because he has already been translated from the Empire of Darkness to the Commonwealth of Love (Col. 1:13).

Precisely because they lack a theology of atonement Liberation Theologians have at last nothing to offer but exemplarism. Rather than being himself the ever-active, triumphant Liberator, Jesus is reduced to the point where his function is merely to offer a paradigm of liberation. He shows us how it should be done, bequeathing to us a praxis and telling us that if we put it into effect liberation will follow. Or, as Sobrino puts it, 'faith in Jesus Christ attains its maximum radicality when we accept his path as normative and traverse it'.[95]

We must not be tempted to respond by denying the importance of the example of Jesus. God's most basic concern is to conform us to the image of his Son (Rom. 8:29), we are under obligation to think the way Jesus thought (Phil. 2:5) and we have to walk in his steps (1 Pet. 2:21). Confronted with such teaching, we have to be concerned for the poor and open our mouths not only to preach the gospel but also to bear witness against injustice and oppression.

But we must immediately add two further considerations.

First, in one crucial area of his praxis, we cannot follow the example of Jesus. When he gave his life as a ransom for the many he personally paid the price and bore the full cost of liberation. We need not and cannot follow him there. The world is already redeemed, not with silver and gold but with the precious blood of Christ (1 Pet. 1:19). This is the triumphant starting-point of all Christian proclamation. The first word is not one which commands us to set up the kingdom, but one which announces that the kingdom has come (Mk.1:15). Here, there is total asymmetry between Jesus' input and ours.

Secondly, he, not we, is the great Liberator. He is not, like Che Guevara or William Wallace, a mere inspiration from the past. He is alive; and he is in control, possessing authority over the whole of heaven and the whole of earth (Mt. 28:18). He *has* liberated; he *is* liberating; and he *will* liberate still. We, to change the metaphor, are mere builder's labourers. He is the great Master Builder. He is not an absent Christ, once active in history but now withdrawn. He is an ever-present one, the great freedom fighter who has already destroyed the powers and who, following his death and resurrection, continues to bring liberation to the world's spiritual slaves.

Our hope for the world rests not with the great stream of Christian pilgrims following in the footsteps of Jesus, but with the living Jesus himself: still able to conquer every potentate and still able to open every heart. Everyone who comes to him finds instant freedom (Mt. 11:29).

All the great Liberation Theologians are orthodox trinitarians and all subscribe, at least formally, to the Christology of Chalcedon. As a result, there is little that is innovative in their Christology as such. What is innovative is the importance they attach to Christ's political activity and to his commitment to liberating people from pain, poverty and injustice. Theirs is a classic example of a theology of overstatement. If we assess it as a balanced description of Christianity as a whole, it fails miserably. But that is not how it asks to be assessed. Acutely and painfully aware of its own Latin American context (largely the result of a heartless orthodoxy) it has recovered a long-neglected vein of New Testament teaching, expounded it with deliberate exaggeration and made the world listen. Had Gutiérrez, Sobrino and Boff inserted all the necessary qualifications, we should never have heard of 'Bias to the poor!' Such has been their success that the church of the future will find it hard to ignore its obligation to defend the oppressed and speak for the dumb. The Liberationist strand will now take its place along with the Kerygmatic, the Charismatic and the Sacramental as an indispensable element in the fabric of Christianity.

But God forbid that it should ever drown out the song of those already redeemed:

Long my imprisoned spirit lay
Fast bound in sin and nature's night;
Thine eye diffused a quickening ray,
I woke, the dungeon filled with light;
My chains fell off, my heart was free:
I rose, went forth, and followed thee.

EPILOGUE

Is the task of Christology completed? Is Chalcedon final? By no means! We cannot content ourselves with merely repeating the words and phrases of the past till the Day of the *parousia*. These very words themselves require to be teased out, using, among other things, the insights of modern psychology and modern genetics. Besides, Christology constantly faces new challenges and each such challenge both changes and enriches us. Even those who cannot always be thanked for their answers must at least be thanked for their questions.

Sometimes, too, there are in the wider theological field paradigm shifts which have profound consequences for Christology. The growing abandonment of the axiom of divine *apatheia* (non-suffering) is one of these. It has allowed us to take seriously the fact that the Son of God who suffers on the cross is *homoousios* with God the Father who sent him; and that, in terms of the concept of *perichoresis*, the Father occupies the same time and the same space as the crucified Son. We still have a long way to go in developing the Christological implications of this revolution.

Finally, there is the need, in every age, to discharge afresh Christology's obligation to preaching. The Formula of Chalcedon has itself to be carried across the great hermeneutical barriers of time, language and culture into the world of today. Nor can it ever be enough merely to clarify it for theologians. It has to be clarified for proclamation. That is no small challenge. How do we translate *homoousios* and *perichoresis* into the plain English of today? The fourth-century theologians ransacked their world for appropriate images. We must find ours in the world of singularities, quarks, black holes and electro-magnetism. He who finds a serviceable new image puts the whole world in his debt.

The task goes on, then. Generations to come will ask different questions and use different language. In that sense Christology never arrives. Born of a living relationship with the Divine Son it remains, eternally, a *Christologia viatoris*. A book such as this is but the mere beginning of a pilgrimage.

Notes

Chapter 1: The virgin birth

[1] W. Pannenberg, *Jesus – God and Man* (London: SCM Press, 1968), p. 35.

[2] K. Runia, *The Present-day Christological Debate* (Leicester: Inter-Varsity Press, 1984), p. 37.

[3] V. Taylor, *The Gospel according to Saint Mark* (London: Macmillan, 1959), p. 152.

[4] C. E. B. Cranfield, *The Gospel according to Saint Mark* (Cambridge: Cambridge University Press, 1959), p. 38.

[5] D. Nineham, *The Gospel of Saint Mark* (Harmondsworth: Penguin Books, 1963), p. 60.

[6] *Ibid.*, p. 56.

[7] C. E. B. Cranfield, *The Epistle to the Romans*, vol. 1 (Edinburgh: T. & T. Clark, 1975), p. 59, fn. 1. *Cf.* R. E. Brown, *The Birth of the Messiah* (New York: Doubleday, 1979), p. 139: 'Joseph, by exercising the father's right to name the child, acknowledges Jesus and thus becomes the legal father of the child.'

[8] This argument is at least as old as the second century. See Justin Martyr, *Dialogue with Trypho*, 67 (*ANF*, vol. I, p. 231).

[9] As Alec Motyer points out, it is not the word itself but its context which

indicates its meaning and 'wherever the context allows a judgement, *'alma* is not a general term meaning "young woman" but a specific one meaning "virgin".' See A. Motyer, *The Prophecy of Isaiah* (Leicester: Inter-Varsity Press, 1993), pp. 84–85.

[10] H. Küng, *On Being a Christian* (London: Collins, 1977), p. 451.

[11] E. Brunner, *The Mediator* (London: Lutterworth Press, 1934), p. 322.

[12] W. Pannenberg, *op. cit.*, p. 143.

[13] E. Schillebeeckx, *Jesus* (New York: Collins, 1979), p. 554.

[14] W. Barclay, *The Plain Man Looks at the Apostles' Creed* (Glasgow: Collins, 1967), p. 81.

[15] J. A. T. Robinson, *The Human Face of God* (London: SCM Press, 1973), p. 144.

[16] J. M. Creed, *The Gospel according to Luke* (London: Macmillan, 1957), p. 19.

[17] J. G. Machen, *The Virgin Birth of Christ* (New York: Harper, 1930), p. 258. For an alternative point of view, arguing for an allusion to the virgin conception, see G. Vos, *The Self-Disclosure of Jesus* (Nutley, N.J.: Presbyterian and Reformed, new edn., 1953), pp. 209–211.

[18] C. E. B. Cranfield, *op. cit.*, vol. 1, p. 59.

[19] J. Orr, *The Virgin Birth of Christ* (London: Hodder and Stoughton, 1907), p. 117.

[20] *Ibid.*, p. 117.

[21] H. Küng, *op. cit.*, p. 456.

[22] E. Brunner, *op. cit.*, p. 325.

[23] J. D. G. Dunn, *Christology in the Making* (London: SCM Press, 1980), p. 51.

[24] *Ibid.*, p. 50.

[25] *Ibid.*, p. 51.

[26] W. Pannenberg, *op. cit.*, p. 143.

[27] E. Brunner, *op. cit.*, p. 325.

[28] *Ibid.*, p. 325.

[29] *Ibid.*, p. 323.

[30] K. Barth, *Church Dogmatics*, IV.1 (Edinburgh: T. & T. Clark, 1956), p. 207.

[31] *Ibid.*, I.2, p. 196.

[32] *Ibid.*, I.2, p. 182.

[33] *Ibid.*, I.2, p. 181.

[34] *Ibid.*, I.2, p. 177.

[35] *Ibid.*, I.2, p. 188.

[36] *Ibid.*, I.2, p. 191.

[37] A. Kuyper, *The Work of the Holy Spirit* (New York and London: Funk and Wagnalls, 1900), p. 82.

[38] Augustine, *On the Merits and Remission of Sins*, II.38 (*NPNF*, First Series, vol. V, p. 60).

[39] K. Barth, *op. cit.*, I.2, p. 192.

[40] Augustine, *op. cit.*, II.38.

[41] J. Calvin, *Institutes of the Christian Religion*, II.xiii.4 (London: SCM Press, 1961, vol. II, p. 481).

[42] See J. Pearson, *Exposition of the Creed* (Oxford: 6th edn., 1877), p. 301; J. Owen, *Works*, vol. III (Edinburgh, 1850–53), p. 168.

[43] W. G. T. Shedd, *Dogmatic Theology*, vol. II (Edinburgh: T. & T. Clark, 1889), p. 59, fn. 1.

[44] *Ibid.*, p. 82.

[45] A. Kuyper, *op. cit.*, p. 87.

[46] John of Damascus, *Exposition of the Orthodox Faith,* IV.xiv (*NPNF*, Second Series, vol. IX).

[47] *Westminster Confession*, VIII, 2.

[48] J. Pearson, *op. cit.*, p. 297.

Chapter 2: The pre-existence of Christ

[1] R. E. Brown, *Commentary on the Gospel According to John, I-XII* (London: Geoffrey Chapman, 1971), pp. 367ff.

[2] *Cf.* C. K. Barrett, *The Gospel According to St John* (London: SPCK, 1965), p. 421.

[3] J. A. T. Robinson, *The Human Face of God* (London: SCM Press, 1973), p. 172.

[4] J. D. G. Dunn, *Christology in the Making* (London: SCM Press, 1980), p. 29.

[5] H. P. Liddon, *The Divinity of our Lord and Saviour Jesus Christ* (London: Longmans, Green and Co., 14th edn. 1890).

[6] J. D. G. Dunn, *op. cit.*, p. 31.

[7] J. B. Lightfoot, *Biblical Essays* (London: Macmillan, 1893), p. 5.

[8] J. D. G. Dunn, *op. cit.*, p. 250.

[9] *Ibid.*, p. 31, italics mine.

[10] J. A. T. Robinson, *op. cit.*, p. 34.

[11] H. P. Liddon, *op. cit.*, p. 209.

[12] *Ibid.*, pp. 209f.

[13] This lecture, along with two others on the same theme, is reprinted in J. B. Lightfoot, *op cit.*

[14] *Ibid.*, p. 23.

[15] C. H. Dodd, *Historical Tradition in the Fourth Gospel* (Cambridge: Cambridge University Press, 1963).

[16] J. A. T. Robinson, *The Priority of John* (London: SCM Press, 1985).

[17] Reprinted in J. A. T. Robinson, *Twelve More New Testament Studies* (London: SCM Press, 1984).

[18] J. D. G. Dunn, *op. cit.*, p. 31.

[19] *Ibid.* All these examples occur on one page, p. 237.

[20] *Ibid.*, p. 42.

[21] *Ibid.*, p. 52.

[22] *Ibid.*, p. 54.

[23] G. K. W. Lampe, *God as Spirit* (London: SCM Press, 1977), p. 123.

[24] J. D. G. Dunn, *op. cit.*, p. 39.

[25] A. Plummer, *A Critical and Exegetical Commentary on the Second Epistle of Paul to the Corinthians* (Edinburgh: T. & T. Clark, 1915), p. 241.

[26] J. B. Lightfoot, *St. Paul's Epistles to the Colossians and to Philemon* (London: Macmillan, 8th edn., 1886), p. 144; and V. Taylor, *The Names of Jesus* (London: Macmillan, 1953), pp. 147f.

[27] J. B. Lightfoot, *St Paul's Epistles to the Colossians and to Philemon*, p. 145.

[28] E. K. Simpson and F. F. Bruce, *Commentary on the Epistles to the Ephesians and Colossians* (Grand Rapids: Eerdmans, 1957), p. 194, fn. 62.

[29] C. E. B. Cranfield, *The Gospel According to Saint Mark* (Cambridge: Cambridge University Press, 1959), p. 66.

[30] *Ibid.*, p. 66.

[31] For reasons of space, I have had to forego thorough consideration of the many issues, critical and theological, raised by the title *the Son of Man*. I am aware that the few comments I do make can be challenged at many points.

[32] C. F. D. Moule, *The Origin of Christology* (Cambridge: Cambridge University Press, 1977), p. 18.

[33] G. E. Ladd, *A Theology of the New Testament* (Grand Rapids: Eerdmans, 1974), p. 241.

[34] See, for example, Barnabas Lindars, *Jesus Son of Man* (London: SPCK, 1983), p. 5: 'It now has to be recognized that a date after the Jewish War is required, because no fragments of the Similitudes have been found in the Qumran literature (deposited in the caves in the year AD 70, or thereabouts, in spite of the fact that Aramaic portions of no less than eleven copies of Enoch have been identified, embracing all parts of the book except the Similitudes.'

[35] J. G. Baldwin, *Daniel: An Introduction and Commentary* (Leicester: Inter-Varsity Press, 1978), p. 142.

[36] Emily Elizabeth Steel Elliott.

[37] G. Vos, *The Self-Disclosure of Jesus* (Nutley, N.J.: Presbyterian and Reformed, new edn., 1953), p. 241.

[38] *Ibid.*, p. 162.

[39] J. A. T. Robinson, *op. cit.*, *passim.*

[40] *Ibid.*, p. 37.

[41] *Ibid.*, p. 54.

[42] C. S. Lewis, *God in the Dock* (Grand Rapids: Eerdmans, 1970), p. 31.

[43] *Hamlet*, V.i.

[44] J. A. T. Robinson, *op. cit.*, pp. 144ff.

[45] A. T. Hanson, *Grace and Truth* (London: SPCK, 1975), p. 67.

[46] *Ibid.*, p. 65.

[47] W. Pannenberg, *Jesus: God and Man* (London: SCM Press, 1968), pp. 150, 154.

[48] J. Knox, *The Humanity and Divinity of Christ* (Cambridge: Cambridge University Press, 1967), pp. 73, 106.

[49] *Ibid.*, p. 73.

[50] *Ibid.*, p. 33.

[51] *Ibid.*, p. 63.
[52] *Ibid.*, p. 110.
[53] *Ibid.*, p. 109.
[54] *Ibid.*, p. 110.
[55] *Ibid.*, p. 110.
[56] G. K. W. Lampe, *op.cit.*, pp. 120–144.
[57] *Ibid.*, p. 140.
[58] Augustine, *On the Trinity*, V.9 (*NPNF*, Second Series, vol. III, p. 92).
[59] P. Davies, *God and the New Physics* (London and Melbourne: J. M. Dent, 1983), p. 18.
[60] G. K. W. Lampe, *op. cit.*, p. 144.
[61] *Ibid.*, pp. 136f.
[62] C. F. D. Moule, *op. cit.*, p. 138.

Chapter 3: Christ, the Son of God

[1] O. Cullmann, *The Christology of the New Testament* (London: SCM Press, 2nd English edn., 1963), p. 287.
[2] *TDNT*, vol. IV, p. 738.
[3] G. Vos, *The Self-Disclosure of Jesus* (Nutley, N.J.: Presbyterian and Reformed, 1953), p. 213.
[4] R. E. Brown, *The Gospel according to John (I-XII)* (New York: Doubleday, 1966), p. 13. *Cf.* B. F. Westcott, *The Gospel according to St John* (London: John Murray, 1896), p. 12.
[5] G. Vos, *op. cit.*, p. 221.
[6] J. M. Creed, *The Divinity of Jesus Christ* (London: Collins, 1964), p. 123.
[7] C. H. Dodd, *The Interpretation of the Fourth Gospel* (Cambridge: Cambridge University Press, 1953), p. 255.
[8] C. K. Barrett, *The Gospel according to St John: An Introduction with Commentary and Notes* (London: SPCK, 1955), p. 78.
[9] Chrysostom, *Homilies on St John*, LXXV.29 (*NPNF*, First Series, vol. XIV, p. 277).
[10] B. F. Westcott, *op. cit.*, p. 213.
[11] J. Pearson, *Exposition of the Creed* (Oxford: 6th edn., 1877), p. 59.
[12] Augustine, *On the Trinity*, I.7 (*NPNF*, Second Series, vol. III, p. 24).
[13] See H. Witsius, *The Economy of the Covenants between God and Man*, trs. W. Crookshank (London, 1822), reprinted with an introduction by J. I. Packer (Escondido, California: 1990), Book II, ch. II, III.
[14] *Ibid.*, Book II, ch. III, XX.
[15] *Ibid.* (Packer's Introduction lacks page numbering).
[16] G. Vos, *The Teaching of the Epistle to the Hebrews* (Grand Rapids: Eerdmans, 1956), p. 80.
[17] See B. F. Westcott, *The Epistle to the Hebrews* (London: Macmillan, 1889), p. 10.
[18] Gregory of Nyssa, *Against Eunomius*, VIII.1 (*NPNF*, Second Series, vol. V).

[19] Chrysostom, *Homilies on the Epistle to the Hebrews*, II.2 (*NPNF*, First Series, vol. XIV, p. 371).

[20] J. Calvin, *Commentary on the Epistle to the Hebrews* (Grand Rapids: Eerdmans, 1963), 1:3.

[21] J. Owen, *An Exposition of the Epistle to the Hebrews* (Edinburgh: Johnstone and Hunter, 1855), vol. III, p. 95.

[22] B. F. Westcott, *The Epistle to the Hebrews*, p. 13.

[23] Hilary of Poitiers, *On the Trinity*, III.23 (*NPNF*, Second Series, vol. IX).

[24] R. P. C. Hanson, *The Search for the Christian Doctrine of God* (Edinburgh: T. & T. Clark, 1988), p. 486.

[25] Even the Cappadocian fathers, who more or less standardized the use of *hypostasis* in the sense of person, recognized that this meaning could not be assumed in Hebrews 1:3. *Cf.* Basil, *Letter* XXXVIII.6–8 (*NPNF*, Second Series, vol. VIII): and see R. C. Hanson, *op. cit.*, p. 690, fn. and p. 724.

[26] B. F. Westcott, *The Epistle to the Hebrews*, p. 13.

[27] Chrysostom, *Homilies on the Epistle to the Hebrews*, II.1.

[28] *Ibid.*, II.2.

[29] J. Calvin, *Commentary on the Epistle to the Hebrews*, 1:3.

[30] Part of the difficulty lies in exegeting Chrysostom himself. In particular, it is by no means clear what he means by *hypostasis*. See *NPNF*, Second Series, vol. XIV, p. 370, fn. 12. Translators appear to choose between three options: substance, subsistence and personality.

[31] *Cf.* Basil, *Letter* XXXVIII.7: 'the object of the apostolic argument is not the distinction of the *hypostases* from one another by means of the apparent notes; it is rather the apprehension of the natural, inseparable, and close relationship of the Son to the Father' (*NPNF*, Second Series, vol. VIII).

[32] J. A. T. Robinson, *The Human Face of God* (London: SCM Press, 1973), p. 156.

[33] J. D. G. Dunn, *Christology in the Making* (London: SCM Press, 1980), p. 52.

[34] J. A. T. Robinson, *op. cit.*, p. 157.

[35] J. D. G. Dunn, *op. cit.*, p. 52.

[36] J. Knox, *The Humanity and Divinity of Christ* (Cambridge: Cambridge University Press, 1967), p. 106.

[37] E. L Mascall, *Theology and the Gospel of Christ* (London: SPCK, 1977), p. 131.

[38] J. A. T. Robinson, *op. cit.*, p. 158.

[39] F. Weston, *The One Christ* (London: Longmans, 2nd edn., 1914), pp. 182–185.

[40] J. A. T. Robinson, *op. cit.*, p. 159.

[41] S. W. Sykes and J. P. Clayton (eds.), *Christ, Faith and History* (Cambridge: Cambridge University Press, 1972), p. 66.

[42] *Ibid.*, p. 66.

[43] L. S. Thornton, *The Dominion of Christ* (London: A. & C. Black, 1952), p. 79.

[44] J. Calvin, *The First Epistle of Paul the Apostle to the Corinthians* (Edinburgh: Oliver and Boyd, 1960), p. 328.

[45] J. D. G. Dunn, *op. cit.*, p. 36.
[46] *Ibid.*, p. 46.
[47] J. A. T. Robinson, *op. cit.*, p. 161.
[48] M. Hengel, *The Son of God* (London: SCM Press, 1976), p. 91.
[49] See C. E. B Cranfield, *A Critical and Exegetical Commentary on The Epistle to the Romans*, vol. 1 (Edinburgh: T. & T. Clark, 1975), pp. 61ff.
[50] *Ibid.*, p. 62.
[51] R. Bultmann, *Theology of the New Testament*, vol. II (ET, London: SCM Press, 1965), pp. 129ff.
[52] R. Bultmann, quoted without precise reference by M. Hengel, *op. cit.*, p. 17.
[53] I. Epstein, *Judaism: A Historical Presentation* (London: Penguin, 1959), p. 307.
[54] M. Hengel, *op. cit.*, p. 18.
[55] *Ibid.*, p. 25.
[56] *Ibid.*, p. 25.
[57] J. G. Machen had already made this point in *The Origin of Paul's Religion* (New York: Macmillan, 1928), pp. 237f.
[58] M. Hengel, *op. cit.*, p. 33.
[59] R. H. Fuller, *The Foundations of New Testament Christology* (London: Lutterworth Press, 1965), p. 69.
[60] M. Hengel, *op. cit.*, p. 41.
[61] R. H. Fuller, *op. cit.*, p. 31.
[62] J. Jeremias, *New Testament Theology*, vol. I (London: SCM Press, 1971), pp. 61ff. and *The Central Message of the New Testament* (London: SCM Press, 1965), pp. 9ff.
[63] J. Jeremias, *New Testament Theology*, p. 66.
[64] J. Jeremias, *The Central Message of the New Testament*, p. 23.
[65] *Ibid.*, pp. 22f.
[66] *Ibid.*, p. 23
[67] J. Barr, '"Abba, Father" and the Familiarity of Jesus' Speech', in *Theology*, vol. 91 (1988), pp. 173–179. See also 'Abba Isn't Daddy' by the same author in the *Journal of Theological Studies*, vol. 39 (1988), pp. 28–47.
[68] K. von Hase, *Die Geschichte Jesu* (1876), p. 422.
[69] R. H. Fuller, *op. cit.*, p. 115.
[70] D. Hill, *The Gospel of Matthew* (London: Marshall, Morgan and Scott, 1981), p. 205.
[71] J. Jeremias, *New Testament Theology*, vol. 1, p. 59.
[72] *Ibid.*, p. 59.
[73] J. A. T. Robinson, *op. cit.*, p. 44: 'As only a father knows his son, so only a son knows his father.'
[74] G. Vos, *op. cit.*, p. 151.
[75] J. B. Mayor, *The Epistle of St Jude and the Second Epistle of St Peter* (London: Macmillan, 1907), pp. 194f.
[76] A. M. Ramsey, *The Glory of God and the Transfiguration of Christ* (London: Longmans, 1949), p. 106.
[77] *Ibid.*, p. 139.

[78] J. Calvin, *Commentary on a Harmony of the Evangelists*, vol. II (Edinburgh: Calvin Translation Society, 1845), pp. 308f.

[79] Anselm, quoted in A. M. Ramsey, *op. cit.*, p. 132. No source is given.

Chapter 4: The Jesus of history

[1] R. Bultmann, *Jesus and the Word* (London: Collins, n. d.), p. 6.

[2] R. Bultmann, *Jesus Christ and Mythology* (London: SCM Press, 1960). 'The New Testament and Mythology', an address delivered in 1941, is reprinted in H. W. Bartsch, *Kerygma and Myth* (New York: Harper and Row, 1961), pp. 1–44.

[3] From 'New Testament and Mythology'. See H. W. Bartsch, *op. cit.*, p. 5.

[4] R. Bultmann, *Jesus and the Word* (London and Glasgow: Collins, 1958), p. 14.

[5] R. Bultmann, *Theology of the New Testament* (ET, London: SCM Press, 1965), vol. 1, p. 3.

[6] See Peter Carnley, 'The Poverty of Historical Scepticism', in S. W. Sykes and J. P. Clayton (eds.), *Christ, Faith and History* (Cambridge: Cambridge University Press, 1972), p. 183: 'the fact that somebody at time t_2 has *grounds for doubting* that *E* occurred does not entail that *E* did not occur, and therefore, it is still possible that *E* did occur. If we admit that it is still possible that *E* did occur, then we may admit that an historian at t_1 could have made absolutely certain that *E* did occur, and could have known with certainty that it did occur ... Clearly it is possible that ... now at t_2 another historian has grounds for believing that *E* might not have occurred ... (but) from a statement of the fact that there are at t_2 grounds for believing that *E* did not occur, it does not follow at all that a person in the past cannot have known with certainty that *E* did occur.'

[7] *Ibid.*, p. 169.

[8] R. Bultmann, *Jesus and the Word*, p. 88.

[9] *Ibid.*, p. 39.

[10] From G. E. Lessing, *On the Proof of the Spirit and of Power* (1777). See H. Chadwick (ed.), *Lessing's Theological Writings* (London: A. and C. Black, 1956), p. 53. *Cf.* C. Brown, *Jesus in European Protestant Thought 1778–1860* (Grand Rapids: Baker, 1985), pp. 16–29.

[11] See P. Carnley, *op. cit.*, p. 177.

[12] E. Hoskyns and F. N. Davey, *The Riddle of the New Testament* (London: Faber, 1958).

[13] M. Hengel, *The Son of God* (London: SCM Press, 1976), p. 41.

[14] Hoskyns and Davey, *op. cit.*, p. 114.

[15] *Ibid.*, pp. 179–182.

[16] J. Calvin, *Institutes of the Christian Religion*, I.vii.4 (ed. J. T. McNeill, London: SCM Press, 1960).

[17] See A. Harnack, *What is Christianity?* (London, 1904): 'The Gospel, as Jesus proclaimed it, has to do with the Father only and not with the Son' (p. 147).

[18] See J. Mackey, *Jesus: The Man and the Myth* (London: SCM Press, 1979),

pp. 230 and 233: 'People are brought into contact with the living God through the faith of Jesus. And they acknowledge that this faith is theirs because it was the faith of Jesus, because Jesus inspired them to such faith ... hence the followers of Jesus felt entitled, indeed obliged, to say that in Jesus they encountered at last the one, true God.'

[19] A. Schweitzer, *The Quest of the Historical Jesus* (London: A. & C. Black, 1910), pp. 368–369.

[20] J. Duncan, *Colloquia Peripatetica* (Edinburgh: 3rd edn., 1871), p. 109.

Chapter 5: The Christ of faith: 'very God of very God'

[1] See further P. Schaff, *The Creeds of the Evangelical Protestant Churches* (New York: Harper, 3rd edn., 1882).

[2] R. Williams, *The Scottish Journal of Theology*, vol. 45, no. 1, p. 102.

[3] See Athanasius, *Discourses Against the Arians* and *Arian History* (*NPNF*, Second Series, vol. IV, pp. 303–431, 266–302); J. N. D. Kelly, *Early Christian Doctrines* (London: A. & C. Black, 3rd edn., 1965), pp. 226–231; J. N. D. Kelly, *Early Christian Creeds* (London: Longmans, 2nd edn., 1960), pp. 231–234; R. P. C. Hanson, *The Search for the Christian Doctrine of God* (Edinburgh: T. & T. Clark, 1988), pp. 3–5; J. H. Newman, *The Arians of the Fourth Century* (London: Longmans, Green & Co., 6th edn., 1890).

[4] R. P. C. Hanson, *op. cit.*, pp. 6–7.

[5] See *ibid.*, p. 16.

[6] Athanasius, *Against the Arians*, II.70.

[7] Tertullian, *Adversus Praxean*, II. See *The Writings of Tertullian*, vol. II, tr. P. Holmes (Edinburgh: T. & T. Clark, 1874).

[8] *Ibid.*, XI.

[9] *Ibid.*, XIII.

[10] *Ibid.*, I.

[11] See G. L. Prestige, *God In Patristic Thought* (London: SPCK, 1952), p. 113, and J. N. D. Kelly, *Early Christian Doctrines*, p. 122.

[12] For Paul of Samosata, see J. N. D. Kelly, *Early Christian Creeds*, p. 248; and G. L. Prestige, *op. cit.*, pp. 201, 205.

[13] Basil, *Letter* LII.3 (*NPNF*, Second Series, vol. VIII).

[14] Tertullian, *Adversus Praxean*, VII, XXIV, XXV.

[15] Augustine, *On the Trinity*, V.10 (*NPNF*, First Series, vol. III). *Cf.* VII.11: 'Why, therefore, do we not call these three together one person, as one essence and one God, but say three persons, while we do not say three Gods or three essences; unless it be because we wish some word for that meaning whereby the Trinity is understood, that we might not be altogether silent, when asked, What three? while we confessed that they are three?'

[16] K. Rahner, *The Trinity* (Tunbridge Wells: Burns & Oates, 1970), p. 57.

[17] K. Barth, *Church Dogmatics*, I.1 (Edinburgh: T. & T. Clark, 1956), p. 411.

[18] E. Brunner, *The Mediator* (London: Lutterworth Press, 1934), p. 234.

[19] See M. Buber, *I and Thou* (1937; Edinburgh: T. & T. Clark, 2nd edn., 1959), pp. 6ff.

[20] D. Waterland, *Eight Sermons in Defence of the Divinity of Our Lord Jesus Christ* (Oxford, 1815), p. lv.

[21] D. Waterland, *Works*, I.II (*A Defence of Some Queries*) (Oxford, 1822), p. 96.

[22] J. MacArthur, *The MacArthur New Testament Commentary: Hebrews* (Chicago: Moody Press, 1983), p. 28.

[23] See D. Waterland, *Works*, I.II, pp. 95ff.

[24] *Ibid.*, p. 115.

[25] Athanasius, *De Synodis*, 42 (*NPNF*, Second Series, vol. IV, p. 473).

[26] Gregory of Nazianzen, *The Fourth Theological Oration*, XX. See *Select Orations of Saint Gregory of Nazianzen* (*NPNF*, Second Series, vol. VII, pp. 185–434).

[27] Athanasius, *Against the Arians*, II.48.

[28] John of Damascus, *Exposition of the Orthodox Faith*, I.viii (*NPNF*, Second Series, vol. IX).

[29] K. Barth, *op. cit.*, I.1, p. 495.

[30] *Ibid.*, p. 487.

[31] Athanasius, *Against the Arians*, II.36.

[32] Gregory of Nazianzen, *The Third Theological Oration*, VIII.

[33] Athanasius, *De Decretis*, 11 (*NPNF*, Second Series, vol. IV, p. 157).

[34] Athanasius, *Against the Arians*, I.28. Compare Gregory of Nazianzen: 'The Father is the begetter and the emitter; without passion, of course, and without reference to time and not in a corporeal manner' (*The Third Theological Oration*, II).

[35] Athanasius, *Against the Arians*, I.14. Compare John of Damascus: 'In treating, then, of the generation of the Son, it is an act of impiety to say that time comes into play and that the existence of the Son is of later origin than the Father' (*Exposition of the Orthodox Faith*, I.viii).

[36] See Gregory of Nyssa, *Against Eunomius*, I.25 (*NPNF*, Second Series, vol.V): 'What exposes still further the untenableness of this view is, that, besides positing a beginning in time of the Son's existence, it does not, when followed out, spare the Father even, but proves that He also had His beginning in time. For any recognising mark that is presupposed for the generation of the Son must certainly define as well the Father's beginning.'

[37] Gregory of Nyssa, *Against Eunomius*, I.42.

[38] Athanasius, *Against the Arians*, I.17.

[39] See Athanasius, *Against the Arians*, IV.30–31. *Cf.* the *Note on agennetos* in *NPNF*, Second Series, vol. V, p. 100.

[40] See Athanasius, *Against the Arians*, I.12; and Gregory of Nyssa, *Against Eunomius*, I.36.

[41] John of Damascus, *Exposition of the Orthodox Faith*, I.viii.

[42] Gregory of Nazianzen, *The Fourth Theological Oration*, XIX.

[43] John of Damascus, *Exposition of the Orthodox Faith*, I.viii.

[44] Gregory of Nazianzen, *The Fifth Theological Oration*, VIII.

[45] *Ibid.*, 10. *Cf.* John of Damascus: 'Likewise we believe also in one Holy Spirit, the Lord and Giver of Life: who proceedeth from the Father and resteth in the Son: the object of equal adoration and glorification with the Father and Son, since He is co-essential and co-eternal' (*Exposition of the Orthodox Faith*, I.viii).

[46] Athanasius, *Against the Arians*, I.9.

[47] John of Damascus, *Exposition of the Orthodox Faith*, I.viii.

[48] Gregory of Nazianzen, *The Third Theological Oration*, X. *Cf.* Athanasius, *Against the Arians*, I.35: 'such as he that begets, such of necessity is the offspring; and such as is the Word's Father, such must be also His Word.'

[49] Quoted by K. Barth, *op. cit.*, I.1, p. 497.

[50] Gregory of Nyssa, *Against Eunomius*, I.34. The same argument was used later by John of Damascus: 'We have an analogy in Adam, who was not begotten (for God Himself moulded him), and Seth, who was begotten (for he is Adam's son), and Eve, who proceeded out of Adam's rib (for she was not begotten). These do not differ from each other in nature, for they are human beings; but they differ in the mode of coming into existence' (*Exposition of the Orthodox Faith*, I.viii).

[51] Augustine, *On the Trinity*, V.5.

[52] K. Barth, *op. cit.*, I.1, p. 495. *Cf.* R. Treffrey, *Inquiry into the Doctrine of the Eternal Sonship of our Lord Jesus Christ* (London, 1837), p. 34: 'divine analogies are only the reflex application to the Deity of such relations among men as have their type in God Himself ... their essential features are to be contemplated as existing in the Deity more really than in those human copies which come under our observation.' Similarly W. Cunningham, *Historical Theology*, vol. I (Edinburgh: 3rd edn., 1870), p. 301: 'We ought to regulate our conceptions of what sonship is and implies, not from the defective and imperfect representations of it given in the relations of fathers and sons among men, but from the original and only true idea of it as subsisting between the first and second persons of the Godhead.'

[53] *Cf.* Athanasius, *De Decretis*, 20: 'the Word must be described as the True Power and Image of the Father, in all things exact and like the Father'. Similarly, *Against the Arians*, II.35: 'For such as he that begets, such of necessity is the offspring; and such as is the Word's father, such must be also His Word.'

[54] Augustine, *On the Trinity*, VI.3.

[55] *Ibid.*, XV.23.

[56] I. Ortiz de Urbina, quoted by J. Galot, *Who Is Christ?* (Rome: Gregorian University Press, 1980), p. 228.

[57] *Cf.* Athanasius, *Against the Arians*, III.5: the attributes of the Father are spoken of the Son.

[58] Gregory of Nazianzen, *The Fourth Theological Oration*, XIX.

[59] John of Damascus, *Exposition of the Orthodox Faith*, I.viii.

[60] K. Barth, *op.cit*, I.1, p. 353.

[61] *Ibid.*, I.1, p. 491.

[62] K. Rahner, *op. cit.*, p. 64.

[63] *Ibid.*, pp. 34ff. *Cf.* John Owen, *Works*, vol. II (Edinburgh, 1850–53), p. 40: 'the fellowship we have with the second person is with him as Mediator – in that office whereunto, by dispensation, he submitted himself for our sakes'.

[64] See R. P. C. Hanson, *op. cit.*, p. 445. Hanson quotes Athanasius, *Ad Afros*, 4 (*NPNF*, Second Series, vol. IV, p. 490), but the translation is uncertain. See further the comments by A. Robertson in his Prolegomena to *Athanasius: Select Works and Letters* (*NPNF*, Second Series, vol. IV), p. xxxii.

[65] Basil, *On the Spirit*, 44, 45 (*NPNF*, Second Series, vol. VIII).

[66] See A. Robertson, *op. cit.*, p. xxxi.

[67] See, for example, Athanasius, *Against the Arians*, III.4: 'So also the Godhead of the Son is the Father's; whence also it is indivisible; and thus there is one God and none other but he.' *Cf.* Gregory of Nazianzen, who spoke of, 'Light thrice repeated; but One Light and One God' (*The Fifth Theological Oration*, III).

[68] J. Galot, *Who Is Christ?*, p. 229.

[69] K. Barth, *op. cit.*, I.1, p. 503f.

[70] Athanasius, *Against the Arians*, I.4.

[71] Gregory of Nyssa, *Against Eunomius*, II.6.

[72] K. Rahner, *op. cit.*, p. 69. Rahner refers to what he calls 'the basic difficulty', namely, 'how two things which are identical with a third are not identical with each other'.

[73] Basil, *Letter* XXXVIII.5.

[74] John of Damascus, *Exposition of the Orthodox Faith*, I.xiv.

[75] See K. Barth, *op. cit.*, I.1, p. 425.

[76] See K. Rahner, *op. cit.*, p. 76: 'Inasmuch as an "activity *ad extra*" (hence the creation of finite reality as distinct from God) is based upon the omnipotence of the one Godhead (upon the divine essence), there is only one outward activity of God, exerted and possessed as one and the same by Father, Son, and Spirit, according to the peculiar way in which each of them possesses the Godhead.'

[77] H. B. Swete, *The Holy Spirit in the Ancient Church* (London: Macmillan, 1912), p. 275.

[78] John of Damascus, *Exposition of the Orthodox Faith*, I.xii.

[79] Augustine, *On the Trinity*, IV.29.

[80] For the history of these developments see J. N. D. Kelly, *Early Christian Creeds*, pp. 358–367; and H. B. Swete, *op. cit.*, pp. 316–355.

[81] See P. Schaff, *History of the Creeds of Christendom* (New York: Harper, 1881), p. 36; J. N. D. Kelly, *The Athanasian Creed* (London: A. and C. Black, 1964); and G. Bray, *Creeds, Councils and Christ* (Leicester: Inter-Varsity Press, 1984), p. 175.

[82] Augustine, *On the Trinity*, IV.29.

[83] *Ibid.*, V.15.

[84] *Ibid.*, XV.47.

[85] B. B. Warfield, *Biblical and Theological Studies* (Philadelphia: Presbyterian and Reformed Publishing Company, 1952), p. 51.

[86] K. Barth, *op.cit.*, I.1 p. 548.
[87] See K. Barth, *ibid.*, pp. 554f.; and G. Watson, 'The Filioque – Opportunity for Debate?' in *Scottish Journal of Theology*, vol. 41, no. 3 (1988), pp. 323ff.
[88] K. Barth, *op. cit.*, I.1, p. 555.
[89] J. Pearson, *An Exposition of the Creed* (Oxford: 6th edn., 1877), p. 239.
[90] H. P. Liddon, *The Divinity of our Lord and Saviour Jesus Christ* (London: Longmans, Green and Co., 1908), p. 202.
[91] G. Bull, *A Defence of the Nicene Creed* (A New Translation, Oxford, 1852), pp. 556f.
[92] J. Calvin, *Institutes of the Christian Religion*, I.xiii (London: SCM Press, 1961, vol. I, pp. 120–159).
[93] *Ibid.*, I.xiii.5.
[94] See Joannis Calvini, *Opera Selecta*, ed. Petrus Barth (Munich: Kaiser, 1926), p. 77: 'Considered as God he is one with the Father, of the same nature and substance or essence, distinguished only as to his person, which he has uniquely and distinctly from the Father' (my translation).
[95] See B. B. Warfield, *Calvin and Augustine* (Philadelphia: Presbyterian and Reformed, 1956), pp. 229–284.
[96] See Calvin's *Letter to Simon Grynee*, May 1537 (in *Letters of John Calvin*, vol. 1, ed. Jules Bonnet, tr. David Constable (Presbyterian Board of Publication, Philadelphia, 1858), vol. 1, p. 55.
[97] See the account in Beza's *Life of John Calvin* in Calvin, *Tracts*, vol. 1 (Edinburgh: Calvin Translation Society, 1844), pp. lxxii–lxxiv.
[98] J. Calvin, *Institutes of the Christian Religion*, I.xiii.25.
[99] J. Calvin, *Letter to Simon Grynee*.
[100] *Ibid.*
[101] J. Calvin, *Institutes of the Christian Religion*, I.xiii.23.

Chapter 6: The incarnation

[1] See *Melanchthon and Bucer*, in *The Library of Christian Classics*, vol. XIX (London and Philadelphia: SCM Press, 1969), pp. 21f.
[2] J. Denney, *Jesus and the Gospel* (London: Hodder and Stoughton, 1908), pp. 386f.
[3] W. G. Blaikie, *David Brown*: *A Memoir* (London: Hodder and Stoughton, 1898), p. 42.
[4] Irenaeus, *Against Heresies*, I. XXVI (*ANF*, vol. I), p. 352.
[5] Tertullian, *Against Marcion*, III.VIII (*ANF*, vol. III), p. 327.
[6] Tertullian, *On the Flesh of Christ*, ch. V. See *The Writings of Tertullian*, tr. P. Holmes (Edinburgh, T. & T. Clark, 1870), p. 174.
[7] G. L. Prestige, *Fathers and Heretics* (London: SPCK, 1940), p. 116.
[8] These fragments were collected by H. Lietzmann in *Apollinaris und seine Schule* (Tübingen, 1904).
[9] See Frances Young, From *Nicea to Chalcedon* (London: SCM Press, 1983), p. 183; and Charles E. Raven, *Apollinarianism* (Cambridge, 1923), p. 167.
[10] Quoted in C. E. Raven, *op. cit.*, pp. 182, 184.

[11] *Ibid.*, p. 230: 'his work was surreptitiously absorbed into the fabric of orthodox dogmatic'.

[12] Quoted in *ibid.*, p. 188.

[13] Quoted in *ibid.*, p. 188.

[14] Quoted in *ibid.*, p. 204.

[15] Athanasius, *Letter to the Church of Antioch*, 7, 11.

[16] The *Letter to Nectarius*, along with other Letters on Apollinarianism, is most conveniently available in E. R. Hardy (ed.), *Christology of the Later Fathers*, in *The Library of Christian Classics*, vol. III (London: SCM Press, 1954), pp. 230–232. See also *Select Letters of Saint Gregory Nazianzen* (*NPNF*, Second Series, vol. VII), p. 438.

[17] Gregory of Nazianzen, *First Letter to Cledonius* [*Epistle 101*]. See E. R. Hardy (ed.), *op. cit.*, p. 219.

[18] Gregory of Nyssa, *Against Eunomius*, II.13 (*NPNF*, Second Series, vol. V).

[19] See *Luther's Works*, vol. 22, *Sermons on the Gospel of John* (St Louis: Concordia, 1957), p. 113.

[20] A. Stewart, *The Tree of Promise* (Edinburgh, 1864), pp. 31f.

[21] See further the discussion on 'Sexuality and God' in E. L. Mascall, *Whatever Happened to the Human Mind?* (London: SPCK, 1980), pp. 128–155.

[22] From 'Some Basic Considerations' in Peter Moore (ed.), *Man, Woman and Priesthood* (London: SPCK, 1978), pp. 23f.

[23] A. Moody Stuart, *Recollections of the late John Duncan* (Edinburgh, 1872), p. 186.

[24] Athanasius, *Against the Arians*, III.43.

[25] Cyril of Alexandria, *Answers to Tiberius*, 4. See *Cyril of Alexandria: Select Letters*, ed. and tr. Lionel R. Wickham (Oxford: Clarendon Press, 1983), p. 151.

[26] Basil, *Letter* CCXXXVI.1 (*NPNF*, Second Series, vol. VIII).

[27] Gregory of Nazianzen, *The Fourth Theological Oration*, 16.

[28] J. Calvin, *Institutes of the Christian Religion*, I.iii.1 (London: SCM Press, 1960).

[29] Athanasius, *Against the Arians*, III.43.

[30] Cyril of Alexandria, *Answers to Tiberias*, 4.

[31] Gregory of Nazianzen, *The Fourth Theological Oration*, 15.

[32] J. Calvin, *Commentary on a Harmony of the Evangelists, Matthew, Mark and Luke*, vol. III (Edinburgh: Calvin Translation Society, 1845), p. 153.

[33] J. Duncan, *Colloquia Peripatetica* (Edinburgh, 3rd edn. 1871), p. 26.

[34] W. Temple, *Christus Veritas* (London: Macmillan, 1925), p. 145.

[35] *Ibid*, p. 145.

[36] B. B. Warfield, *The Person and Work of Christ* (Philadalphia: Presbyterian and Reformed, 1950), p. 93.

[37] J. Calvin, *The Epistle of Paul the Apostle to the Hebrews and The First and Second Epistles of Peter* (Edinburgh: Oliver and Boyd, 1963), p. 55.

[38] J. Calvin, *Commentary on a Harmony of the Evangelists*, vol. III, p. 227.

[39] *Ibid.*, pp. 228, 230.

[40] See R. E. Brown, *The Gospel according to John (I–XII)* (New York: Doubleday, 1966), p. 426.

[41] See C. K. Barrett, *The Gospel according to St John* (London: SPCK, 1955), p. 332.

[42] B. B. Warfield, *op. cit.*, p. 116. *Cf.* R. E. Brown, *op. cit.*, p. 435: 'he was angry because he found himself face to face with the realm of Satan which, in this instance, was represented by death'.

[43] B. B. Warfield, *op. cit.*, p. 145.

[44] J. Calvin, *Commentary on a Harmony of the Evangelists*, vol. III, p. 227.

[45] Cited in V. Taylor, *The Gospel according to St Mark* (London: Macmillan, 1952), p. 552.

[46] J. B. Lightfoot, *Saint Paul's Epistle to the Philippians* (London: Macmillan, 4th edn., 1879), p. 123.

[47] So D. Nineham, *The Gospel of Saint Mark* (Harmondsworth: Penguin Books, 1963), p. 391.

[48] K. Barth, *Church Dogmatics*, IV.1 (Edinburgh: T. & T. Clark, 1956), pp. 267f.

[49] See D. Guthrie, *The Letter to the Hebrews* (Leicester: Inter-Varsity Press, 1983), p. 129: 'The loud cries and tears seem to be an undeniable allusion to the agony of Jesus in the garden of Gethsemane, where his prayer was accompanied by sweat of blood, revealing the inner intensity of the struggle through which he passed.'

[50] Quoted in C. E. B. Cranfield, *The Gospel according to Saint Mark* (Cambridge: Cambridge University Press), p. 431.

[51] In Hebrews 2:9, many fathers, both Eastern and Western, read *choris theou* ('without God') in place of *chariti theou* ('by the grace of God'). This variant is almost certainly inauthentic, but it does express an important theological truth. See B. Metzger, *A Textual Commentary on the Greek New Testament* (London and New York: United Bible Societies, 1975), p. 664.

[52] See A. Moody Stuart, *op. cit.*, p. 105.

[53] From the hymn, *Fulangas Chriosd* ('The Suffering of Christ'), in Donald Maclean (ed.), *The Spiritual Songs of Dugald Buchanan* (Edinburgh, 1913), p. 8.

[54] H. Martin, *The Shadow of Calvary* (Glasgow: Free Presbyterian Publications, new impression, 1956), p. 24.

[55] M. Luther, *Lectures on Galatians*, on Gal. 3:13. See Luther, *Works*, vol. 26 (St Louis: Concordia, 1963), p. 277.

[56] *Ibid.*, pp. 277f.

[57] K. Barth, *op. cit.*, IV.1, pp. 246, 253.

[58] J. Calvin, *Institutes*, II.xvi.10.

[59] J. Calvin, *Commentary on a Harmony of the Evangelists*, vol. III, p. 319.

[60] See P. Schaff, *The Creeds of the Greek and Latin Churches* (London: Hodder and Stoughton, 1877), p. 72; and T. H. Bindley, *The Ecumenical Documents of the Faith* (London: Methuen, 4th edn., 1950), pp. 197, 205.

[61] For the Monothelite controversy the most accessible treatment is that of R. L. Ottley, *The Doctrine of the Incarnation* (London: Methuen, 5th edn., 1911), pp. 447–456.

[62] J. Calvin, *Commentary on a Harmony of the Evangelists*, vol. III, p. 233.

[63] K. Barth, *op. cit.*, IV.2, p. 50.

Chapter 7: Chalcedon: 'perfect in godhead, perfect in manhood'

[1] See particularly J. F. Bethune-Baker, *Nestorius and His Teaching: A Fresh Examination of the Evidence* (Cambridge: Cambridge University Press, 1908).

[2] *Ibid*, p. 17.

[3] Frances Young, *From Nicea to Chalcedon* (London: SCM Press, 1983), p. 231.

[4] The letter is quoted in *ibid.*, p. 242.

[5] Cyril of Alexandria, *First Tome Against the Blasphemies of Nestorius.* See *St Cyril of Alexandria: Against Nestorius,* in *A Library of Fathers of the Holy Catholic Church*, translated by Members of the English Church (Oxford: James Parker, no date), p. 10.

[6] The *Formula of Reunion* is contained in Cyril's *Epistle to John of Antioch.* See L. R. Wickham, *Cyril of Alexandria: Select Letters* (Oxford: Clarendon Press, 1983), p. 222. Alternatively, see T. H. Bindley, *The Ecumenical Documents of the Faith* (Westport, Connecticut: Greenwood Press, 4th edn., 1950), p. 221.

[7] See L. R. Wickham, *op. cit.*, pp. 31, 49.

[8] J. N. D. Kelly, *Early Christian Doctrines* (London: A. & C. Black, 3rd edn., 1965), pp. 331f.

[9] The *Letter to Flavian* is commonly referred to as *Leo's Tome*. For the text, see T. H. Bindley, *op. cit.*, pp. 168ff. (English translation, pp. 224ff.); or *NPNF*, First Series, vol. XII, *Letter* XXVIII, pp. 38–43.

[10] For the text of the Chalcedonian Definition of the Faith, see T. H. Bindley, *op. cit.*, pp. 191–193 (Greek); pp. 232–235 (English translation).

[11] Cyril, *Second Letter to Nestorius*, 3. *Cf.* K. Barth, *Church Dogmatics*, IV.2 (Edinburgh: T. & T. Clark, 1956), p. 43: 'the God who acts in the incarnation is God in His mode of being as the Son ... it is He and not the Father who becomes flesh – the one God in this second and not the first mode of being'.

[12] K. Barth, *op. cit.*, IV.2, p. 40.

[13] K. Rahner, quoted in J. Galot, *Who Is Christ?* (Rome: Gregorian University Press, 1980), p. 269.

[14] See T. H. Bindley, *op. cit.*, p. 221; L. R. Wickham, *op. cit.*, p. 222.

[15] K. Rahner, *Theological Investigations*, vol. I (London: Darton, Longman and Todd, 2nd edn., 1965), p. 129.

[16] See *ibid.*, p. 203f.: 'this Motherhood is a free act of the Virgin's faith. One comes about by the other, and both together form a unity. Mary's consent in faith ... is part of the saving history of humanity, not a pious, edifying idyll

from someone's private life ... She is Mother personally, not just biologically. Looked at in this way, her personal divine Motherhood precedes – this is rather a bold way of putting it, admittedly – her Son's divine sonship ... she became Mother of God in the freedom of faith.' Compare K. Barth, *op. cit.*, IV.2, p. 45: 'It was not, however, Israel or Mary who acted, but God – acting towards Israel, and finally (in fulfilment of the promise given with its election) towards Mary ... Even the *fiat mihi* of Mary is preceded by the resolve and promise of God. It confirmed His work, but it did not add anything at all to it.'

[17] Rahner, having stressed that Mary is 'the perfect, exemplar (sic), pure case of redemption in general' adds: 'redemption does not necessarily and in every case presuppose a temporally earlier condition of being unredeemed, of sin and alienation from God. Someone who is preserved in grace is just as radically delivered and redeemed, if not more so' (*op. cit.*, p. 211).

[18] Cyril, *Against Nestorius*, in *A Library of Fathers of the Holy Catholic Church*, p. 23.

[19] L. R. Wickham, *op. cit.*, p. xxxiv.

[20] K. Barth, *op. cit.*, IV.2, p. 60.

[21] See Cyril's *Second Letter to Nestorius* (4): 'The point is that it was not the case that initially an ordinary man was born of the Virgin and then the Word simply settled on him – no, what is said is that he underwent fleshly birth united from the very womb, making the birth of his flesh his very own' (in L. R. Wickham *op. cit.*, p. 7).

[22] This analogy is sanctioned by Calvin: 'If anything like this very great mystery can be found in human affairs, the most apposite parallel seems to be that of man, whom we see to consist of two substances. Yet neither is so mingled with the other as not to retain its own distinctive nature. For the soul is not the body, and the body is not the soul ... Such expressions signify both that there is one person in man composed of two elements joined together, and that there are two diverse underlying natures that make up this person. Thus, also, the Scriptures speak of Christ' (*Institutes*, II. xiv.1).

[23] D. Baillie, *God Was in Christ* (London: Faber, 1948), pp. 106–132. For a critique see K. Barth, *op. cit.*, IV.2, pp. 55–60.

[24] D. Baillie, *op. cit.*, p. 129.

[25] It is significant that John Hick cites Baillie's use of the paradox of grace as an example of the modification in recent Christian theology of 'the monolithic character of the traditional doctrine of the uniqueness of Christ'. See further E. L. Mascall, *Theology and the Gospel of Christ* (London: SPCK, 1977), p. 125.

[26] The title of Baillie's book is taken from 2 Corinthians 5:19 as rendered by the King James Version. This is a misuse of Paul's statement, however. The apostle was not making a Christological statement ('God was in Christ') but a soteriological one ('God was reconciling the world to himself in Christ').

[27] J. Baillie, *Our Knowledge of God* (London: Oxford University Press, 1939), p. 94.

[28] K. Barth, *op. cit.*, IV.2, p. 57.

[29] *Ibid.*, IV.2, p. 59.

[30] C. Gore, *The Incarnation of the Son of God* (London: John Murray, 1898), p. 219.

[31] Compare J. Galot, *op. cit.*, p. 334: 'Jesus does not have a single divine-human consciousness, since the two activities, like the two natures, are distinct, "without any commingling', as Chalcedon says.'

[32] John of Damascus, *Exposition of the Orthodox Faith*, III.iii. See further the discussion on Maximus the Confessor and pseudo-Cyril in G. L. Prestige, *God in Patristic Thought* (London: SPCK, 1952), pp. 292–296. These fathers use the principle of reciprocity and interchange to explain how the two natures produce a single action.

[33] T. M. Bindley, *op. cit.*, p. 226.

[34] Cyril of Alexandria, *On the Creed*, 14 (in L. R. Wickham, *op. cit.*, p. 111).

[35] See Leo's *Tome* (4): 'He who is invisible in what belongs to Himself was made visible in what belongs to us, the incomprehensible willed to be comprehended, He who continued to exist before time began to exist in time, the Lord of the universe took upon Him a servant's form shrouding the immensity of His majesty, the impassible God did not disdain to be passible man, nor the Immortal to be subject to the laws of death' (T. H. Bindley, *op. cit.*, pp. 226f.).

[36] Quoted in H. Heppe, *Reformed Dogmatics* (1950; Grand Rapids: Baker, 1978), p. 445.

[37] K. Barth, *Church Dogmatics*, IV.2, p. 51. *Cf.* E. L. Mascall, *op. cit.*, p. 181: 'all the acts of the incarnate life are, in various ways, theandric, acts of a divine person in a human nature'.

[38] See H. Heppe, *op. cit.*, pp. 434–438.

[39] J. Owen, *Works*, vol. I (Edinburgh, 1850–53), p. 93.

[40] Calvin, *Institutes*, II.xiv.2.

[41] Quoted in H. Heppe, *op. cit.*, p. 444.

[42] W. G. T. Shedd, *Dogmatic Theology*, vol. II (Edinburgh: T. & T. Clark, 1889), p. 323.

[43] K. Barth (*op. cit.*, IV.2, p. 77), summarizing the Lutheran theologian, Hollaz.

[44] J. T. Mueller, *Christian Dogmatics* (St Louis: Concordia, 1955), p. 275.

[45] Cyril was emphatic that neither nature was changed in the incarnation. For example, in his *Second Letter to Succensus* he writes, 'the Word's nature has not been transferred to the nature of the flesh or that of the flesh to that of the Word' (in L. R. Wickham, *op. cit.*, p. 89).

[46] W. G. T. Shedd, *op. cit.*, vol. II, p. 327.

[47] See H. M. Relton, *A Study in Christology* (London: SPCK, 1934), p. 11.

[48] Cyril of Alexandria, *Third Letter to Nestorius*, 8 (in L. R. Wickham, *op. cit.*, p. 25).

[49] See G. K. W. Lampe, *A Patristic Greek Lexicon* (Oxford, 1961), p. 164.

[50] H. Heppe, *op. cit.*, p. 416. *Cf.* John Owen, *Works*, vol. 1, p. 233.

[51] R. C. Moberley, *Atonement and Personality* (London: John Murray, 1901), p. 93.

[52] H. R. Mackintosh, *Doctrine of the Person of Christ* (Edinburgh: T. & T. Clark, 2nd edn., 1913), p. 207.

[53] D. Baillie, *op. cit.*, p. 86. See also J. A. T. Robinson, *The Human Face of God* (London, SCM Press, 1973), p. 39; and Sydney Cave, *The Doctrine of the Person of Christ* (London: Duckworth, 1925), p. 113.

[54] H. Heppe, *op. cit.*, p. 417.

[55] A. N. S. Lane in H. Rowdon (ed.), *Christ the Lord* (Leicester: Inter-Varsity Press, 1982), pp. 272ff. Lane's essay is entitled, 'Christology Beyond Chalcedon'.

[56] D. Baillie, *op. cit.*, p. 89.

[57] See G. K. W. Lampe, *op. cit.*, p. 486.

[58] H. M. Relton, *op. cit.*, p. 77. This work contains a summary of the theology of Leontius (pp. 69–83). See further R. L. Ottley, *The Doctrine of the Incarnation* (London: Methuen, 5th edn., 1911), pp. 443–447.

[59] John of Damascus, *Exposition of the Orthodox Faith*, III.iii.

[60] K. Barth, *op. cit.*, IV.2, p. 49.

[61] T. F. Torrance (ed.), *The Incarnation: Ecumenical Studies in the Nicene-Constantinopolitan Creed* (Edinburgh: Handsel Press, 1991), p. 139.

Chapter 8: *Kenōsis*: making himself nothing

[1] See H. R. Mackintosh, *The Doctrine of the Person of Jesus Christ* (Edinburgh: T. & T. Clark, 2nd edn., 1913), pp. 267f.

[2] Quoted, but not attributed, in J. Carpenter, *Gore: A Study in Liberal Catholic Thought* (London: The Faith Press, 1960), p. 156.

[3] C. Gore, *The Incarnation of the Son of God* (London: John Murray, 2nd edn., 1898), p. 266.

[4] *Ibid.*, p. 158.

[5] C. Gore, *Dissertations on Subjects Connected with the Incarnation* (London: John Murray, 2nd edn., 1896), pp. 94f. *Cf.* Gore, *The Incarnation of the Son of God*, p. 158: 'He so emptied Himself as to assume the permanent characteristics of the human or servile life: He took the *form* of a servant.'

[6] C. Gore (ed.), *Lux Mundi: A Series of Studies in the Religion of the Incarnation* (London: John Murray, 12th edn., 1902), p. 265.

[7] P. T. Forsyth, *The Person and Place of Jesus Christ* (London: Hodder and Stoughton, 2nd edn., 1910), p. 296.

[8] *Ibid.*, p. 317.

[9] *Ibid.*, p. 318.

[10] *Ibid.*, p. 319.

[11] See R. R. Redman Jr., 'H. R. Mackintosh's Contribution to Christology and Soteriology in the Twentieth Century' in the *Scottish Journal of Theology*, vol. 41, no. 4, pp. 517–534.

[12] H. R. Mackintosh, *op. cit.*, pp. 466f.

[13] *Ibid.*, p. 479.

[14] *Ibid.*, p. 473.

[15] *Ibid.*, p. 477.

[16] *Ibid.*, p. 477.

[17] *Ibid.*, p. 480.

[18] See A. B. Bruce, *The Humiliation of Christ* (Edinburgh: T. & T. Clark, 1876), pp. 212–247; W. Temple, *Christus Veritas* (London: Macmillan, 1926), pp. 141–145; D. M. Baillie, *God Was In Christ* (London: Faber, 1948), pp. 94–98.

[19] W. Temple, *op. cit.*, p. 142ff.

[20] *Ibid.*, p. 144.

[21] A. Ritschl, quoted in Mackintosh, *op. cit*, p. 485.

[22] See H. P. Liddon, *The Divinity of our Lord* (London: Longmans, Green and Co., 14th edn., 1890), pp. 461–480.

[23] *Ibid.*, p. 462.

[24] K. Barth, *Church Dogmatics* (Edinburgh: T. & T. Clark, 1956), I.2, pp. 507ff.

[25] D. Mackinnon, in an essay, '"Substance" in christology – a cross-bench view', in S. W. Sykes and J. P. Clayton (eds.), *Christ, Faith and History* (Cambridge: Cambridge University Press, 1972), p. 297.

[26] H. A. Kennedy, *The Epistle to the Philippians*, in *The Expositor's Greek Testament*, vol. III (London: Hodder and Stoughton, 1903), pp. 435f.

[27] R. P. Martin, *Carmen Christi* (Cambridge: Cambridge University Press, 1967), pp. 99–120.

[28] H. A. Kennedy, *op. cit.*, vol. III, p. 435.

[29] R. P. Martin, *op. cit.*, p. 108.

[30] H. A. Kennedy, *op. cit.*, vol. III, p. 436.

[31] See R. P. Martin, *op. cit.*, pp. 134–164. For bibliography see Peter T. O'Brien, *The Epistle to the Philippians: A Commentary on the Greek Text* (Grand Rapids: Eerdmans, 1991), pp. 186–188.

[32] C. F. D. Moule, 'The Manhood of Jesus in the New Testament', in S. W. Sykes and J. P. Clayton (eds.), *op. cit.*, p. 97.

[33] D. A. Carson, *The Gospel according to John* (Leicester: Inter-Varsity Press, 1991), p. 462.

[34] J. Owen, *Works*, vol. 1 (Edinburgh, 1850–53), p. 324.

[35] See the suggestive comments in Hans Urs Von Balthasar, *The Glory of the Lord: A Theological Aesthetics* (Edinburgh: T. & T. Clark, 1989), pp. 142–161.

[36] *Ibid.*, p. 146.

[37] Augustine, *On the Trinity*, VII.5.

[38] John Knox, for example, cites Philippians 2:7–8 as one of two passages where Paul uses 'the language of docetism': 'we cannot easily pass by the suggestion of unreality conveyed in *homoiōma* and *schēma*' (J. Knox, *The Humanity and Divinity of Christ* [Cambridge: Cambridge University Press, 1967], pp. 31ff.).

[39] J. Calvin, *Commentary on the Epistle to the Philippians*, 2:7. See Calvin, *Commentaries on the Epistles to the Philippians, Colossians, and Thessalonians* (Edinburgh: Calvin Translation Society, 1851), pp. 56f.

[40] Luther, quoted in E. Brunner, *The Mediator* (London: Lutterworth, 1934), p. 331.

[41] H. U. Von Balthasar, *op. cit.*, p. 144. *Cf.* W. Pannenberg: 'The surrender of Jesus to the Father ... was not surrender to a mission lived out in full clarity and accepted wholeheartedly. Rather, it was surrender to the will of God amid all the obscurity surrounding his path to the cross, and the cross represents the complete failure of Jesus' mission.' Cited in J. Sobrino, *Christology at the Crossroads* (London: SCM Press, 1978), pp. 336f.

[42] J. McLagan (reputedly), in an anonymous sermon appended to M. Dods, *On the Incarnation of the Eternal Word* (London, 1831), p. 300.

[43] *Ibid.*, p. 302.

[44] C. Gore, *The Incarnation of the Son of God*, p. 158.

[45] H. Martin, *The Shadow of Calvary* (Edinburgh, 1875; new impression, Glasgow, 1956), p. 26.

Chapter 9: The sinlessness of Christ

[1] C. F. D. Moule, 'The Manhood of Jesus in the New Testament', in S. W. Sykes and J. P. Clayton (eds.), *Christ, Faith and History* (Cambridge: Cambridge University Press, 1972), p. 102.

[2] See *The Doctrine of the Incarnation Opened in Six Sermons* (London, 1828); *The Orthodox and Catholic Doctrine of our Lord's Human Nature* (London, 1830); *The Opinions Circulating Concerning our Lord's Human Nature* (London, 1830); and *Christ's Holiness in Flesh* (Edinburgh, 1831).

Views similar to Irving's were prevalent among the Spanish Adoptionists of the eighth century. They also featured in the preaching of Gottfried Menken of Bremen in the nineteenth century. But there is little likelihood that Irving had any knowledge of either of these sources. See A. B. Bruce, *The Humiliation of Christ* (Edinburgh: T. & T. Clark, 1876), pp. 269ff.

In 1887, an American Presbyterian minister, Rev. John Miller (son of Dr Samuel Miller of Princeton) set forth a more extreme position than Irving in a brief monograph, *Was Christ in Adam?* (Princeton, 1887). A footnote to the Preface makes plain that he had come to his position quite independently of Irving.

Miller's position is summarized in the following statement: 'Christ, therefore, was of guilty parentage, though only of a woman: he was of a wicked nature by right of descent; its wickedness, though not its infirmity, being cut off from him by the Holy Ghost: nevertheless he had to keep that holiness, and win it further, by hard trials of temptation: and herein lay his torture' (p. 12).

[3] Robert McCheyne, for example, noted in his *Diary* for November 9, 1834: 'Heard of Edward Irving's death. I look back upon him with awe, as on the saints and martyrs of old. A holy man in spite of all his delusions and errors. He is now with his God and saviour, whom he wronged so much, yet, I am persuaded, loved so sincerely.'

[4] *The Collected Writings of Edward Irving*, vol. V (London, 1865), pp. 126, 129, 137.

[5] *Ibid.*, p. 116.
[6] *Ibid.*, p. 126.
[7] *Ibid.*, pp. 115ff.
[8] *Ibid.*, p. 128.
[9] *Ibid.*, p. 170.
[10] Quoted in C. G. Strachan, *The Pentecostal Theology of Edward Irving* (London: Darton, Longman and Todd, 1973), p. 27.
[11] *Ibid.*, p. 28.
[12] See M. Dods, *The Incarnation of the Eternal Word* (London, 1831); A. B. Bruce, *The Humiliation of Christ* (Edinburgh: T. & T. Clark, 1876), pp. 269–275; H. R. Mackintosh, *The Doctrine of the Person of Jesus Christ* (Edinburgh, T. & T. Clark, 2nd edn., 1913), pp. 276f.; D. Baillie, *God Was in Christ* (London, 1948), pp. 16f.
[13] K. Barth, *Church Dogmatics*, I.2 (Edinburgh: T. & T. Clark, 1956), p. 154.
[14] *Ibid.*, I.2, p. 153.
[15] C. E. B. Cranfield, *The International Critical Commentary: A Critical and Exegetical Commentary on the Epistle to the Romans*, vol. I (Edinburgh: T. & T. Clark, 1975), pp. 379ff.
[16] T. F. Torrance, *The Mediation of Christ* (Grand Rapids: Eerdmans, 1983), p. 48.
[17] J. B. Torrance, 'The Vicarious Humanity of Christ', in T. F. Torrance (ed.), *The Incarnation* (Edinburgh: Handsel Press, 1981), p. 141.
[18] For Gregory of Nazianzen see *NPNF*, Second Series, vol. VII, p. 440.
[19] See L. R. Wickham, *Cyril of Alexandria: Select Letters* (Oxford: Clarendon Press, 1983), pp. 173f.
[20] Augustine, *On the Trinity*, XIII.23.
[21] See T. H. Bindley, *Ecumenical Documents of the Faith* (Westport, Connecticut: Greenwood Press, 4th edn., 1950), p. 227. Referring to the Chalcedonian phrase, 'like us in all things, sin apart' (*choris hamartias*), Bindley comments, 'This phrase is equivalent to Rom. VIII.3, in the likeness of sinful flesh. Our Lord took perfect manhood, not fallen manhood. His was not "flesh of sin", but like it in every respect, except its sinfulness' (*ibid.*, p. 196).
[22] E. Irving, *Collected Writings*, vol. V, p. 117.
[23] M. Dods, *op. cit.*, p. 31.
[24] E. Irving, *Collected Writings*, vol. V, p. 137.
[25] *Ibid.*, p. 128.
[26] John of Damascus, *Exposition of the Orthodox Faith*, III.xx.
[27] E. Irving, *Collected Writings*, vol. V, p. 565.
[28] *Ibid.*, pp. 563, 565.
[29] A. B. Bruce, *op. cit.*, p. 271.
[30] Jonathan Edwards, *On the Freedom of the Will*, III.II. See *The Works of Jonathan Edwards*, vol. I (1834), pp. 42f.
[31] W. G. T. Shedd, *Dogmatic Theology*, vol. II (Edinburgh: T. & T. Clark, 1889), p. 334.

[32] J. A. Mackay, *A Preface to Christian Theology* (London: Nisbet, 1942), pp. 27–54.

Chapter 10: No other name: the uniqueness of Christ in modern theology

[1] J. A. T. Robinson, from an essay, 'Need Jesus Have Been Perfect?' in S. W. Sykes and J. P. Clayton (eds.), *Christ, Faith and History* (Cambridge: Cambridge University Press, 1972), p. 39.

[2] A. Schweitzer, *The Quest of the Historical Jesus* (London: A. & C. Black, 3rd English edn., 1954), p. 3.

[3] J. Knox, *The Humanity and Divinity of Christ* (Cambridge: Cambridge University Press, 1967), p. 100.

[4] D. Cupitt, from an essay, 'The Christ of Christendom', in J. Hick (ed.), *The Myth of God Incarnate* (London: SCM Press, 1977), p. 134.

[5] J. Hick, from an essay, 'Jesus and the World Religions', in J. Hick (ed.), *op. cit.*, p. 178.

[6] R. Bultmann, *Jesus and the Word* (London and Glasgow: Collins, 1958), pp. 16ff.

[7] *Ibid.*, p. 18.

[8] R. Bultmann in 'The New Testament and Mythology' (first published in 1941), reprinted in H. W. Bartsch, *Kerygma and Myth* (New York: Harper and Row, 1961), p. 41.

[9] H. W. Bartsch, *op. cit.*, p. 37.

[10] *Ibid.*, p. 41.

[11] See Bultmann's comment in 'The New Testament and Mythology': 'The saving significance of the cross is not derived from the fact that it is the cross of Christ: it is the cross of Christ because it has this saving efficacy' (H. W. Bartsch, *op. cit.*, p. 41).

[12] J. Hick (ed.), *op. cit.*, p. 178.

[13] D. Nineham, in his *Epilogue* to J. Hick (ed.), *op. cit.*, p. 190.

[14] C. F. D. Moule, *The Origin of Christology* (Cambridge: Cambridge University Press, 1977), p. 2.

[15] *Ibid.*, p. 135.

[16] J. Hick (ed.), *op. cit.*, p. 172.

[17] *Ibid.*, p. 176: 'because of the inherent conservatism of religion, the way in which the significance of Jesus was expressed in the mythology and philosophy of Europe in the first three centuries has remained the normative Christian language which we inherit today'.

[18] *Ibid.*, p. 170.

[19] See Oliver O'Donovan, *Resurrection and Moral Order* (Leicester: Apollos, 2nd edn. 1994).

[20] See J. Hick and P. F. Knitter (eds.), *The Myth of Christian Uniqueness* (London: SCM Press, 1988). *Cf.* G. D'Costa (ed.), *Christian Uniqueness Reconsidered: The Myth of a Pluralistic Theology of Religions* (New York: Orbis, 1990).

[21] See H. Cotterell, *Mission and Meaninglessness* (London: SPCK, 1990), pp. 40–52. The Second Vatican Council gave considerable attention to this issue and expressed an inclusivist position in such documents as *Lumen Gentium*. See Austin Flannery (ed.), *Vatican Council II: The Conciliar and Post-Conciliar Documents* (1981), pp. 366–369.

[22] See J. Hick's article, 'Jesus and the World Religions', in J. Hick (ed.), *The Myth of God Incarnate*, pp. 167–185.

[23] *Ibid.*, p. 180.

[24] Besides the works of Cotterell and D'Costa already cited see, for example, L. Newbigin, *The Gospel in a Pluralist Society* (London: SPCK, 1989) and H. A. Netland, *Dissonant Voices: Religious Pluralism and the Question of Truth* (Grand Rapids: Eerdmans, and Leicester: Apollos, 1991). For a briefer but perceptive treatment see A. E. McGrath, 'The Challenge of Pluralism for the Contemporary Christian Church', in *Journal of the Evangelical Theological Society* (September 1992), pp. 361–373.

[25] J. Calvin, *Commentary on the Gospel of John*, vol. 1 (Edinburgh: Calvin Translation Society, 1847), p. 38.

[26] J. Hick begs the question when he suggests that the doctrine of the incarnation must be rejected precisely because it implies Christian exclusivism: 'If Jesus Christ was God incarnate … then the only doorway to eternal life is Christian faith. It would follow from this that the large majority of the human race so far have not been saved' (J. Hick [ed.], *The Myth of God Incarnate*, p. 180).

[27] L. Newbigin, *op. cit.*, p. 7.

[28] It was with reference to these theologians that E. L. Mascall declared: 'a great deal of modern Christology is inspired by a mainly unconfessed and certainly uncriticized mixture of Unitarianism and Adoptionism' (*Theology and the Gospel of Christ* [London: SPCK, 1977], p. 121).

[29] M. Wiles in J. Hick (ed.), *The Myth of God Incarnate*, pp. 2–6.

[30] J. Knox, *The Humanity and Divinity of Christ* (Cambridge: Cambridge University Press, 1967), p. 106.

[31] G. K. W. Lampe, *God as Spirit* (Oxford: Clarendon Press, 1977), p. 138.

[32] *Ibid.*, p. 157.

[33] *Ibid.*, p. 208.

[34] E. L. Mascall, *op. cit.*, p. 121.

[35] G. K. W. Lampe, *op. cit.*, p. 228.

[36] M. Wiles in J. Hick (ed.), *op. cit.*, p. 9.

[37] G. K. W. Lampe, *op. cit.*, pp. 180–181.

[38] According to A. M. Ramsey, the leading representatives of this tendency were W. R. Inge, Hastings Rashdall, J. F. Bethune-Baker and H. D. A. Major (see A. M. Ramsey, *From Gore to Temple: The Development of Anglican Thought between Lux Mundi and the Second World War 1889–1939* [London: Longmans, 1960], pp. 66–73).

[39] H. D. A. Major, quoted in A. M. Ramsey, *op. cit.*, p. 73.

[40] G. K. W. Lampe, *op. cit.*, p. 138.

[41] J. A. T. Robinson, *op. cit.*, p. 179.

[42] *Ibid.*, p. 165.

[43] M. Wiles in J. Hick (ed.), *The Myth of God Incarnate*, p. 8. *Cf.* G. K. W. Lampe: 'it is a fact that although we need not think that the overall impression which we derive from the Synoptic Gospels is simply misleading, we are unable to determine with complete certainty that the tradition behind any particular saying or story contained in these Gospels goes back to the historical Jesus himself. On the principle that a chain cannot be stronger than its individual links we must at least be cautious about making it take the heavy strain of supporting the decisive centrality of Jesus in the history of the human race' (*op. cit.*, p. 102).

[44] J. A. T. Robinson, *op. cit.*, p. 161.

[45] *Ibid.*, p. 162.

[46] G. K. W. Lampe, *op. cit.*, p. 208.

[47] *Ibid.*, p. 206.

[48] *Ibid.*, p. 100.

[49] *Ibid.*, p. 115.

[50] T. F. Torrance, *The Mediation of Christ* (Grand Rapids: Eerdmans, 1983), p. 69.

[51] J. A. T. Robinson, *op. cit.*, p. 180.

[52] O. Cullmann, *The Christology of the New Testament* (London: SCM Press, 2nd English edn., 1963), p. 266.

[53] *Ibid.*, p. 267.

[54] See 'The Reply of Professor Cullmann to Roman Catholic Critics', in *Scottish Journal of Theology*, vol. 15, no.1 (March 1962), pp. 36–43.

[55] J. A. T. Robinson, *op. cit.*, pp. 162, 166.

[56] G. K. W. Lampe, *op. cit.*, p. 228.

[57] K. Barth, *Church Dogmatics*, I.1 (Edinburgh: T. & T. Clark, 1956), pp. 349, 358, 362.

[58] W. Pannenberg, *Jesus – God and Man* (London: SCM Press, 1968), p. 127.

[59] *Ibid.*, p. 129.

[60] *Ibid.*, p. 130.

[61] See further I. Howard Marshall, 'Incarnational Christology in the New Testament', in H. Rowdon (ed.), *Christ the Lord: Studies Presented to Donald Guthrie* (Leicester: Inter-Varsity Press, 1982), pp. 1–16.

[62] See J. Hick (ed.), *The Myth of God Incarnate*, p. 4: 'the setting in which the process took place was one in which the idea of supernatural divine intervention was a natural category of thought and faith, in a way that is no longer true of the main body even of convinced believers today'. In an earlier article Wiles had expressed his aversion to an approach 'which looks for some specific creative act of God within the evolutionary process even though not as part of it' and endorsed the comment of Audrey Moore, 'A theory of occasional intervention implies as its correlative a theory of ordinary absence' (S. W. Sykes and J. P. Clayton [eds.], *Christ, Faith and History* [Cambridge: Cambridge University Press, 1972], p. 5).

[63] G. K. W. Lampe, *op. cit.*, pp. 33, 208, 96 (respectively).

[64] For Rashdall and Bethune-Baker, see A. M. Ramsey, *op. cit.*, ch. V.

[65] N. Pittenger, *The Word Incarnate* (Welwyn: Nisbet, 1959), p. 99.

[66] *Ibid.*, pp. 155f.

[67] *Ibid.*, p. 184. From a non-Anglican point of view similar sentiments are expressed by Ruth Page, who regards the idea of divine intervention as inconsistent with the freedom of creation (*The Incarnation of Freedom and Love* [London: SCM Press, 1991], pp. 5, 8).

[68] B. L. Hebblethwaite, 'The Appeal to Experience in Christology', in S. W. Sykes and J. P. Clayton (eds.), *op. cit.*, p. 276: 'Given belief in God, it is far from clear how any experience, ancient or modern, can dictate how he is to relate to the world or make himself present in the world.'

[69] J. Polkinghorne, *Science and Christian Belief* (London: SPCK, 1994), p. 78.

[70] *Ibid.*, p. 78.

[71] J. Sobrino, *Christology at the Crossroads: A Latin American Approach* (London: SCM Press, 1978), p. 37.

[72] *Ibid.*, p. 35.

[73] See *ibid.*, p. 275: 'We gain access to him only through a specific kind of praxis, which the gospels describe as the "following of Jesus" or "discipleship".'

[74] G. Gutiérrez, *A Theology of Liberation: History, Politics and Salvation* (London: SCM Press, 1974), pp. 155, 157.

[75] J. Sobrino, *op. cit.*, p. 92.

[76] *Ibid.*, p. 275.

[77] *Ibid.*, p. 278.

[78] See Y. Congar, *Jesus Christ* (London: Geoffrey Chapman, 1966), pp. 66–85. *Cf.* David Sheppard, *Bias to the Poor* (London: Hodder and Stoughton, 1983).

[79] See G. Gutiérrez, *op. cit.*, pp. 225–232. *Cf.* O. Cullmann, *The State in the New Testament* (London: SCM Press, 1957), pp. 8–49.

[80] L. Boff, quoted in J. Sobrino, *op. cit.*, p. 139.

[81] J. Sobrino, *op. cit.*, p. 92.

[82] J. Moltmann, *The Crucified God* (London: SCM Press, 1974), p. 24.

[83] D. Bonhoeffer, *Letters and Papers from Prison* (London: SCM Press, 1971), p. 17.

[84] *Cf.* Gutiérrez: 'In the liberation approach sin is not considered as an individual, private, or merely interior reality ... Sin is regarded as a social, historical fact, the absence of brotherhood and love in relationships among men, the breach of friendship with God and with other men ... Sin is evident in oppressive structures, in the exploitation of man by man, in the domination and slavery of peoples, races and social classes' (*op. cit.*, p. 175).

[85] L. Boff, *Trinity and Society* (Tunbridge Wells: Burns & Oates, 1988).

[86] *Ibid.*, pp. 6–7.

[87] Y. Congar, *op. cit.*, p. 68.

[88] R. Page, *op. cit.*, p. 17.

[89] J. Sobrino, *op. cit.*, p. 60.

[90] For an exposition and defence of this Realized Eschatology see, for example, C. H. Dodd, *The Parables of the Kingdom* (London: Collins, revised edn., 1961), pp. 29–61.

[91] J. Sobrino, *op. cit.*, pp. 179–235.

[92] *Ibid.*, p. 224.

[93] *Ibid.*, p. 226.

[94] *Ibid.*, p. 218.

[95] *Ibid.*, p. 108.

For Further Reading

A. B. Bruce, *The Humiliation of Christ* (Edinburgh: T. & T. Clark, 1876). This book is out of print, but it remains one of the best overall studies.

A. E. McGrath, *The Making of Modern German Christology 1750–1990* (Leicester: Inter-Varsity Press, 2nd edn., 1994).

I. H. Marshall, *The Origins of New Testament Christology* (Leicester: Apollos, 2nd edn., 1993).

E. L. Mascall, *Whatever Happened to the Human Mind?* (London: SPCK, 1980)

C. F. D. Moule, *The Origin of Christology* (Cambridge: Cambridge University Press, 1977).

H. H. Rowdon (ed.), *Christ the Lord* (Leicester: Inter-Varsity Press, 1982).

K. Runia, *The Present-day Christological Debate* (Leicester: Inter-Varsity Press, 1984).

S. W. Sykes and J. P. Clayton (eds.), *Christ, Faith and History* (Cambridge: Cambridge University Press, 1972).

B. B. Warfield, *The Person and Work of Christ* (Philadalphia: Presbyterian and Reformed, 1950).

Index of Biblical References

Index of Names

Index of Subjects